Oceanus

Bel Videre

C

B

Palatium pape

A

I

D

Tiberis fl.

Q

THE BORGIAS

MARION JOHNSON

THE BORGIAS

MACDONALD
MACDONALD FUTURA PUBLISHERS
LONDON

*On behalf of the late Marion Johnson,
the producers of this book would like
to thank all those who gave help and
advice on the text, the illustrations
and the captions.*

First published in 1981 in Great Britain by
Macdonald · London and Sydney

Macdonald Futura Publishers
Paulton House
8 Shepherdess Walk
London N1 7LW

This book was designed and produced by
George Rainbird Ltd
36 Park Street
London W1Y 4DE

House editor: Erica Hunningher
Assistant house editor: Clarinda Roothooft
Picture research: Harriet Berry
Designer: Yvonne Dedman

ISBN 0 354 04791 4

Text set and illustrations originated by
W. S. Cowell Ltd, Ipswich
Printed and bound by
Dai Nippon, Hong Kong

ENDPAPERS Woodcut of Rome in the early
sixteenth century.

FRONTISPIECE The Borgia arms in the Sala delle
Scienze e delle Arti Liberali, the Borgia Apartment.

CONTENTS

Maps and Genealogical Tables

CHAPTER ONE
BORGIA BEGINNINGS: THE ROAD TO ROME

WITHIN A SHORT TIME THE NAME WAS JUDGED AND damned. From obscure beginnings the family arose like a malign meteor, infecting the body politic with its influence, before it blazed away into darkness. For fear of the infamy, bones were scattered, the epitaphs destroyed, the monuments razed. The stink of abomination remains to this day. History has shown the Borgias as fallen men and women in a bad era. But the condemnation has been too absolute; behind the gaudy horrors lie people of real talent and achievement, possessors, even, of moderate virtues.

Alfons de Borja – Borgia is the Italian version of the Spanish Borja – was born in 1378, the only son among five children. His father, Domingo, lived at Torre de Canals, a fortified manor near the ancient hill town of Játiva, a stronghold of Roman origin which still frowns over the plains of Valencia. In the collegiate church of Játiva, Alfons was baptized. In later times, to add grandeur to their cause, the Borgias claimed descent from the Atares, the old royal house of Aragon. That was a fabrication; but neither was it true, as opponents and detractors said, that the Borgias were a peasant family who clawed their way out of servitude by deceit and violence. The family came originally from further north in Spain, taking their name from the town of Borja in the Ebro valley. Early members of the family, soldiers and adventurers, followed King Jaime I of Aragon when he undertook the reconquest of Valencia from the Moors. And when that task was done, the Borjas received, in 1240, extensive lands and jurisdiction in the reconquered territory round Játiva. There they stayed, multiplied and prospered. In the fourteenth century we read of a Borja who owned a dye works in Játiva, and another who kept a brothel in the port of Valencia. Obviously a vigorous family of some local importance.

The castle near Játiva in Valencia where Alfons de Borja was born in 1378.

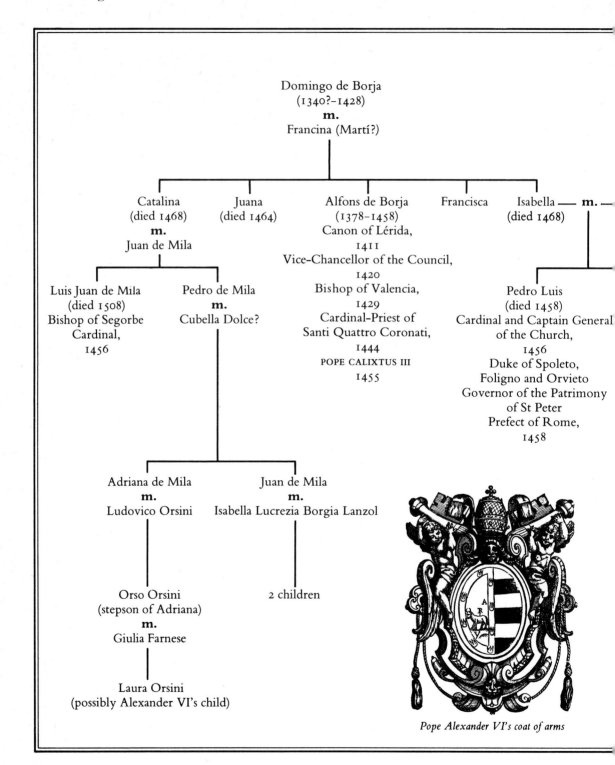

Domingo de Borja
(1340?–1428)
m.
Francina (Martí?)

Catalina
(died 1468)
m.
Juan de Mila

Juana
(died 1464)

Alfons de Borja
(1378–1458)
Canon of Lérida,
1411
Vice-Chancellor of the Council,
1420
Bishop of Valencia,
1429
Cardinal-Priest of
Santi Quattro Coronati,
1444
POPE CALIXTUS III
1455

Francisca

Isabella —— **m.** ——
(died 1468)

Luis Juan de Mila
(died 1508)
Bishop of Segorbe
Cardinal,
1456

Pedro de Mila
m.
Cubella Dolce?

Pedro Luis
(died 1458)
Cardinal and Captain General
of the Church,
1456
Duke of Spoleto,
Foligno and Orvieto
Governor of the Patrimony
of St Peter
Prefect of Rome,
1458

Adriana de Mila
m.
Ludovico Orsini

Juan de Mila
m.
Isabella Lucrezia Borgia Lanzol

Orso Orsini
(stepson of Adriana)
m.
Giulia Farnese

2 children

Laura Orsini
(possibly Alexander VI's child)

Pope Alexander VI's coat of arms

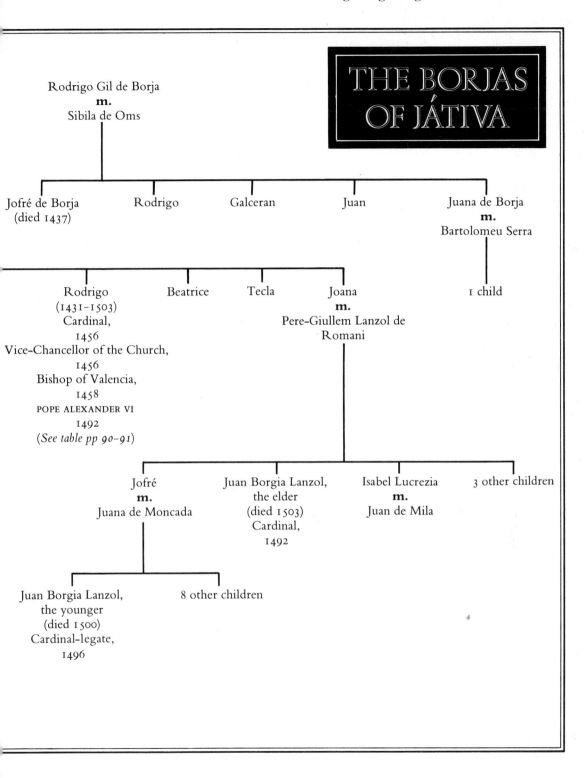

THE BORJAS OF JÁTIVA

Rodrigo Gil de Borja
m.
Sibila de Oms

- Jofré de Borja (died 1437)
- Rodrigo
- Galceran
- Juan
- Juana de Borja **m.** Bartolomeu Serra

- Rodrigo (1431–1503) Cardinal, 1456 Vice-Chancellor of the Church, 1456 Bishop of Valencia, 1458 POPE ALEXANDER VI 1492 (*See table pp 90–91*)
- Beatrice
- Tecla
- Joana **m.** Pere-Giullem Lanzol de Romani
- 1 child

- Jofré **m.** Juana de Moncada
- Juan Borgia Lanzol, the elder (died 1503) Cardinal, 1492
- Isabel Lucrezia **m.** Juan de Mila
- 3 other children

- Juan Borgia Lanzol, the younger (died 1500) Cardinal-legate, 1496
- 8 other children

'*Un bon home*', say the documents of Alfons' father, but add the quali-
fication '*laurador*': petty landholder, from the junior branch of the
family and in reduced circumstances. The way up for the son of such
a man was the harder, for there was far to go and little influence to help
him on his road. Trade or the work of an artisan was, in general, not
for him. In Spain, the poorest landholder, though living in a decaying
hovel with the animals underfoot, still clung to the aspirations of his
caste, of the *hidalgo*. The thousand useful occupations of a middle class –
traders, shopkeepers, craftsmen – were left largely to *conversos*, Moors
and Jews who had been assimilated into Christian society and kept the
ordinary business of life running along. For the well-born, no matter
how poor, there was 'Church, or sea, or the royal house', as an old
proverb put it. The chief business of the *hidalgo* had always been the
profession of arms, in the service of the king, driving the Moors from
Spain in the Reconquest, and then, after 1492, taking possession of the
New Lands opened up by the voyages of the navigators. Conquest was
the great task; and for those who could not come up to that pitch there
was always the Church.

Alfons de Borja avoided a military career, but whether from choice
or through force of circumstance there is no knowing. In his maturity
he was of a scholarly and peaceful disposition, and perhaps an inclina-
tion towards the study came to him early. In any case, at the age of fourteen he was enrolled at Lérida University, a student of canon and civil
law. Well-born Spaniards, bred for war, tended to despise learning.
The cultivated Marqués de Santillana, trying to recommend books to
a young prince of Castile, wrote in some despair that 'knowledge does
not blunt the iron of the lance nor weaken the sword in a knight's hand'.
But the common aristocratic opinion was against him. The pursuit of
letters, said Fernandez de Navarrete, reflecting on fifteenth-century
Spanish history,

> usually engenders a certain melancholy that weakens the spirit by opposing
> the cheerful impulsiveness with which dangerous adventures are under-
> taken . . . For the peoples that indulge excessively in the pleasure of learning
> easily forget the practice of arms. Spain has examples enough of this, for as
> long she struggled to rid the land of the Saracens' heavy yoke, she was raw
> and lacking in letters, and to remedy this the king founded the universities
> and schools.

The king, expanding his power into new territory, discovered that his forceful but ignorant knights lacked the training and the qualities that make for effective government. So a bright young student of good birth had every chance to rise. Places in the royal administration awaited a man trained in logic, with a command of Latin and vernacular languages, and some knowledge of affairs. The bureaucracy of the Church welcomed a good canon lawyer with open arms.

Inevitably, young Alfons was directed towards the Church. The medieval university was in the main a training ground for the clergy. Churchmen were employed indiscriminately by state and Church alike, for they were the learned in an unlettered age. The kings needed them; so also did the universal Church, if not for spiritual welfare at least for teaching, for diplomacy, for administration. After taking doctorates in both canon and civil law, Alfons remained at Lérida as a lecturer. By the age of thirty he had begun to rise. In 1408 he became assessor and bailiff to the Lérida diocese. Three years later he was a canon of Lérida. At the same time it is very likely that he took minor orders, though he was not ordained priest for another eighteen years. He had caught the eye. St Vincent Ferrer, it is said, noted his talent and forecast for Alfons 'the highest authority to which moral man can attain'. Did that mean the papacy, the See of St Peter itself?

St Vincent Ferrer healing a possessed woman. Vincent Ferrer foretold Alfons de Borja's election to the 'highest authority to which moral man can attain'. In 1455, as Pope Calixtus III, Alfons was responsible for the canonization of St Vincent.

And certainly, at this time, the Church was in bad disarray, and the papacy lacked the 'authority of the moral man'. In 1378, the year of Alfons de Borja's birth, the Great Schism in the Church had begun. The partiality of the western nations tore apart the pretensions of a universal Christendom. The papacy found itself more and more in conflict with, and helpless against, nationalism and the brutal self-interest of kings. In the fourteenth century the powerful French monarchy had led the popes away from Rome into the 'Babylonish captivity' at Avignon. The conclave of cardinals that met on the death of Gregory XI, in 1378, faced a Roman mob, beating on the walls of the Vatican: 'Give us a Roman pontiff, or we'll kill you all.' After a riotous and scandalous assembly, the frightened cardinals managed to elect, if not a Roman, at least an Italian. This fierce old man, Urban VI, was upright, well-intentioned and energetic. He was determined to stamp out Church corruption and to restore the authority of the papacy against the inter-ference of kings, specially the meddling of the French king. But he set about this task like an elemental force, as random and destructive as a thunderbolt. Even good people who supported his aims, like St Catherine of Siena, were aghast at his violence and want of tact. The large and important French faction in the Curia – the papal court and administration – was immediately antagonized. The influential car-dinal of Amiens was publicly derided as an idle scoundrel. 'In the name of Our Crucified Saviour,' St Catherine implored the fiery pope, 'moderate your impetuous temper.' All was in vain. In the face of this turbulent, uncompromising Italian pope the French party in the Church planned a revolt. In August 1378, thirteen cardinals, under the protec-tion of French troops, declared the election of Urban null and void, and gave the Church another pope in the person of Clement VII, who promptly withdrew to French territory at Avignon.

Thus began the reign of two popes (for a few lamentable years there were three). The support of pope or anti-pope became a calculation of national policy. Spain declared herself for the anti-pope at Avignon and, in 1394, had the satisfaction of seeing one of her own sons, Pedro de Luna, elected to the succession at Avignon and reigning there as Benedict XIII. In the shadow of Luna, this 'moon pope', the talented canon lawyer Alfons de Borja began to be noticed. From Benedict XIII he collected his first benefice. And when a Church Council met at

Medal of King Alfonso V of Aragon; the reverse shows the young king hunting wild boar. In 1417, Alfons de Borja represented the diocese of Lérida in financial negotiations with the king and was taken into the royal service. He was King Alfonso's secretary and chief councillor until 1444.

Constance to try to reconcile the claims of pope and anti-pope, Alfons was chosen to go there, in 1416, to represent the diocese of Lérida. But he did not go, for in the same year young Alfonso V came to the throne of Aragon and would not support the work of the Council. Instead, Alfons went to Barcelona where the king presided over an assembly of the Aragonese Church. In 1417 he was once more before the king, entrusted by his diocese with delicate financial negotiations. No doubt he handled the task well. Certainly King Alfonso was impressed, for he immediately took this astute lawyer into his retinue and made him his secretary.

Despite all difficulties, the Council of Constance had judged the rival popes (there were now three of them), and deposed them all. At the subsequent conclave the aristocratic Roman, Cardinal Ottone Colonna, was elected Pope Martin V, with a clear mandate to heal divisions in the Church and a strong desire to establish the authority of the pope in Rome. But the Spaniard Pedro de Luna refused to accept the decision of the Council, and still calling himself Benedict XIII, retired to the jutting castle of Peñiscola in Aragon. In self-righteous austerity he claimed a papal jurisdiction that hardly extended beyond the hilltop of his fortress. Here, safe from attack, he constituted a problem for the young king of Aragon. A problem, but also a valuable property, a pawn which the king, in the manner of the time, intended to advance in the long game played out between state and papacy. Alfonso V was only twenty, wise beyond his years but lacking experience; no doubt he looked to his new secretary, the wily canonist Alfons de Borja, to help him along the path of Church intrigue.

The scene was set for a familiar confusion of the times. Alfons de Borja was a churchman. True, he was not a priest, but he was in minor orders, a holder of Church benefices, a canon lawyer, Church trained, and for many years in the employment of a diocese. Now he was the secretary of a king. Where did his loyalty lie? To the well-being of Christendom, obedient to the Roman pontiff? To the Spanish Church of Aragon? Or to his master the king whose struggle for power and revenue so often went against the interests of the Church? These hard questions were unresolved in the late Middle Ages, when churchmen held the positions of power in the secular courts, and the aims of nationalism battered down the ideals of Christendom. Lawyers are practical people, even Church lawyers, and Alfons took the pragmatic view. He looked after the business in hand to the best of his ability. That was his duty to the king; it was also in his own interest, for Alfons knew that the king was the fount of all privilege and reward within his realm. Larger ideals, or questions of conscience, gave way before business of the moment.

So when Cardinal Adimari, the papal legate, arrived in Spain to force the deposition of Benedict, the king and his secretary were well-prepared to make what capital they could out of the stubborn old schismatic. Alfonso V was in dispute with Rome over the control of Spanish Church funds, so the pope's answer on this point would determine the king's conduct towards the errant Benedict. In no hurry to meet the legate, Alfonso sent his secretary on a secret mission to prepare the ground. Alfons was to tell Adimari that the honour of Aragon was impugned by the appointment of an Italian bishop to be Collector General for the Papal Treasury in the Spanish domain. This powerful and sensitive post the king wanted for his own man, Francisco Martorell, and Alfons de Borja was therefore instructed to speak 'most secretly and affectionately' to the legate, to ensure that 'Don Francisco Martorell *and no one else*' held this vital appointment.

Control of Church funds, and the rights to clerical appointments, went to the heart of the long-running contest between monarchs and the papacy. In a matter of such profound importance, it was never likely that Alfons de Borja could achieve all that his master desired. But the king was well-pleased. He had gained a little against Rome, and he still held the schismatic Benedict in play. He felt there was still more to be won, for he knew the very keen wish of Pope Martin to rid himself of the imposter, 'to ensure that Don Pedro de Luna, as a notorious schismatic, should be forced to accept obedience to the true universal pastor'. But Alfonso also knew that Benedict was more stubborn than any Spanish mule and was, moreover, impregnable at Peñiscola, protected by the sea on one side and formidable defences on the other. The solemnities of the game commenced. A royal mission was dispatched to Peñiscola, studded with Church dignitaries and theologians. Arguments of all kinds were put forward, theological, legal, practical, seductive. Generous bribes and incentives were offered. Benedict answered everything with a stony 'No'. The legate Adimari, at the best of times an impatient man, fretted at the delay. The suave young king smiled and shrugged: what more could he do? Adimari convened a council at Lérida and tried to force through a condemnation of Benedict. The Spanish clergy, most of whom had already dropped their allegiance to the schismatic, nonetheless resented this Roman interference with the rights of the Church in Aragon, and dug in as stubbornly as Benedict himself. All paths seemed to be blocked. But soon rumours went about that another way had been tried, a peculiarly Roman method of cutting knots.

Benedict liked sweets, the indulgence of an austere old man. One hot July day, just before the midday siesta, he summoned his Groom of the Chamber and asked for the candied peel, the quince preserve and the sugared biscuits that he loved. He ate a few and lay down to sleep. Later, he woke in violent pain, trembling and vomiting. For ten days he was at death's door, then gradually he recovered.

The Groom of the Chamber, Domingo Delava, was a new man at Peñiscola. Formerly a lecturer at Toulouse with a reputation for brilliance, he had been offered a place at Benedict's court, but soon found his ambition unsatisfied in the isolated little congregation around the abandoned anti-pope. After a while Delava was in touch with enemies beyond the castle gate who were familiar with men in Adimari's mission. From there, a monk set out with a packet for Delava, containing two small samples of arsenic, in the white powder form and also in the disulphide known as realgar. Delava and the monk set about doctoring Benedict's sweetmeats. The reddish-coloured realgar was concealed in the rind of candied citron, while the biscuits were coated with a paste made up of arsenic powder mixed with egg and sugar. In all, arsenic roughly equivalent in volume to a hazelnut was hidden in the comfits, which were kept in the box entrusted to Delava. The work done, Delava fled. But Benedict, against expectations, recovered. Poisoner and accomplice were pursued and brought back to face trial in Peñiscola, where the proceedings were broadcast to all the inhabitants. After torture, the prisoners confessed. They were condemned to death and handed over to the secular arm for execution. Among those who witnessed the trial was a certain Juan Claver, and it is from his letter to the Bishop of Valencia, dated 22 October 1418, that we know the details of the attempt. Claver did not discover whether Adimari himself, or a zealous official, instigated the poisoning, but this Italian method was no surprise to Juan Claver; poisoning, he commented, was 'part of the manners and custom of Italy'.

King Alfonso expressed his horror, no doubt on this occasion genuine enough. The legate Adimari left Spain in some confusion, and Benedict continued in lonely eminence at Peñiscola. He lived out the rest of his life undisturbed and died in 1422, from natural causes. The young King Alfonso had also come successfully through his first clash with Rome. He had resisted papal interference in the Aragonese Church, and had fortuitously acquired, through the misfiring of the poison plot, a moral ascendancy over papal representatives. 'Poisoning', said the king, 'is, before God and man, and especially to Spaniards, one of the most abominable crimes.'

These events gave Alfons de Borja his first lesson in the affairs of state. From the backwater of the Lérida diocese, he had been pitched suddenly into the tidal flow of history. He saw at first hand the drift of the age – the irreconcilable aims of kings and pope, the enmity between Rome and national churches, the power and ambition of great men, and the dangerous means they were prepared to use towards an end. He was a man of forty, of mature judgment, and he assimilated the lesson with equanimity. As the royal secretary, he took the king's cards and played them to the best advantage of his master. As a diplomat and negotiator he was all that King Alfonso could wish for, patient, learned, subtle, and perpetually unsurprised. When in 1420 Alfonso V stepped out into the whirlwind of Mediterranean politics, tempted by the weakness and the disputed succession in Naples to add that Italian realm to the kingdom he already owned in Sicily, he had such confidence in his secretary that he raised Alfons to be Vice-Chancellor of the Royal Council, serving the Regent, Queen Maria. It was an extraordinary honour for a man who had been but three years in the royal service.

So far, no personal scandal had touched Alfons de Borja. Though not an unworldly man, he was cool of temperament, something of an ascetic, a scholar. His life as secretary was arduous and regular, devoted to royal business. But soon, in his new-found power, he showed one deep fault, a failing that lies at the root of the entire Borgia tragedy: he showed a strong compulsion to advance the interests of his family against any opposition.

Alfons' sister, Isabella, had married her relative Jofré de Borja, the heir to the main line of the Borja family in Játiva. That choice alone seemed excessively clannish. On the night of 20 October 1420, Jofré and his brother-in-law Bartolomeu Serra, together with three henchmen, murdered Folo de Montferrat. Montferrat was on his way to Játiva to lay charges against Serra, accusing him of misuse of his feudal powers. Montferrat was waylaid and slaughtered, and in such a brutal and cowardly manner that the Governor of Valencia himself came to Játiva to preside over the trial. All the conspirators were condemned to death, and in addition ruinous fines were imposed on their families; but before sentence could be carried out, all the accused had escaped and fled from Aragon. In their absence, their property was valued and a judicial order made for the sale on 21 March 1421. On the following day, however, the Regent, Queen Maria, abrogated the judgment and herself assumed jurisdiction over the case. The families of Borja and Serra had appealed against the 'irregularity' of the sentence. There can be no doubt that the Vice-Chancellor, Alfons de Borja, was behind this development. The murder was notorious, and the judiciary at Valencia strongly defended its rights and its sentence, but could make no way against the influence of the Vice-Chancellor. King Alfonso, away on his Mediterranean wars, would not intervene. In 1422 he wrote to the queen commending 'Micer Alfons de Borja, our beloved councillor and Vice-Chancellor,' who had, the king said, 'undertaken great mission, at peril to his own person.' Two years later Queen Maria decreed that the whole trial was null and void, and the sentence invalidated 'as if it had never been passed'.

The episode was ominous for the Borgia future. It had demonstrated, in one branch of the family, violently uncontrolled passions leading to murder; and in the other branch, a moral blindness that caused a respectable Church lawyer to deny all justice. Jofré de Borja, the murderer, came out of hiding and prospered. In 1436 he became castellan of Capdet, a position given to him, as the grant brazenly said, 'out of consideration for' his brother-in-law the Vice-Chancellor. In the following year Jofré died, leaving five children, all minors, in the care of their mother and her brother Alfons. Among those children were two boys, Pedro Luis and Rodrigo – Borgias soon to be known only too well in Italy, the Church and the papacy. It is certain that these children would receive from the Vice-Chancellor the same solicitous and partial consideration that he had given to their father.

But in these years the king's business pressed hard, and not even care for family could make Alfons de Borja forget his master's service. King Alfonso was away in Naples, and the burden of government in Aragon fell on the Vice-Chancellor. The king's adventure abroad had begun fortunately. He had occupied Sardinia and had then received an appeal from Joanna II of Naples to help her against Louis, Duke of Anjou. The childless queen of Naples, a slothful woman with outrageous morals and a capacity for double-dealing, even offered to name Alfonso as the heir to her throne. Alfonso did not hesitate. Naples, the jewel on which his heart was set, seemed about to fall into his lap. He arrived in Naples in the summer of 1421 and immediately the hornets of Italian dissension buzzed about his ears. Pope Martin V feared to see a strong Spanish kingdom just south of Rome. The pope, moreover, had no reason to love Alfonso in whose territory the anti-pope Benedict still lived. Martin was feudal suzerain of the kingdom of Naples and would need very strong political reasons to confirm the Spaniard on that throne. In Naples itself, the people hated Spaniards, Catalans in particular, who had a reputation for greed and brutality. One of the queen's lovers conspired with the populace against Alfonso, and another, the *condottiere* Attendolo Sforza, besieged Alfonso in the Castel dell'Ovo. In 1423 the unstable Joanna revoked her adoption of Alfonso, who decided to withdraw to Spain, leaving his brother John of Navarre in charge of the Aragonese forces.

Driven out of Italy, at least for the time being, the king also faced troubles at home. One matter still to be cleared up, which stood between him and the pope, was the question of the anti-pope at Peñiscola. Benedict XIII had died in 1422 and a new schismatic, Clement VIII, was elected in his place. Another papal legate, Cardinal de Foix, was awaiting the king's permission to enter his realm, but Alfonso would not receive him. The last legate, Alfonso complained, had done 'nothing but upset the consciences of his subjects, despoil the clergy of his realms, and administer potions'. Legates such as Adimari were 'ravening wolves rather than evangelical pastors', and Paul de Foix was very likely another 'from the same fountain'. Alfonso ordered his subjects to recognize Clement VIII 'as the true Vicar of Christ', a move that so enraged

Naples, the fickle Italian kingdom, finally fell to the Spaniards in 1443. King Alfonso took up residence in Castel Nuovo, overlooking the wide bay.

Pope Martin in Rome that he threatened Alfonso with his anathema. The time had come to bend, so the king, with good grace, agreed to receive the legate. Hard bargaining was about to begin, and the chief negotiator on the king's side was Alfons de Borja, Vice-Chancellor and expert on canon law.

Cardinal de Foix was arrogant and obtuse. Negotiations were long and difficult, and finally the two parties could only agree to differ. But with great skill Alfons de Borja devised a way to save appearances on both sides, yet still leave ground for future accommodation. He drew up for the pope two documents, setting out the points at issue. The legate's memorandum stipulated that the king's claim to Naples and Apulia should be 'submitted to the judgment of impartial persons, to be appointed by His Holiness the Pope'. This cunning formula implicitly allowed, first, that Alfonso had some valid claim to Naples and Apulia; and second, that in submitting it to the arbitration of Martin V, Alfonso recognized him as the true pope. And to underline this point still further, the king's memorandum formally asked Martin to hand back to Aragon the castle of Peñiscola, which had been 'given to the Church of Rome for Don Pedro de Luna'. This also was a tacit admission of Martin's status, for if he had the castle to dispose of, he was necessarily true Head of the Church of Rome. The documents were signed at Valencia in October 1427 and the legate left hurriedly for Rome. In May 1429 Cardinal de Foix returned to Barcelona with agreement more or less assured. One delicate task remained, so once more the king's trusty Vice-Chancellor was sent out on a secret mission. He went to persuade Clement VIII to abdicate, and at last he succeeded. Clement took off the papal robes and appeared in the plain habit of a secular doctor. Pope Martin V was left in undisputed possession of the See of St Peter.

The result of this difficult negotiation was a triumph for Alfons de Borja. He had shown great qualities as lawyer and diplomat, and his success benefited both Aragon and the Church. He now began to rise in the favour of Rome, while still retaining the confidence of the king. Pope Martin, recognizing the service to Church unity, made him Bishop of Valencia. And on the day before consecration, Cardinal de Foix, whose mission could hardly have succeeded without the Vice-Chancellor, personally ordained him as priest. Priest and bishop almost in a moment. The man who had lived for so long, as it were, on the fringe of a vocation, more administrator, bureaucrat and lawyer than servant of God, was at last drawn fully into the compass of the Church.

The diocese of Valencia had been one of the last strongholds of the schism. The clergy were split; allegiance was divided, faith was uneasy and practice lax. The new bishop, with his long experience of royal administration, was the ideal man to repair the organization and restore efficiency. But he also saw that something more was needed, some spiritual event, some symbol, that would rub out hatreds and stir up a common devotion. He found what he needed in the bones of St Louis of Torlosa, which Alfons brought to Valencia with the greatest cere-mony and pomp. Such a theatrical flair was unexpected in a dry lawyer, but it was a family trait that all Borgias would use to advantage, and it certainly helped the new bishop. Animosities were reconciled in re-ligious carnival. Celebration and new enterprise went hand in hand; a new chapel was planned to receive the relics of the saint. More than fifty years later, in 1486, the chapel begun by Alfons de Borja was com-pleted by his nephew Rodrigo Borgia.

Few had been so well-placed to see the dangers of schism as the new Bishop of Valencia. He knew at first hand what temptations for political meddling – hard to resist at the best of times – confronted kings and popes alike when divisions rent the papacy. The mature reflection of the fifty-year-old canonist, now graced with a bishopric, confirmed him as a supporter of Church unity, an upholder of the universal rule of the Roman pontiff. Alfons had begun his career as the possessor of small benefices granted by the schismatic Benedict, but these he had given up – in a manner highly unusual for the age – when he entered the king's service. One master at a time seemed to be his principle. That alone made him extraordinary in a notorious age of pluralism and simony. Now Alfons had been called by the Church, and he responded with characteristic care and intelligence. With the king, a conflict of duty was always possible for the future, but Alfons, ever the pragmatist, would deal with that problem when it arose.

For three years Valencia had the care of its bishop. Then, in 1432, King Alfonso was drawn once more towards unfinished business in Naples. And since the conquest and retention of the fickle Italian kingdom required the concentration of all the powers of the Aragon state, it is no surprise that the king very soon sent for his most trusted and experienced minister, Alfons de Borja. A royal summons could not be denied. But for two short visits to his homeland, Alfons spent the rest of his long life in Italy. He began to create the fortunes, and misfortune, of the house of Borgia in a characteristic Italian setting. For a dozen years or so history loses sight of Alfons the individual, though certain acts of the minister are recorded. In 1436 he travelled to Spain to collect Ferrante, King Alfonso's illegitimate son, and became a tutor to this

Ferrante, illegitimate son of King Alfonso. Alfons de Borja became tutor to this future king of Naples and as Pope Calixtus resisted Ferrante's succession to the throne.

future king of Naples. When Naples at last fell to the Spaniards, Alfons reorganized the judiciary and the administration and was, until 1444, president of the Sacro Consiglior and the Royal Council. Quite clearly he was in the good graces of the king and was as prudent as ever in the difficult government of a difficult kingdom. But what did Alfons de Borja make of the potent Italian air, which seduced and then unnerved so many Spaniards?

King Alfonso was under the spell of this siren land; no Spaniard gave way to Italian influence more thoroughly than this engaging and spirited monarch whom history calls 'the Magnanimous'. From the death of Queen Joanna in 1435 until the final triumph eight years later, Alfonso's path to the Neapolitan throne was stony and tortuous. But he trod the labyrinth of Italian intrigue with a resolution, a dignity and a generosity that won most hearts. Dashing and precipitous in success, he was nonetheless calm and undismayed in defeat. When Filippo Maria Visconti took him prisoner, in 1435, the king argued so persuasively for a Spanish, and against a French, succession in Naples that Visconti released him immediately, to the amazement of contemporaries. Even his vices seemed attractive. His reckless extravagance seemed the natural outpouring of a kingly generosity, while his headlong passion for the beautiful young Lucrezia d'Alagno elicited sympathy rather than derision. The personality that charmed the faithless princes of the Italian states quite bowled over the scholars, poets and artists who clustered around him. 'This is not to pay you,' said Alfonso, handing the historian Fazio a present of 1500 ducats, 'for your work is worth more than the fairest of my cities; but in time I hope to satisfy you.' 'My last crust,' he told Giannozzo Manetti, 'I will share with you.'

No spot pleased this energetic monarch more than the library in the castle at Naples, where the window opened over the wide bay, and the airs wafting in from sea and mountain would ruffle the edge of a manuscript page. And in the hurry of his many campaigns he always gave time to study, when he was not to be disturbed, even by the sound of music. His love of letters and antiquity was so great that he begged from the Venetians what was claimed to be the arm bone of Livy and received it in Naples with superstitious splendour. Indeed, there was something consciously imperial and Roman about the scope and execution of his life. And when at last he made his entry into Naples, to claim his new

Detail of the Aragonese arch, Castel Nuovo, Naples, commemorating King Alfonso's triumphal entry into his new kingdom in February 1443.

kingdom in February 1443, he came in triumphal style, riding through the breached walls in a gilded chariot drawn by four white horses. Even the Neapolitans, traditional enemies of all things Catalan, could not withhold a cheer.

But the other side of magnificence is debt. Moneylenders were soon as familiar as poets in the court of Naples. The king, whose good heart had relieved his poorest subjects of several heavy taxes, was driven in time by his improvidence to high-handed extortion. Money was wrung from the clergy under pretext of a crusade. Jews stayed unmolested only on payment of regular fees. A community in the Abruzzi, decimated by an earthquake, was still dunned for the unpaid taxes of the dead. What did a man like Alfons de Borja, prudent governor and minister of orderly society, make of this gallantry, this spendthrift excess? In the crowd around the throne there were humanists and writers of real talent and achievement. Men like Lorenzo Valla, Poggio Bracciolini and George of Trebizond have their place in the history of the mind, and Alfons treated them with friendship and respect. But the

The cloisters of the medieval palace of Santi Quattro Coronati in Rome. Cardinal Borgia's residence stood in an unfrequented stretch of country between the Colosseum and the Lateran.

20,000 gold florins a year that King Alfonso spent on artistic patronage –
was that wisely done? There was something in Italian airs that unhinged
the traditional austerity of the Spanish *hidalgo*. The raptures of the king's
historians Panormita and Fazio must have seemed despicable to Alfons,
the evidence of a cynical, changeable and essentially frivolous society.
Amid these Italian vapours it was hard to hold on to the great verities
of settled state power and a unified Church.

There is no doubt that in Italy the Bishop of Valencia, though always
loyal, was no longer the king's creature, and dared to stand against
Alfonso, especially in Church affairs. Pope Martin had died in 1431. His
successor, Eugenius IV, immediately had to contend with a Church
Council at Basle and with the possibility of another schismatic pope.
Alfonso, who was trying to force the papacy to recognize his claim to

Naples, dallied once more with the anti-Roman conciliar party, and wanted to send Alfons to represent him in Basle. But Alfons refused to go, judging that the cause of Church unity overrode his duty to the king. But in 1439, when in the face of the Turkish threat to Constantinople a new council was convened in Florence, to reconcile Christians of East and West and to warn the princes of Europe against the danger from the infidel, Alfons took his rightful place in the assembly as Bishop of Valencia and leader of the Aragonese delegation. The Council of Florence failed. But in notable company, which included such champions of unification and reform as the Greek Patriarch Johannes Bessarion and Cardinal Giuliano Cesarini, Alfons made a mark. There was talk of a nomination to the College of Cardinals.

But Alfons de Borja still owed service to the king and, despite some independent views, was not to be seduced into the enemy camp. In 1442 Alfonso finally made good his claim to the Neapolitan throne and Eugenius, stubborn though he was, could no longer withhold recognition. A powerful Spanish kingdom now existed on the southern border of papal lands and mutual interest now pointed to a pact between Alfonso and the pope. In 1443 the papal legate Cardinal Scarampo came to an agreement with the king's representative Alfons de Borja at Terracina. Pope Eugenius agreed to confirm Alfonso as King of Naples, and in return Alfonso at last formally recognized Eugenius as the true pope. Alfonso also promised to protect the papal states from the ravages of Francesco Sforza who, with his rival mercenaries, the *condottieri* Niccolò Piccinino and Fortebraccio, was rapidly turning all central Italy into a battlefield. In return, the pope invested Alfonso with the papal cities of Terracina and Benevento for life.

Alfons de Borja now had his reward. In 1444 he was elevated to the Sacred College, becoming Cardinal-Priest of Santi Quattro Coronati in Rome.

ALPHONSVS BORGIA. VALEN
NVS SETAB.ITANVS. A MARTINO
PP. S. VALENTINVS EPISCOP'
ELECTVS FVIT ANNO DÑI
1429. QVI AB EVGENIO 4°

CARDINALIS CREATVS TAN
DEM AD SVMMI PONTIFICA
TVS APICEN PERVENIT NV
CVPATVS CALIXTVS TER
TIVS ANNO. 1455.

CHAPTER TWO
CALIXTUS III: FOUNDER OF THE BORGIA FORTUNES

I N 1445 CARDINAL ALFONS BORGIA – AS HE WAS NOW known to his Italian colleagues – arrived in Rome and took his place in the Sacred College. He was in his sixty-seventh year, an elderly man by any account in this age of war and famine and plague. But it was a vigorous old age; his health was good, apart from attacks of the gout, and his strong frame was not undermined by debauchery. The portraits show a sturdy figure with the well-known Borgia features: a head of receding curves, domed forehead, prominent nose, heavy jowl, teeth slightly protruding, and the chin in retreat. Not a handsome face, but the watchful grey eyes suggested steady judgment and clear thought. The titular church of Quattro Coronati was attached to a medieval palace, standing in vineyards and gardens, a quiet, almost rural place, within the city walls but far from the Vatican and the papal court. A place of repose, it must have seemed, for the retirement of a world-weary statesman.

Rome too seemed old but, unlike the cardinal, without vigour, a city of ruins, broken-backed, suffering with the sufferings of the papacy. For over a century the pontiff had deserted Rome for Avignon. Without its master, the city declined, a dilapidated huddle of medieval tenements around crooked alleyways, without order or beauty. 'The most noisome of cities,' Petrarch had called it, 'the sink of iniquity, the cesspit of the world.' The antiquities of the classical age had been lost or shattered. Marble from the Capitol was crushed and burned for lime. The Lateran palace was in ruins, the Vatican in urgent need of repair. Pope Martin V, who restored the papacy to the city, for eleven years wandered from building to building, seeking a habitable palace. The population had dwindled to about 25,000. Most of the large area within the Aurelian wall had reverted to rough pasturage. 'Owing to the absence

Alfons de Borja was elected Pope Calixtus III eleven years after his arrival in Rome.

of the pope,' wrote the biographer of Eugenius IV, 'the city had become like a village of cowherds; sheep and cattle wandered through the streets to the very spot now occupied by the merchants' stalls.' The Capitol and the Forum had become Monte Capra and Campo Vaccino – 'Goat Hill' and 'Cow Field' – their origins and history completely neglected. The inhabitants, booted and cloaked like peasants, looked to foreigners no better than rustic herdsmen.

Pope Martin, himself a Roman from the powerful, patrician family of the Colonna, began the work of repair. The city walls were patched up and some of the bridges over the Tiber made serviceable. Eugenius, in his turbulent, angry pontificate, managed to keep some restoration going on. A few streets and piazzas were paved. The hucksters and their stalls were removed from the Portico of the Pantheon, and the building restored. In a gesture of confidence Eugenius commissioned from

Rome, a city of ruins where animals grazed in the Forum, had been without effective government for nearly a century when the new cardinal of Santi Quattro Coronati arrived there in 1445.

The martyrdom of St Peter, detail from the bronze doors of St Peter's Basilica by Antonio Filarete, commissioned by Pope Eugenius IV. The doors were installed in the year of Cardinal Borgia's arrival in the Eternal City and were the first Renaissance works of art to be seen there.

Filarete the bronze doors for St Peter's Basilica, completed and installed in the year of Cardinal Borgia's arrival. But prosperity in Rome depended too much on the presence of the papal court, a dronelike city almost without industry or manufactures, living dangerously off imported wealth. Factions competed strenuously for influence and power. The great families, the most important being the Orsini and the Colonna, carried on a dedicated rivalry, facing up to each other from their estates on either side of the Tiber. And among the Roman populace there had always been a violent, unruly republican element, which clung to the ancient freedoms guaranteed by the city's communal constitution, and threatened intermittent danger to popes and patricians alike. Gangs of bully boys prowled the streets; beatings, robbery, rape, murders were the commonplace; bodies were washed ashore on the river banks, awaiting identification.

The pope was never quite safe in this city that depended on him, nor was Rome secure under the pontiff's cloak. The papal states, weakly organized but strategically placed, in a belt across the middle of Italy, were a mark for every upstart or ambitious prince. Mercenary generals, the *condottieri*, pulled by land hunger or the hope of treasure, harried the environs of Rome and threatened the city itself. Angry citizens, subjected to violence or siege, turned on their master. In June 1434, a citizens' uprising drove Pope Eugenius from the city, forcing him to flee down river in a boat, hidden under a shield to avoid the missiles. For nine years the pope was in exile from Rome while the Patrimony of St Peter and the Campagna reeled under the blows of contending generals. The terrible warrior-priest Giovanni Vitelleschi undertook to subdue the city and the countryside on the pope's behalf and instituted a spectacular bloodletting. He reduced the opposing barons by alliance or by force. He made treaties with those he could not reach, but any he could touch he utterly destroyed by fire and sword. He executed the Prefect Jacopo of Vico head downwards in his own castle. Another fighting baron whom Vitelleschi overtook was strung up casually on a handy olive tree. In the Alban hills he set about the Savelli family and left their stronghold an utter ruin. That should have served as a warning. When the important Colonna town of Palestrina surrendered, Vitelleschi ordered the whole place to be razed, the houses thrown down block by block, even to the stones of the cathedral. Then he turned on Rome, which received him with olive branches, with gifts and with terror. He entered in armour, the city elders leading his horse by the bridle, while twelve youths held a golden canopy above his head. He prayed at San Lorenzo, then got down to vengeance. Poncelletto, leader of the populace against Eugenius, was dragged through the city from the Capitol, torn apart with red-hot pincers and then quartered in the Campo dei Fiori.

Vitelleschi fell as many tyrants have done, through the jealousy and fear of his own party. He was tricked and poisoned, so it is said, by the pope's new favourite, Cardinal Scarampo. For Rome, to exchange Scarampo for Vitelleschi was no great advantage. Though hideously cruel, Vitelleschi had a certain stern probity about him, and upheld a savage justice. The new tyrant possessed most of the vices of the old, and perhaps fewer virtues. No wonder the city and the lands around

Five powers dominated the Italian peninsula: Venice, Milan, Florence, Naples and the papacy.

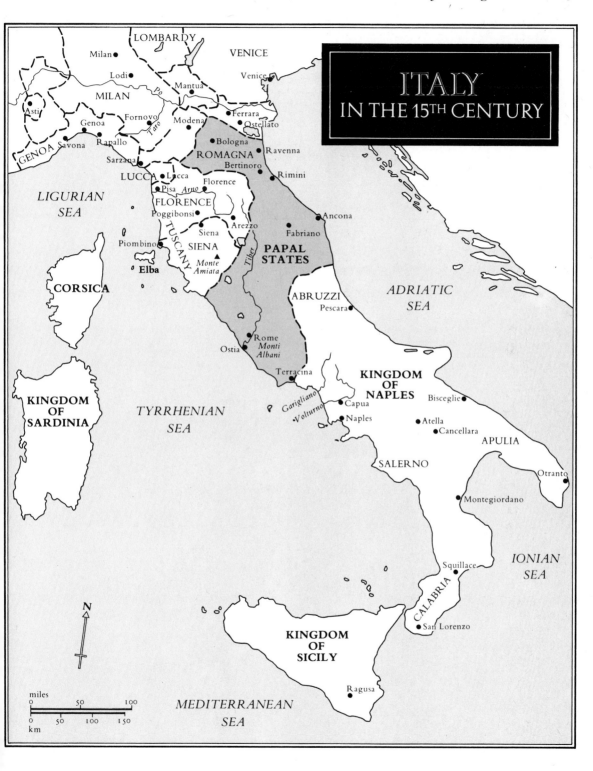

ITALY
IN THE 15TH CENTURY

THE PAPAL
STATES

Po

Bologna

Imola

Faenza

Forlì

ROMAGNA

Cesena

Via Flaminia

Pesaro

Fano

Urbino

Senigallia

Ancona

*ADRIATIC
SEA*

Pisa

Arno

Florence

Siena

Via Cassia

Pienza

Perugia

Assisi

THE MARCHES

Camerino

Fermo

Foligno

Ascoli

Todi

UMBRIA

Spoleto

Orvieto

Tiber

Narni

Lake Bolsena

Montefiascone

Capodimonte

Soriano

Orte

Viterbo

Bassanello

PATRIMONY
OF ST PETER

Civita Castellana

Nepi

*Monte
Argentario*

SABINA

Tolfa

*Lake
Bracciano*

Trevignano

Civitavecchia

Bracciano

Anguillara

Cerveteri

Ceri

Vicovaro

Monte Mario

Tivoli

Subiaco

Rome

Genazzano

Ostia

*Monte
Cavo*

Palestrina

Velletri

CAMPAGNA

LATIUM

Via Appia

Sermoneta

Fossanuova

Terracina

*TYRRHENIAN
SEA*

Benevento

Naples

miles
0   20   40

0   40   80
km

called out for the return of the pope. An observer surveying the country-side counted more than thirty castles destroyed, the estates in ruins, and hardly a poor peasant in sight. Poggio, writing of Eugenius' time, saw a 'country scourged by war, the depopulated and ruined towns, the devastated fields, the roads infested by robbers, more than fifty places partly destroyed, partly sacked by armies, a prey to every species of revenge. Many destitute citizens have been sold into slavery; many have died of hunger in prisons.' Such was the inheritance to which Pope Eugenius returned in September 1443. And such was the forlorn state of Rome that greeted the arrival of Cardinal Alfons Borgia in 1445.

At first, it seemed that the new cardinal was seeking the quiet life appropriate to his age, insulated among the meadows of Quattro Coronati from Roman turmoil and Church intrigue. Though he now answered to the Italianized name of Borgia, that was the only Italian thing about him. His servants and retinue were all Spaniards. Tucked away in his old fortified palace between the Colosseum and the Lateran, he looked for no preferment and seemed to avoid the papal court. For a prince of the Church he was not rich. His only income came from his bishopric in Valencia, and amounted to 6500 Aragonese pounds a year. Nor did he alter the rule of his life, which bound him to one benefice at a time. Most great churchmen were enthusiastic pluralists, collecting as many profitable benefices as they could lay hands on. But Alfons would not hold an office *in commendam*, milking the revenues of places he would never even visit. The humanist Platina praised him for this unusual devotion to canon law; Alfons Borgia, he said, was 'a very upright man, and to be applauded for one thing above all: when he was a bishop or a cardinal he never kept any benefice *in commendam*. Because he said he would be content with one wife, and that a virgin – his Church of Valencia – as canon law ordains.' The humanist praised him, but these foreign, sober ways were not likely to please many of his fellow cardinals. Such honest behaviour reproved their luxury and immorality. Nor was he likely to please the Roman populace; for among the things that they hated most were Spaniards, rectitude and a lean purse.

In the last years of his reign, the sick Pope Eugenius saw one matter that marred a successful conclusion to his troubled and obstinate pontificate. The question of papal supremacy was not quite settled. The anti-Roman faction still held sway in the unfinished business of the Council

The pope, as temporal head of the papal states, was one of the most important princes of the Italian peninsula. His dominion, a disorderly network of semi-independent cities and provinces, stretched across central Italy from Terracina in the south to Ancona on the Adriatic coast and as far north as Bologna.

of Basle; a schismatic pope Felix V lived, neglected, in Lausanne; and
the German Empire under Frederick III had not yet acknowledged
obedience to Rome. The instinct of the German Church had been to
win a freedom from Roman interference such as the French and
English Churches already possessed, and many of the electors who ruled
the German principalities were hostile to papal claims. But Frederick,
trying to maintain his position over the wayward electors of his chaotic
empire, had as much interest as the pope in the idea of a central authority,
and eventually, by a mixture of bribes and argument, he was won over
to the papal cause. The electors and the papal legates agreed on a
declaration of obedience, subject to certain conditions, at Frankfort in
1446. In Rome, a commission of cardinals met to examine the grounds
of the German treaty. Strong opposition came from within the commission, especially from the two elderly Spaniards, Juan de Torquemada
(uncle of the infamous inquisitor) and Borgia. To them, the Frankfort
declaration seemed to give too much away to the German Church. A
long wrangle began between the papal legates, practitioners of the
political art of the possible, and the majority of the cardinals, upholders
of a stricter authority. But Eugenius was dying and very anxious to have
the matter settled. The opposition among the cardinals gave way. On
7 February 1447, the pope received the German Church into obedience.
On 23 February he died, but not before he had dictated a protest that
the concessions to Germany had been wrung from a mind darkened by
illness, and might be considered null and void if found to contradict the
teaching of the Fathers or the rights of the Pontiff.

'An old age full of majesty,' wrote Cardinal Aeneas Sylvius Piccolomini of Eugenius; 'he despised money, loved virtue; he knew no
fear; stern and hard towards enemies, he was benign towards those in
his confidence.' Aeneas Sylvius Piccolomini, whose career owed much
to Eugenius, did not add that the pope was obstinate, rash, meddlesome
and politically incompetent, that his reign had seen schism, wars, flight,
exile, continuous trouble. No doubt the cooler-headed Alfons Borgia,
a newcomer to Roman politics, instead of triumph saw the infinitely
tangled skein of rival interests that all but ensnared the central offices
of the Church. He would have noted the limits of papal action, the
necessity to pander to kings, the insecurity of the pope's lands, the confusion of temporal and spiritual, the ever-present temptation to fight

secular battles with spiritual weapons and an impoverished treasury. And when one pope died, all had to be begun again, while the princes circled like beasts of prey.

So the predators gathered when Eugenius died, and chief among them was Borgia's former master, King Alfonso, who in the last days of the dying pope had sprung from Naples to Tivoli, posing as protector of the papal states, but in reality seeking to influence the election of the new pope. These hopes were dashed by one of the shortest conclaves in history. After only two days, a small, skinny, ugly Italian emerged as Pope Nicholas V. Tommaso Parentucelli was a good choice. He was a simple, unaffected man, no friend to pomp and luxury. He was a good speaker with a wry and ready wit, sometimes sharpened by fierce attacks of gout. He was a famous scholar, so learned that it was said of him 'if he does not know, then it is unknown to human knowledge'. Cosimo de' Medici was his friend, the humanist writers and scholars were his colleagues, all the world of intellectual curiosity was his province. He was the first humanist to occupy the chair of St Peter, the first Renaissance pope.

But best of all, from the point of view of the papal cause, Tommaso Parentucelli had given no hostages to fortune. He was the son of an ordinary doctor and no factions gathered about his name, as they did around the great princes of the Church, the Orsini, the Colonna and the like. He himself had been a cardinal for only two months and owed nothing to any of the warring parties within the Sacred College. 'It will disturb the pride of many', the new pope remarked, 'that a priest who was only good for ringing bells has become pope.' If his election was as a result of compromise, then it was a good compromise. 'Storms are gathering round,' Piccolomini told Nicholas, 'the sailors will soon be tested by the waves.' If the ship of the Church was running in heavy seas, at least the new captain was an able, experienced mariner.

Alfons Borgia had taken his part in the election of the new pope, but his modest role rated no comment from the chroniclers. Nor had they much to say about his Spanish establishment living quietly in the far reaches of Santi Quattro Coronati. We know, however, that by 1449 three young Spanish blades were evident about town. These were the nephews of the Spanish cardinal: the sons of his sister Isabella, Pedro Luis and Rodrigo, and their cousin Luis Juan de Mila. The year of their arrival is not certain. Jofré de Borja, the intemperate father of the brothers, had died in 1437, leaving his widow for the time being in poor circumstances. It was natural enough for the lads to leave Aragon for their uncle's household in Rome, where chances for preferment were good. The eldest boy, Pedro Luis, was marked out, according to Spanish custom, for a military career; the two younger boys were destined for the Church. In 1449 the youngest, Rodrigo, was eighteen. They were all, said one reporter, 'most splendid young men, devoted to one another'. Rodrigo, the future pope, was schooled by Gaspare da Verona before going on to the University of Bologna, a student of canon law like his uncle before him. Young Rodrigo had the Borgia intellect and practical ability, but something else besides not seen in the old cardinal. 'He is well-formed', Gaspare wrote of his pupil, 'and speaks with honeyed eloquence. His attraction for beautiful women, and the manner in which he excites them – and they fall in love with him – is quite remarkable. He attracts them more powerfully than a magnet does iron.' This appeal to women was the more remarkable because Rodrigo had the Borgia features in full measure: the moonlike head, the plump cheeks, the beak of a nose, the receding chin.

The story of fifteenth-century Rome was a chronicle written by the humanists, and they gave most credit to those who shared their ideals. Alfons Borgia was not counted among this number. A casual inspection revealed an elderly church lawyer, of severe aspect, and a Spaniard to boot, a race judged in Italy to be bloodthirsty, greedy and ignorant. Cardinal Borgia was indeed what training and long experience had made him – a dry administrator – and he gave few signs that he shared the humanists' passion for antiquity and for the revival of ancient learning. But he was a man of strong intelligence and admired intellectual power in others. In so many ways authoritarian and conservative, he had a strange liking for daring minds. Lorenzo Valla had risked a trial for heresy by exposing the fraudulent nature of the Donation of Constantine, a document on which the pope's temporal claims rested. Alfons had met him at King Alfonso's court and remained on affectionate terms with him ever after. Later, when he had the power, he gave Valla preferment and honours. And to show that his respect for brains was without prejudice, Alfons was also a friend and supporter of Poggio Bracciolini, the fierce scholarly opponent of Valla.

OPPOSITE Alfons de Borja kneeling before St Idelfonsus. King Alfonso sent his court painter Jaime Baco, or Jacomart, to see his old Vice-Chancellor in Rome where he received a commission to paint a retable for the Borgia family chapel at Játiva. The central panel of Jacomart's retable was destroyed in this century but the side panels survived, including this earliest known portrait of a Borgia. The likeness is certainly authentic, as Alfons' features appear little changed in Sano di Pietro's portrait (facing page 37), painted some eight years later.

OVERLEAF 'The Disputation of St Catherine' by Bernardino Pinturicchio. One of a series of frescoes in the Borgia Apartment in the Vatican commissioned by Pope Alexander VI. The story depicted is of Catherine of Alexandria disputing before the pagan emperor Maximinus. Cesare and Lucrezia were probably the models for the central figures of emperor and saint and, on the right, the mounted horseman is thought to be Juan Borgia. The boy and girl in the foreground, standing in front of a bearded man, are thought to be Jofré and Sancia.

O PASTOR · dE NIO · AL MIO · POPOL · XPIANO
A TE · di · SIENA · ORMAI · LA CURA · RENdo
FA · CH · AI LEI · VOLA · OGNI · TUO · SENSO HUMANO

VERGINE · MADRE · A CIO · FAR A · CONSORTE
SE L TUO · CALISTO · E dENIO · A TANTO · dONO
A SIENA · NÕ · TORAMI · ALTRO · CHE · MORTE

CALISTVS · III · SANVS · PETRI · dE SENIS · PIXE

So the Spanish youths, the three nephews of Cardinal Borgia, came to maturity in the Roman air permeated not only with the old stench of corruption, deceit and bloodshed, but also with new and sweeter aromas hinting of love and courtliness and intellectual curiosity. In the early years of Nicholas' pontificate, the world looked fortunate for Rome and the papacy. The passage of time, and papal diplomacy, had resolved troubles with a certainty that seemed triumphant. The limping progress of the Council of Basle was finally halted and the Church reconciled under papal authority. In the same year, 1449, Felix V – the last anti-pope – surrendered his tiara. The jubilee year of the mid-century was approaching, with an expectation of renewed religious fervour and a great influx of pilgrims to Rome, bringing with them gifts and donations to replenish the papal coffers. Rome itself was pacified for the moment. Nicholas had recognized the city's autonomy and taken clerical hands off the municipal taxes. The rulers of the Italian states were in a rough equilibrium. In the papal states Nicholas quickly set about a reform of administration and taxation. The papal treasury, deep in debt for so long, began to fill up. And not least of his many achievements, Nicholas attracted to Rome the best artists, the best builders, the best scholars, and put them all to work.

The jubilee year of 1450 found a city at peace. The pilgrims came to Rome like clouds of starlings, as one observer wrote, or like swarms of ants. It is reported that over a thousand inns were kept busy. In the streets, the press of the throng was so great that the weak or the unwary were in danger of their lives. On one occasion more than a hundred people were thrust off the bridge of Sant' Angelo, a tragedy commemorated by two chapels erected at the entrances to the bridge. In the overcrowded city, the pope himself became so afraid of the ever-present risk of the plague that he fled to Fabriano and shut himself behind locked doors. But in Rome the offerings flowed into the chests of the Camera Apostolica and at last the funds were available to begin the great work of artistic creation by which Nicholas hoped to transform Rome from a city of ruins to a place of imperial splendour, the visible emblem of a mighty and triumphant papacy.

Craftsmen and artists came cheerfully from all corners of Christendom, and magnificent plans were unveiled. Public works were put in hand – streets cleared and paved, buildings restored, aqueducts patched

Sano di Pietro's portrait of Pope Calixtus III, as protector of the city of Siena, commissioned by the Sienese in gratitude for the pope's intervention against Jacopo Piccinino whose breach of the Italian League threatened the peace of the peninsula.

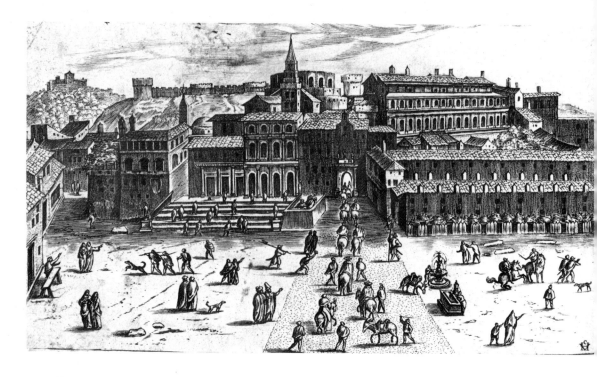

up, fountains erected. Walls and fortifications were renewed and strengthened. Under the influence of the great architect Leon Battista Alberti, Nicholas planned a vast unity of buildings around the Vatican which would incorporate the pope's palace, the Citadel and the Basilica of St Peter. A start was made. Venerable old buildings were swept away by the impetuous new enthusiasm. With an equal hurry the painters and scholars were at work. Fra Angelico began the frescoes in the papal chapel of San Lorenzo. To accommodate all the writers and scholars, positions in the Curia were multiplied dangerously so that any minor pedant with a taste for Latin or Greek and an introduction to papal circles could be given a profitable berth. Nonetheless, the valuable work of recovery and translation went on. Under Nicholas V the Vatican Library grew into the storehouse of European knowledge, a depository for the classical inheritence of the western mind.

'If the authority of the Holy See were visibly displayed in majestic buildings,' said Nicholas on his deathbed, 'all the world would revere it.' It was a noble impulse, to raise up the Chair of St Peter on monuments of the imagination. But this secular ideal of grandeur had little to do with the necessary reform of the Church. A resplendent papal

Old St Peter's and the Vatican, Rome. Nicholas V's ambitious plans for a vast unity of buildings around the Vatican, reflecting the power of the pope, were only partly implemented during his pontificate. He added the new wing to the Vatican that houses the Borgia Apartment.

court still reigned over too much clerical sloth and apathy, too many greedy, immoral and ignorant priests. The familiar abuses abounded. The flowering at the centre distracted attention from the disease in roots and branches. Nicholas, an honest, moral and upright pope, made Rome the intellectual and artistic capital of the west; yet in this world a man was often esteemed more for learning than sanctity, more for wit than morality. At the highest level, the way in the Church was opened for worldly men, and they entered in abundant numbers. The dangers and limits of this secular vision of the papacy were soon made clear. In 1453 Stefano Porcari, a well-born Roman whose enthusiasm for ancient learning had received rewards and every encouragement from the pope, became so infatuated with the republicanism of his classical reading that he decided to rid Rome once and for all of the authoritarian theocracy which the papacy had imposed upon the city. Porcari proclaimed himself to be the man who 'would for ever deliver the city from the yoke of priests'. He made plans to arrest the pope and set fire to the Vatican during High Mass, and it was said that he had brought a gold chain to fetter Pope Nicholas. But the plot failed and Porcari, prophet of Roman freedom, was discovered hiding in his sister's linen chest. When the news of the revolt spread about, atrocious rumours terrified the clergy. Porcari was hurried to trial and rushed from there to his execution, hanged before dawn in a tower of the Castel Sant'Angelo.

Porcari was an inept revolutionary, with little of the demented grandeur of Cola di Rienzo, his republican predecessor in Rome. But even such a weak uprising might have warned the papal court. Not only ambitious republicans resented the ostentatious secular power of the pope and the Curia. Plain citizens throughout Christendom objected to a corrupt and venal lower clergy too often unchecked by the great men of the Church, whose lives demonstrated more worldly luxury than spiritual fervour. The Porcari revolt warned of the dangers of the drift towards secular power; a far more serious event showed the limits of that power. Five months after the Roman uprising, on 29 May 1453, Constantinople, the great city of the Eastern Empire, fell to the Turks of Mohammed II. The Moslem army was at the gate of Europe and showed every intention of pushing on. The papacy, which had not managed to stir the princes of Europe into any action to avert the threat, now failed to take any action to put right the tragedy. Frederick III of Germany, whom Nicholas had recently crowned Holy Roman Emperor, caught birds on his country estate. Domestic troubles ensnared the other kings of Europe as surely as the nets of Frederick trapped the birds. Pope Nicholas V was accused of regretting the loss of Greek classical manuscripts more than the loss of Greek religion and Greek land.

When the dying Nicholas reviewed his reign, he found it necessary to justify his works. He pointed to the splendour of Rome, to the advancement of learning, to the strength of the papal states, to the amity of the Italian princes, to the general well-being of the land, and he concluded that the Church 'had emerged from her time of trouble and entered into the period of her triumph'. When he died, in March 1455, this seemed a plausible conclusion, and he was sincerely mourned by a great many in Rome and in the Church. It was an odd pontificate. Neither Nicholas nor his humanist followers knew quite what they had done. Nicholas had celebrated a secular triumph, and thereafter the pope was condemned to follow the path of the Italian Renaissance prince, condemned to get down in the dirt where secular politics were played and besmirch an already stained Church with the muck of princely ambition.

'He who enters the conclave a pope,' says the old Roman proverb, 'leaves it a cardinal.' On the death of Nicholas, fifteen cardinals entered the conclave, of whom seven were Italians. Intrigue had begun long before, during the illness of the pope, and the knowledgeable agreed that the contest once again would be between Orsini and Colonna. Preliminary manoeuvres had seemed to favour the Colonna faction, but the pope's long sickness gave the Orsini time to rally, and their astute leader, the wordly Cardinal Orsini, had won the support of Venice and King Alfonso of Naples. So the conclave began in deadlock. For a time opinion swayed towards Cardinal Capranica, a very worthy choice; but he was a Roman, a Colonna supporter, and therefore objectionable to Cardinal Orsini. Since the Roman factions blocked each other, attention turned next to an outsider. The name of Cardinal Bessarion began to attract votes, for he was another pious and learned man. Moreover, as a Greek and a representative also of the Eastern Church, he was the man most likely to set in motion a crusade against the all-conquering

Turks. But Bessarion still wore a flowing beard in the Eastern fashion, and this evidence of Greek practice stirred up ancient rancour in some jealous hearts of the West. 'Shall a newcomer and a Greek have the Latin Church?' sneered a French cardinal. 'Bessarion has not yet shaved his beard, and shall we make him our head?'

Time passed. Coffers of food bearing the cardinals' arms went back and forth before the bowing populace, but no word came from the conclave. The Roman watchers grew impatient. The ambassadors sent in urgent messages, pressing for an early decision. Rome was unsettled and the *condottiere* Piccinino threatened. The third scrutiny yet again failed to reveal the necessary majority. Finally, in some desperation, eyes turned on a man to whom no one could object. The Cardinal of Quattro Coronati was a foreigner, it is true; but he was an austere figure of good reputation, he was a follower of no important Church faction, and best of all he was unlikely to reign long. He was seventy-seven and no longer in very good health. On 8 April 1455, Alfons Borgia was elected pope, taking the name Calixtus III.

'See what the indecision of our Italians has brought us to,' the Florentine envoy complained to Piero de' Medici. 'The Catalans rule here now, and God knows how it will suit their nature.' Italian national feeling was hurt. Florence, Venice and Genoa bewailed the choice. Spaniards were not popular at the best of times, and no one could forget that the new pope had spent much of his life in the service of Alfonso of Naples. The possible conjunction between a Spanish pope and an ambitious Spanish monarch who ruled the lower half of Italy brought fear to other Italian rulers. Gloomy voices prophesied an influx of detested Catalans, a removal of the papal court from Rome, another schism. On the other hand, for Calixtus himself there was generally favourable comment. 'An old man of honourable and virtuous life,' the Procurator reported to the Grand Master of the Teutonic Order. 'His nature is peaceable and kindly' wrote a representative from Siena.

On 20 April, the day of Calixtus' coronation, Roman unease broke out into a factional brawl. In the morning, the new pope walked in solemn procession from the Vatican Palace to St Peter's. Before him went the emblem of earthly frailty, the priest with the burning tow, chanting 'Holy Father, thus does the glory of the world pass away.' Calixtus celebrated Mass, then stepped out to an open-air platform where the aged Cardinal Colonna was waiting to replace the mitre with the tiara: 'Receive the tiara ornamented with three crowns, and know that you are the father of princes and kings, guide of the terrestial orb and Vicar of Christ on earth.' Afterwards, the newly crowned pope rode to the Lateran, to take possession of his temporal power and to be enthroned as Bishop of Rome. This ceremonial progress showed the pope to the city for the first time, and was traditionally done with great splendour. Eighty bishops accompanied the pope, robed in white and mounted on horses with white trappings. Behind them came the nobles, the city fathers, the ambassadors of all Europe, and a vast host of citizens, walking to the sound of trumpet and drum, while twenty grooms leading white horses brought up the rear. From St Peter's the route went over the bridge of Sant'Angelo, winding into the streets of the old city.

Woodcut of Rome as it was in the early sixteenth century, showing the landmarks Calixtus passed on his ceremonial route through the city after his coronation in St Peter's.

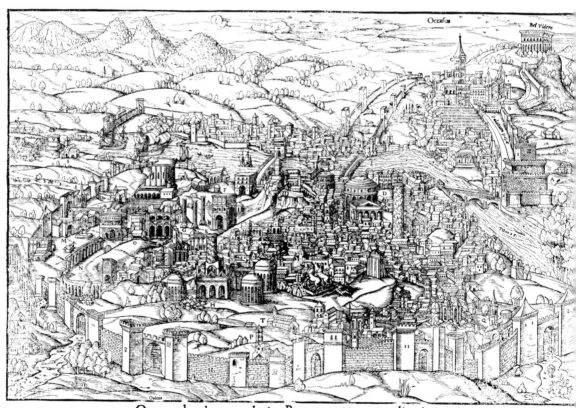

Quorundam locorum huius Romanæ picturæ explicatio.

A Moles Adriani, hodie Castellum S. Angeli.
B Palatium papæ.
C Ecclesia S. Petri.
D Columna Antoniana, & è regione eius, Maria rotunda.
E Columna Adriani.
F Arcus Septimij.
G Templū pacis, ubi quoq̃ stare debuerat Colloßen ingēs ædificiū, sed loci angustia exclusit.
H Thermæ Diocletianæ.
I Pons Sixti.
K Capitoliū.
L S. Bartholomei insula, iuxta pontem Sixti.
M S. Iohannes Lateranus.
N Aquæductus.
O Arcus Titi & Vespasiani.
P S. Susanna.
Q S. Maria de populo.
R S. Laurentius.
S S. Sebastianus.
T S. Vitalis.
V Caput bouis.

Leaving the Capitol, it traversed the deserted Forum, passed under the Arch of Titus on the way to the Colosseum, and from there went on to the Lateran.

All was well until the procession reached Monte Giordano, an Orsini enclave standing at the edge of the Jewish quarter. Here, according to custom, the rabbi offered Calixtus a bible, which the pope took and dropped with the traditional words: 'We recognize the Law, but not your interpretation of it.' The crowd, as usual, jostled to retrieve the richly bound volume, and fights developed. The pope's horse reared and nearly threw him, but he dismounted and took refuge in a house, resting a little before he went on to the Lateran. Meanwhile, the brawl spread and soon engulfed the neighbourhood. City factions, full of time-honoured hatreds, pitched in, and the brawl became a battle. Napoleone Orsini took the chance to rally his supporters and attack an old enemy, the followers of the Count of Anguillara. The battle surged towards the Lateran, where cries of resentment against a foreign pope mingled with the war chants of the factions. Inside the Basilica, din and confusion so disturbed the ceremonial that Calixtus had to order Cardinal Orsini to curb his unruly family. In the streets, houses were sacked and set on fire and several people killed. The reign began sourly, and for this Calixtus did not forgive the Orsini clan.

But Calixtus was careful, at first, to do nothing provocative, and the fears raised by his election soon died away. A letter from the Archbishop of Florence noted the change for the better:

> The minds of men have been reassured by more mature reflection, and by the reputation which he bears for goodness, penetration and impartiality. Moreover, Calixtus has bound himself by a solemn document – a copy of which I have seen – to devote all his powers, with the advice of the cardinals, to the war against the Turks and the reconquest of Constantinople.

For a man in his dotage, Calixtus had made an energetic beginning, and the Crusade against the Turks became the dominating passion of his pontificate. 'I was elected', reads one of his inscriptions, 'to annihilate the enemies of the faith.' The task that, in the years before 1453, Eugenius IV had neglected for wars and politics, and Nicholas V neglected for art and learning, Calixtus took up, even though the burden was almost impossible, with the single-mindedness of the

Spanish, whose national destiny had been determined by the Reconquest of Spain from the infidel Moors.

From the start the case seemed desperate. Mohammed II, an intelligent, ambitious young prince, was not content to stop at Constantinople. His armies threatened to overwhelm the Balkans. Already, Turkish control of Mediterranean sea routes had led to a stagnation of trade. No help could be expected from the major powers of Europe, preoccupied with local affairs, seeking wealth and national aggrandizement at the expense of neighbours. The seafaring republics of Venice and Genoa preferred to compromise with the Turks for the sake of trade. For all Europe the crusading ideal was a bad dream, a memory of centuries of failure, of fruitless suffering in barren lands far from home. Only the papacy had the stature and the conviction to lead the defence of Christendom. Nothing in the life of Calixtus was so noble or tragic as this stubborn enterprise. In his darkened room the old pope, bedridden with gout, dictated by candlelight, and with frantic haste dispatched his appeals and his legates to every part of Europe. 'If I forget thee, O Jerusalem, let my right hand be forgotten. Let my tongue cleave to my jaws if I do not remember thee.' Never had the biblical promise been so sincerely meant. Mendicant sandals stirred the dust on a thousand roads, taking the message to marketplace and pulpit. The bells of Christian churches rang out three times a day, a continual reminder of the need for prayer. Tithes were levied for the Crusade, and indulgences sold. The papal treasury, well-stocked from the prudent management of Nicholas V, was drained. The pope's own resources were thrown in. His household was run with the utmost simplicity and everything saved went to the great cause. 'Sell them for the Crusade,' he is said to have exclaimed, seeing the silver salt cellars of Nicholas, 'earthenware is good enough for me.' The most gorgeous papal tiara was sold; jewels, treasure, Church estates were disposed of. For reasons of economy, the myriad of minor humanists introduced by Nicholas were thrown out of their soft places in the Curia, and the artists were diverted to martial business. Painters designed battle standards and sculptors carved marble cannon balls.

In May 1455, within a few weeks of his election, Calixtus was already hiring galleys. Then, as cash flowed in, he established a shipbuilding yard on the Ripa Grande, right in the heart of Rome. Towards the end of the year the first squadron was ready and placed under the command of the Bishop of Tarragona. But this cleric was nothing but a piratical rogue who betrayed his trust by lending his forces to King Alfonso for a raid on Genoa. The bishop was speedily replaced by the bellicose Cardinal Scarampo, who had proved his fighting ability under Pope Eugenius. In May 1456, Scarampo set out from Ostia with the pope's blessing and a fleet of sixteen galleys and twenty-five other ships. Alfonso had promised reinforcements for the Crusade, but his action against Genoa had shown where his true interest lay, so Scarampo, having lingered in Naples too long, was forced to leave for the Aegean with little help from Alfonso. The duplicity of the king whom Calixtus had formerly served so well enraged the pope, and led to a bitter enmity on both sides. Scarampo, however, lived up to his tough reputation. Using the island of Rhodes as a base, he attacked in the Aegean, clearing Turkish garrisons from Lemnos, Thassos and Samothrace, and defeating the Turkish fleet at Mytilene. If reinforcements had been sent, it might have been possible to blockade the Dardanelles, striking at the heart of the Turkish empire. But nothing came, neither troops nor ships. Only in eastern Europe, in the lands directly in the path of the Turkish advance, was there temporary success. A triumvirate of notable men – Cardinal Carvajal, the papal legate, Fra Capistrano, the preacher,

The Roman port of Ostia, on the mouth of the Tiber, from which Cardinal Scarampo set out for the crusade against the Turks.

and John Hunyadi, the Hungarian general – combined to halt the Turks. In July 1456, Hunyadi broke the Moslem army before the walls of Belgrade. This, and the determined resistance of the Albanian hero Scanderbeg, gave Calixtus some hope. For him, Scanderbeg was 'the Athlete of God' and Hunyadi was 'the greatest man seen in the world these last 300 years'; in his joy Calixtus instituted the Feast of the Transfiguration, so it is said, to celebrate these Christian victories. The relief was short-lived. In August, Hunyadi caught the plague from the pestilential bodies rotting in the Belgrade streets, and died; two months later the valiant old friar Giovanni Capistrano followed him to the grave. Athens fell to the Turks in 1458; Serbia and most of the Balkans went in the next two years. The Greek islands tumbled one by one. In 1470 Venice lost her Aegean trading stronghold at Negroponte. Ten years later Italy had the shock of seeing a Turkish raiding force at Otranto on the Calabrian coast. 'The pope calls for help', wrote Aeneas Sylvius Piccolomini with sad truth, 'and no one listens to him; he threatens and no one is afraid.'

Bitterly frustrated in his crusading zeal, Calixtus found little relief in Italy. His reign had begun fortunately. The Italian zones of influence had been marked out at Lodi, in 1454. The adventurer Francesco Sforza was confirmed as Duke of Milan, and Milan, Venice and Florence were bound together in the Holy League, to keep the peace within Italy and to resist attack from without. Peace, however, meant that the formidable Venetian *condottiere* Jacopo Piccinino was out of a job. He had a mercenary army to support and an ambition to satisfy. He had seen how the *condottiere* Sforza had risen to a dukedom, and he expected great things for himself also. First, he turned his eye on Bologna and the Romagna, but being strongly opposed there, crossed the Appenines and made for Siena, the weakest of the Tuscan republics. Calixtus, angry that the peace should be broken by this marauding freebooter, sent the papal forces to the defence of Siena, while King Alfonso of Naples, ever anxious to exploit a weakness among rivals, gave help to Piccinino. The campaign dragged on, a matter for general aggravation and ruinous expense. The twist of plot, insinuation, argument and counter-argument was as tortuous as ever in Italian politics. At last, on receipt of a large bribe, which went towards the upkeep of his army, the brigand Piccinino agreed in May 1456 to leave Siena alone and withdraw to

Alfonso's lands in the south. 'You have a pope', Piccolomini wrote to the Sienese, 'who is very attached to your republic; you should seek to profit from this, because his energy is as great as his generosity, and nothing is dearer to him than justice.' But the agreement to buy off Piccinino had cost the Camera Apostolica 20,000 florins, and exacerbated still further the dislike between the pope and King Alfonso. Only the Sienese gave thanks, and in gratitude to Calixtus they commissioned from Sano di Pietro the portrait of the pope that still hangs in the Pinacoteca in Siena.

Nothing went right now between Alfonso and the pope. They shared the rancour of an old friendship gone sour, for which each held the other to blame. In the crooked paths of Italian polity, Alfonso's shifts and turns were no more devious or reprehensible than those of other rulers. He was not filled with the crusading spirit; neither was any other prince, inside or outside Italy. He was a foreign king ruling a volatile people in a notoriously changeable land. His aims were simple: to secure himself against enemies, to increase his power and territory at the expense of rivals, and to secure the succession. The failure of Calixtus to help towards these ends seemed stark ingratitude from a man who owed the king everything. Calixtus saw matters differently. When he had entered the service of the Church he ceased to be the king's man. And now he had assumed the office of Pontiff, he saw the good of Church and papacy overriding the wishes of the king. 'Let the King of Aragon', he admonished one envoy, 'rule his own kingdom, and leave us to administer the supreme Apostolate.' He had to endure peremptory orders or insults from the royal ambassadors. He saw the king's policy meddling in his crusading plans, the work of his heart. He was enraged by Alfonso's support for Piccinino. He feared an agreement between Naples and the Sforzas of the powerful Milanese duchy, which Alfonso attempted to seal by a double marriage alliance. The delicate balance of the Italian states, which the papacy since the days of Martin V had tried so hard to preserve, seemed likely to be broken by Alfonso's acts.

So Calixtus set himself against the king. He would not appoint the king's eleven-year-old grandson to be Bishop of Saragossa. The lad was the illegitimate son of the bastard Ferrante, and canon law debarred him from the priesthood. 'His Majesty should be aware', Calixtus wrote with haughty severity, 'that the pope may depose a king.' 'Let His

Holiness know', the king replied with hidden threat, 'that a king, if he wishes, can find a way to get rid of the pope.' When Lucrezia d'Alagno, Alfonso's young and beautiful mistress, came to Rome in 1457, the pope received her with great state, pronouncing the papal blessing in the presence of all the cardinals. But when Lucrezia, who wished to marry the king, begged the pope to annul the marriage between Alfonso and Queen Maria, Calixtus was adamant, protesting that he was bound to refuse 'so as not to go to hell with her'. And finally, as a last thrust at the enemy, Calixtus opposed the succession of Ferrante to the throne of Naples. Alfonso, the pope said, had been a constant torment to the papacy: 'Therefore, when he dies I will do my utmost to deliver my successor from such bondage by preventing the succession of Don Ferrante, the king's illegitimate son.'

The refusal to advance the interests of Alfonso's family contrasted very sharply with the pope's notorious partiality for his own clan. The nephews who had lived with him at Quattro Coronati were still in his household when he moved to the Vatican, and within months of his election Calixtus was looking for ways to reward them. In a secret consistory he announced his intention to make cardinals of Rodrigo and Luis Juan de Mila. The Sacred College was scandalized: the candidates were mere youths, hardly weaned from their university studies, as yet distinguished only in being the pope's kin; moreover, they were Spaniards. A year later, in 1456, when the late summer heat had emptied the city, Calixtus made the appointments and brought the two young cardinals – one was twenty-five, the other a little older – triumphantly from university at Bologna. Pedro Luis, the eldest nephew and the one marked out for a military career, was already commandant of the papal fort of Castel Sant'Angelo. Now he was advanced to become Captain General of the Church. This piece of Spanish nepotism was in no way mitigated in Italian eyes when it was seen that at least two of the Spanish *nipoti* were young men of ability. Calixtus immediately sent Rodrigo to be papal legate in the March of Ancona, a fractious part of the papal states where the ubiquitous hand of King Alfonso stirred up trouble. Rodrigo was a success. He recaptured Ascoli, pacified the region, and proved himself a good and popular administrator. His brother Pedro Luis had an equally difficult task to accomplish around Rome. Allied to the Colonna, he set about bringing the hated Orsini family to order.

By gaining control of strategic castles to the north of Rome, he prevented the Orsini from dominating the northern routes into the city, and thus kept them in check.

Heartened by the evidence of talent, Calixtus gave full rein to family feeling and piled his nephews with honours. Rodrigo became a commander in the papal army, President of the Sacra Rota – the ecclesiastical high court – and Vice-Chancellor of the Church, effectively the second man in the hierarchy of the Curia. Pedro Luis did as well from secular appointments. He collected the governorship of several small, strategic towns around Rome. He became Duke of Spoleto, Foligno and Orvieto. He became Governor of the Patrimony of St Peter, and in 1458 Prefect of Rome. Such a hectic progress was scandalous even by the standards of the time, and the general rumour whispered that Calixtus intended to carve out an Italian principality for his favourite. And the rumour seemed well-founded when Calixtus revived the ancient custom of crowning the Roman Prefect with a gold circlet. The admiring city fathers, well-rehearsed, burst out with perfect sycophancy that they hoped to see their new Prefect become King of Rome. Pedro Luis, an arrogant and cynical young man, gravely assured them that he studied to become Italian and wished to live in their fair country all his life.

The pope's nephews gained the most, but Calixtus also distributed certain key posts among minor members of the family. Juan de Borja, a galley captain, commanded the Roman port of Ostia. Miguel de Borja, another ex-sailor, held the castles of Orte and Soriano, while Galceran de Borja was Governor of Spoleto. The three nephews, in the forefront of Roman fashion, had a reputation for luxury and insolence, but in fact all the Borgia clan, great and small, was cordially detested by the Italians. Pedro Luis was considered particularly overbearing, a handsome, riotous adventurer, who attracted a parcel of Spanish desperadoes, and with them rode down justice, decency and good order. Catalans, as the Spaniards were generally called, got a bad press. 'Every day', wrote the chronicler, 'there were murders and brawls in the streets, and nothing but Catalans to be seen.' Spiteful anti-Spanish libels were broadcast. Vespasiano da Bisticci reported, quite untruthfully, that the papal jewels were to be seen decorating the stockings of Pedro Luis.

Nepotism was nothing new. The careful placing of *nipoti* was a calculated part of papal strategy, designed, in particular, to hold papal lands secure from the grasping hands of surrounding rulers. A pope, chosen from among elderly men, was unlikely to reign long. On his election he inherited, at best, governors and administrators only cautiously committed to his interests, and at worst, men downright inimical to him and all his works. In the short years of his pontificate, he strove to replace these men with others closer to his heart, and few answered this purpose better than members of his own family. Pope Martin V, the man who restored the papacy to Rome and gave the papal states their characteristic Renaissance form, made shrewd use of his Colonna relatives. In later years of the fifteenth century, the warlike Sixtus IV would carry nepotism far beyond anything that Calixtus had practised. Sixtus used his family as a bludgeon to break completely the clutch of robber barons whose unruly ambitions perpetually threatened the papal lands.

Calixtus, however, was a foreigner and needed his *nipoti* for reasons beyond policy. Stranger in a hostile city, he needed the affection of family to ease the loneliness of an old bachelor heart. Many years before, in Spain, the disreputable affair with his criminal brother-in-law Jofré had indicated just how strongly Calixtus was bound by the ties of the Borja family. In the years of his pontificate, when he was old and sick, wearing out spirit and health in a hopeless crusading cause, he needed the comfort of his native tongue and the strength of Spanish tradition, the steely spirit of the Reconquest, to sustain him against the mockery of kings and the indifference of the people. His nephews, surely, had excellent qualities – intelligent, persuasive, debonair. It was hard for the pope to refuse them; and were they not as worthy to occupy high places as Italian *nipoti* of former papal reigns? The indulgence of a fond uncle passed over incipient vices that others saw. We know, too, that the bedridden and harried pope was deliberately left ignorant of his nephews' worst excesses. The tragedy of this pontificate came not so much from the common fact of nepotism, but from the nature of the men honoured. Pedro Luis showed every sign of being a slippery self-seeker, and it was as well for the Church and the Borgias that he died young. Rodrigo, however, prospered. He was a man of easy charm and easy morals, but of great ability. He went steadily along the primrose path on which his uncle had set him. He was neither the first nor the worst churchman to confuse secular aims with the mission of the Church. But as a libertine in the City of God, he hastened the drift of the papacy towards worldly ends, and at the end of that road there stood eventually the appalling figure of his son Cesare, another *nipote*, a rod to flay the backs of Church and state alike.

Shut in the darkened room, with his ideals gone awry, Calixtus suffered a great weariness. In the summer of 1458, the plague swept Rome, as it did so often in that century. All who could fled the city, but the pope stayed, pondering his defeats, watching the slow decay of King Alfonso, old friend and master, now his most bitter antagonist. On 27 June, the celebrated king died. 'The bond is broken,' Calixtus exclaimed, 'and we are free.' For the last time he summoned those remarkable powers of concentration and decision that he had shown throughout his long career. At once, he ordered the arrest of the Neapolitan ambassador, but the wily envoy had bolted. Pedro Luis hastened to the frontier of Naples with an army. A papal bull of 12 July declared the kingdom of Naples escheated to the Holy See. The pope, so the gossip said, intended to give the kingdom to Pedro Luis. Florence and Milan, thoroughly alarmed, at once voiced their opposition. With the border between Naples and the papal states closed, the usual supply of food for the unproductive Romans began to dwindle. Prices rose in the city; murmurings of discontent were heard on all sides; a list of grievances was attached to the door of St Peter's.

Towards the end of July, laid low by another attack of gout, Calixtus was forced to stop work. He was eighty, and Rome did not think he could last long. As always, the last days of a pope caused turmoil in the city, intensified on this occasion by the general hatred felt for the Catalans. The fury of the mob turned on all Spaniards and their property. Lives were lost and houses sacked. A correspondent of Francesco Sforza saw a man hacked down in the street while the crowd bayed 'Catalan, you must die'. Rodrigo, who had been at Tivoli, hurried back to Rome and found his uncle a little recovered: strong enough, unfortunately, to fan popular rage by investing Pedro Luis with the papal cities of Benevento and Terracina. The Milanese envoy reported that the cardinals did not dare stand against the pope lest the peremptory old Spaniard should imprison them in Castel Sant'Angelo. Affairs became so desperate, however, that several of the more independent members of the

Sacred College decided to do something about Pedro Luis. With the help of Rodrigo, who had some influence over his wayward brother, the cardinals persuaded the Captain General to sell several of his castles to the Sacred College, and in particular the Castel Sant'Angelo, the key to the security of Rome. Passions within the city were so inflamed that now the chief problem was how to get Pedro Luis away to safety. On every side the Orsini were gathering to block the escape. With courage and generosity, Cardinal Barbo agreed to help. An escort of 3000 cavalry and 200 infantry was assembled, then Pietro Barbo and Rodrigo took Pedro Luis towards the old Milvian bridge. But at the Porta del Popolo, the cardinals with the disguised Pedro Luis doubled back with a small guard to the Porta San Paolo, from where Pedro Luis escaped by road to Ostia. In the port, surrounded by a multitude of treasures, he awaited a ship that never came. At last, a fishing boat took him to Civitavecchia where, on 26 September, he died of malaria, still expecting the ship for Spain.

Rodrigo, who had acted bravely and swiftly throughout, stayed in Rome. Though his palace had been sacked and he was in danger of his life, he went to St Peter's to pray for his dying uncle. He was at the bedside when Calixtus died, on the evening of 6 August 1458 – the Feast of the Transfiguration, the celebration of the one transitory success of the pope's Crusade. Outside in the streets of the city the Roman mob, led by the Orsini, howled and looted, as they had done on the day of the pope's coronation.

The Vatican and Castel Sant'Angelo. The castle commanded the major bridge over the river Tiber, combining impregnability with close proximity to the heart of Rome.

OPPOSITE On Calixtus' death, the Roman mob, led by the Orsini, howled and looted as they had done on the day of the pope's coronation.

The calumny of the chroniclers has done Calixtus III much harm. Damned for his nepotism, he has been equally damned for his name. Many of the scandals attributed to him came from the bitter pens of men like Francesco Filelfo and Vespasiano, humanists driven from profitable positions in the Curia by Calixtus' economies. Far from wanting, as these writers alleged, to destroy the glory of the Roman papacy so carefully nurtured by Pope Nicholas, Calixtus did what he could, within the straightened circumstances imposed by the Crusade, to conserve and extend the work of Nicholas. The priceless Vatican Library was not dispersed, as enemies said; rather it was put in the charge of Cosimo de Montserrat, a most conscientious keeper. Calixtus maintained a modest programme of restoration, with particular emphasis on early Christian churches. He even had a surprising care for pagan Roman antiquities, placing a fine of 25 florins on those who despoiled ancient monuments. His old friends Valla and Poggio, worshippers of the past, approved these measures; and at least Calixtus did not forget them, for like any astute ruler of the time he knew the power of the humanists with their talent for propaganda. Once when Piccinino threatened him, he replied scornfully that the Church had more than 3000 scholars whose advice and wisdom could confound even the greatest kings. Calixtus had cause to know. Did not malicious, backbiting rumours attempt to father him with a couple of bastards?

The tomb of Pope Calixtus III. On his death in early August 1458, Calixtus' body was laid to rest in Santa Maria delle Febbre. Later his body was removed to the church of Santa Maria di Moserrato.

Though the nepotism of his last days was a sad fall from the high principles of Alfons de Borja's earlier years, there was something impressive about this serious and capable pontiff. And he seemed most grave and noble in the forlorn pursuit of his Crusade. No doubt the attempt to resurrect this universal Christian ideal was a serious error in a selfish age of rising national monarchies. But the passionate defence of Christendom undertaken by a man of seventy-seven cried heroically in the face of Western indifference. 'If only a few Christian galleys', Calixtus wrote with despair, 'had shown themselves in the neighbourhood of Ragusa. O, traitors! your ships might have discomfited the Turks, raised up the Christians of the East, and delivered Hungary from her dangers.' And again: 'O Almighty God, it is thy will that I should wear myself out and die for the general good. So be it! Nothing will induce me to leave Rome, not even if I, like so many others, fall victim to the plague. Mahomet, the enemy of our faith, compels me to remain.' And the last cry of wounded nobility: 'The vengeance of God and of the Holy See will surely overtake you. Alfonso, King of Aragon, help Pope Calixtus!' Not Alfonso, nor any other prince, heard him.

CHAPTER THREE
CARDINAL RODRIGO: THE BORGIA DYNAST

THE STORY WAS TOLD BY AENEAS SYLVIUS PICCO-lomini: on 16 August 1458, in the heat of the Roman summer, the Sacred College met in conclave to elect a new pope. In a building of the Vatican Palace the windows were boarded, and only the thin light of candles pierced the constant gloom. In the hall, wooden partitions had divided the space into narrow cells, each with bed, table and stool. Here, for the period of the conclave, the cardinals lived, slept and ate. Only through the guarded wicket gate was there a glimpse of the outside world, and through this gate passed the food hampers of the prelates, each one, for fear of poisoning, privately prepared by the cardinal's own household. Off the hall with the wooden cells there was a chapel furnished with high-backed stalls each bearing a cardinal's coat of arms. Here the cardinals deliberated and voted, and drew up the 'capitulations' by which they sought to bind whoever should be elected pope to a general statement of policy. On the death of Calixtus, the forerunners for the new pope had seemed to be Domenico Capranica and Guillaume d'Estouteville. But the saintly Cardinal Capranica died two days before the conclave, and the way seemed clear for Estouteville, the immensely rich Cardinal of Rouen and cousin of the French king. The first ballot was held on the third day of the conclave, and to general surprise it was seen that only two cardinals had won a significant vote: Calandrini of Bologna and his friend Picco-lomini, the impecunious Cardinal of Siena.

Estouteville and his party refused to take part in the discussion that followed the ballot. Estouteville, with the calculated discourtesy of the over-proud, made his position quite clear to his colleagues: 'Will you give us this Aeneas for pope, a man lame in both feet and poor besides? How will this sick man cure our sickness? Shall we put a poet in Peter's

Aeneas Sylvius Picco-lomini created Cardinal of Siena by Pope Calixtus III. Cardinal Piccolomini became a close associate of Calixtus' nephew Rodrigo and his election as Pope Pius II in 1458, due to Rodrigo's courage in being the first to declare his vote for Piccolomini, strengthened his link with the Borgias.

chair?' He then set out to canvass support for his own cause, pointing
to his seniority, his royal blood, his wealth, his influential friends, and
particularly to the plethora of rich benefices he had to distribute to well-
wishers. That night, surrounded by the whispers of the bargainers,
Aeneas Sylvius retired to bed in disgust. Calandrini woke him in the
small hours with disturbing news. He had just come hot-foot from the
latrines, which Estouteville had chosen as 'a secluded and retired place'
to put together a pact. Eleven cardinals, said Calandrini, had pledged
their vote to the Frenchman, and if Aeneas hurried he might yet be in
time to offer his vote and collect the reward. But Aeneas Sylvius replied
that the latrines were an appropriate place for such a foul bargain, and
went back to sleep.

Piccolomini, however, was the most wily diplomat in the Church's
service. In a long career throughout Europe, he had put together count-
less treaties, changed sides on numerous occasions, always, it seemed,
judging men and the times to a nicety. He had the most extensive knowledge of the Church's international affairs, and the widest acquaintance
of high churchmen in all countries. He knew the strength and weakness
of all the cardinals, and how to touch each one. At dawn, he was quickly
up and at work to undermine the plans of the arrogant and unpopular
Estouteville. Significantly, he began with Rodrigo Borgia, the junior
cardinal but the one likely to lose all that his uncle had given him. The
exchange was brisk, as between men who understood business. 'Have
you sold yourself to Rouen?' Aeneas enquired, to which Rodrigo
answered frankly that he had, for Estouteville had promised to let him
keep the very important and profitable Vice-Chancellorship. 'Young
fool!' Aeneas reproved him, 'will you put an enemy of your nation in
the Apostle's Chair? Do you expect a Frenchman to favour a Catalan
above another Frenchman? You will have your promises and Alain of
Avignon will have the Chancellorship.' And so Piccolomini went on
down the list of cardinals, promising favours, threatening retribution,
playing on national antipathies and national pride, suiting the argument
expertly to each listener. When the second ballot was taken, it was seen
that he had done great things, but not quite enough. He had broken the
Estouteville clique, and gained himself a clear majority of nine votes;
but he had failed by three to get the two thirds majority needed to
elect a pope.

The decision now was to vote by accession in a full meeting. For one cardinal publicly to change his vote was very probable, for he would reap the benefit of being the pope-maker; but there were long odds against three men being brave enough to make that public accession. 'All sat pale and silent, as if entranced,' wrote Aeneas, remembering that scene so well. 'For some time no one spoke, no one opened his lips, no one moved any part of his body except the eyes, which kept glancing all about. It was a strange silence and a strange sight, men sitting there like their own statues. Thus they remained for some time, those of lesser rank waiting for their superiors to begin.' At last, the most junior, Rodrigo Borgia, rose and said: 'I accede to the Cardinal of Siena.' It was a brave move, and on it rested the Vice-Chancellor's career. The utterance was 'like a dagger in Rouen's heart, so pale did he turn'. Two French supporters immediately excused themselves and disappeared to the latrines, 'with the purpose of escaping the fate of that day'. No one followed, so they returned just in time to hear the Cardinal of St Anastasia also accede to Piccolomini. And now the way was open for the third man to declare himself with safety. Cardinal Prospero Colonna stood up. As he did so Estouteville and Bessarion seized him and tried to drag him from the hall, but they could not smother the cry: 'I too accede to the Cardinal of Siena, and I make him pope!'

Colonna thought he would have the 'glory of announcing the pope'. But that credit properly belonged to the twenty-seven-year-old Cardinal Borgia. Colonna, the patrician of vast experience and influence, the friend of Aeneas Sylvius, lacked the courage of the young, unpopular Catalan. And it is a mark of Piccolomini's astuteness that the first man he approached in the dawn light outside the latrines was Borgia. Two capable men came together and understood each other. Rodrigo's future was in the balance. He had been the favoured *nipote* of a doting pope. Now he was a detested Spanish upstart alone amid jealous enemies. His family had dispersed. Pedro Luis was awaiting flight to Spain in Civitavecchia; Luis Juan de Mila had returned to his bishopric of Segorbe in Spain. Rodrigo looked likely to lose all – office, benefits and sources of income. He made his judgment and bravely played his hand; the balance tipped and came down on his side. Aeneas Sylvius Piccolomini, the new Pope Pius II, had the papacy, and Rodrigo Borgia had the Vice-Chancellorship.

'A man of versatile intellect', said a contemporary of Rodrigo, 'and of great sense and imagination; an eloquent speaker and learned in a rather general way; he has a warm nature, but above all is brilliantly skilled in conducting affairs.' Rodrigo was, when all allowances had been made for his philandering, for his love of show and pomp, for his attachment to riches, as capable as any man in Rome to run the office of the Vice-Chancellor and be the chief administrator of the papal Curia. He was Vice-Chancellor for thirty-five years, and it is said that he never missed a consistory in that time, unless ill or away from Rome. He carefully tended the source of his power and used it to the very best advantage. It was in the interest of the Church to have an efficient administrator; but of course the chief beneficiary of the position was Rodrigo himself. His office gave him a rather modest income, about 8000 ducats a year, but afforded him – and this was more important – an almost limitless opportunity to collect rich benefices. In 1458 his uncle Calixtus had installed him as Bishop of Valencia, a see by then almost a part of Borgia family property. Rodrigo then added the bishoprics of Cartagena and Majorca, and several other Spanish bene-fices besides. For all the success of his Italian achievements, Rodrigo never forgot that he was a Spaniard. The members of his household in Rome were mainly his own countrymen, and he spoke Catalan or Castilian for preference; it was quite natural for him to secure a strong base in his homeland. But he protected his Italian interests with equal success. He understood very well that the key to safety in Rome was some controlling hand in the turbulent country around the city, in the Campagna to the south, and in the Patrimony of St Peter in the north. By careful dealing, collecting various benefices and abbey lands, which he held *in commendam*, he got possession of castles which dominated the Via Flaminia and Via Cassia to the north and the Via Appia to the south, old Roman roads that were the vital arteries of the city.

But these later successes were the fruits of time. For the moment, re-confirmed in his valuable office, young Cardinal Borgia seized the day. The new pope was well-disposed towards him, and since Pius II was a man of imagination, spirit and abundant humour, the papal court looked forward to lively entertainment. 'Father Pius,' wrote the Man-tuan chronicler, 'a rosy little man, arrived with many ambassadors.' In 1459 the pope had invited the crowned heads of Europe to a Congress

eneas Sylvius Picco-
mini as Pope Pius II,
man of imagination,
pirit and abundant
umour. He confirmed
odrigo in the office of
ice-Chancellor.

in Mantua, where he intended to spur them, or shame them, to a new crusade against the Turks. For the twenty years or so before his pontificate, Aeneas Sylvius Piccolomini had been the indispensable acolyte of great men, flexible, evasive, accommodating. He had allied wit and real rhetorical skill to a keen judgment of people and events. He had a word for every ear and was at ease with the best minds of the time. But scintillating though he was, there seemed something unprincipled about his brilliance. He was the master of adaptability, the poor scholar clutching for the next rung of the ladder to preferment. 'I fear continence', he had said when he reluctantly took Holy Orders, leaving behind the sportive but poverty-stricken young writer of love stories and beginning the worthy and profitable trudge through the hierarchies of the Church. All that changed. The guileful man found constancy and purpose in the frightening responsibilities of the Supreme Pontiff. Fifty-three years old, broken in health by travel, dissipation and the papal complaint of gout, Pope Pius II renounced the past. '*Aeneam rejicite, Pium recipite,*' he wrote: I renounce the frivolity of the humanist, and take on the burden of the Church.

Of the manifold burdens that awaited him, one in particular took up his energy and intelligence. The diplomatic humanist that he had been might have warned Pius that the crusading ideal was dead. But his new dignity drove him, surprisingly, into the impossible task. After a stately progress through Italy, the papal court descended on Mantua in May 1459, and settled down to await the arrival of the secular princes. In the restless summer, as time fidgeted by, the eye of the Mantuan chronicler watched the papal court in action. Cardinals and their retinues went to and fro from the consistories. The arrogant Estouteville, 'a handsome man of sixty, fat but good-looking', swept in with 300 horsemen. Orsini, on the other hand, was 'about seventy, grey and old, small and thin, and not much to look at'; the horses of his followers were also 'thin and sad', numbering only seventy, and the whole household looked 'in great need of ducats'. Then there was the bold Patriarch of Aquileia, 'a little black, hairy man of sixty, very proud', who rode in the town 'with magnificent chargers clearing the way for him, and his entourage numbered at least 400.' And there also was Rodrigo Borgia, assiduously present at every consistory. 'The Vice-Chancellor', the chronicler wrote, 'is twenty-five [he was in fact twenty-eight] and

Ludovico Gonzaga, Marchese of Mantua, with his wife Barbara of Brandenburg, their children and attendants. The marchesa – a woman of impeccable reputation – enjoyed a warm friendship with Cardinal Borgia.

looks capable of every wickedness; when he goes to the pope's court he is accompanied by 200 or 250 horses and great pomp.'

Rodrigo was too worldly a realist to expect anything from negotiations with reluctant princes. He begged the Marchesa of Mantua to find him lodgings with a little garden, for the work of the Chancellery kept him indoors all day and he longed in the evening to take the air in his own grounds, as he was used to doing in Rome. Barbara, Marchesa of Mantua – a lady of impeccable reputation – shared with Rodrigo a common love for hunting and sport, and gave her Spanish friend presents of falcons and hunting dogs. And when there was no time for the hunting field, Rodrigo escaped the overcrowded city by boating on the lagoon. In the consistories, speeches of classical eloquence followed one another, all to no purpose. The European princes either stayed away from Mantua, or listened and did nothing.

Ill and deeply discouraged, Pius brought the congress to an end. He retreated to Siena, the city of his family, arriving with a sense of relief on 2 February 1460, the Feast of the Purification. In a consistory called to announce the names of six new cardinals, Pius faced the usual obstructive criticism from the Sacred College, from men who feared that extra numbers meant the dilution of their profitable benefices. The pope, who understood their motives so well, let all the rage and frustration

OPPOSITE Hunting and sport eased Rodrigo's boredom in Mantua, enabling him to escape the tedious consistories that he knew would do little to help Pius's crusade.

of the past year burst out in a violent condemnation of immoral prelates. They were to blame for the state of the Church, cried the accusing pontiff:

> You who do not preserve the dignity and sanctity belonging to this eminence. Judging from your manner of life, you seem not to have chosen to govern the State of the Church, but to enjoy pleasure. You do not abstain from hunting or games, or from intercourse with women; you give dinners of unseemly magnificence; you wear costly clothes; you have an abundance of gold and silver plate, and you keep more horses and servants than any man can need.

No names were mentioned, but just how well the cap fitted was very soon shown.

After Easter the pope left Siena. He was suffering from neuralgia and rheumatic pains, and spent most of the spring and early summer at the sulphur baths of Petriolo. Here word reached him of a scandalous event. Young Cardinal Borgia and ageing Cardinal Estouteville had disported themselves in a most licentious way, at a christening party held in a Sienese garden on 7 June. On the 11th Pius sent Rodrigo a severe reprimand:

ALTENPO

> We have learned that your Worthiness, forgetful of the high office with which you are invested, was present from the 17th to the 22nd hour, four days ago, in the gardens of Giovanni de Bichi, where there were several women of Siena, women wholly given over to worldly vanities. Your companion was one of your colleagues, whose years, if not the dignity of his office, ought to have reminded him of his duty. We have heard that the dance was indulged in, in all wantonness; none of the allurements of love was lacking, and you conducted yourself in a wholly wordly manner. Shame forbids mention of what took place, for not only the things themselves but their very names are unworthy of your rank. In order that your lust might be all the more unrestrained, the husbands, fathers, brothers, kinsmen of the young girls were not invited; you and a few servants were the leaders and inspirers of this orgy. It is said that nothing is now talked of in Siena but your vanity, which is the subject of universal ridicule. Certain it is that here at the baths, your name is on everyone's tongue. Our displeasure is beyond words.

The city of Siena welcomed Pius's return in February 1460; the squares were strewn with scented herbs and flowers.

Three days later the pope wrote again: perhaps he had been overhasty; the first reports seemed to be exaggerated, magnified by the idle gossip of the baths at Petriolo. Nonetheless, he, Pius, knew Rodrigo

well enough, and the christening party was not an isolated incident. Did the cardinal really think it was consonant with his place 'to court young women, to give those whom you love presents of fruit and wine, and to give no thought to anything but sensual pleasure'? And Pius was not wrong in finding Rodrigo's behaviour notorious. The Mantuan envoy, Bartolomeo Bonatti, reported to his master that he had been denied access to the christening, but had played the Peeping Tom, and 'By God, if the children born within the year arrive dressed like their fathers, many will appear as priests and cardinals.' In a letter to the Marchesa Barbara, Bonatti recalled with enthusiasm the pleasures of that Sienese summer, 'in the company of the most triumphant cardinal and the most beautiful woman that ever·was'. The most beautiful woman was the courtesan Nachine, and her liaison with the triumphant Cardinal Borgia was evidently common knowledge.

Reprimanded by the pope, Rodrigo did not moderate his sensual appetite but learned instead to be discreet. So discreet in fact that the mother, or mothers, of his first three children are unknown. A boy, Pedro Luis, named after the brother who had died at Civitavecchia, was born in 1462; two girls, Isabella and Girolama, followed between 1467 and 1471. Around the year 1473, Rodrigo began a long and comfortable affair with Vanozza dei Catanei, an accommodating Roman beauty of great practical ability who pandered to the desires of Rodrigo's warm and sensual heart for the best part of ten years. He had four children by Vanozza. The eldest, Cesare, was born in 1475; then came Juan in 1477, Lucrezia in 1480, and another son Jofré in 1481. And to complete this roll-call of a prodigious clerical appetite, Rodrigo had one, and possibly two more children after he became pope in 1492.

The prevalence of bastards, which often scandalized foreigners, raised few eyebrows in fifteenth-century Italy. Where the establishment of power in nearly every Italian state had been, at some time, a gigantic exercise of illegitimate force, the mere fact of illegitimate birth did not disturb the conscience. In Italy, every ruling house acknowledged bastards, even in the direct line; the worth and seniority of a person so often outweighed legitimacy. During the progress to Mantua, in 1459, eight bastards of the house of Este had ridden out from Ferrara to greet Pope Pius II, and among them were the duke himself and two bastard sons of his illegitimate brother. In Italy it could happen that a *condottiere*, bastard-born from some menial loins and wielding the illegitimate power of a mercenary army, might carve out a territory, founding a dynasty in his own right and be considered no worse for doing so. He would stand on equal footing with all other Italian princes. Was the great Federigo of Urbino a true Montefeltro? It did not matter for he was a wise ruler and a magnificent patron. And as for Ferrante, bastard son of Alfonso of Naples, he had such a peculiar and swarthy aspect that many questioned any blood link at all with the Spanish king. Yet he inherited the Neapolitan throne, and few would have contested his right on the grounds of illegitimacy alone.

As the Roman papacy and Curia became more and more secularized, so the common attitudes of Italian polity infected the princes of the Church. Indeed, cardinals and then popes, in their capacity as men of affairs with complicated temporal and dynastic ambitions to uphold, soon came to regard children as a positive blessing, to be placed in key posts or to be married off in advantageous alliances. Rodrigo Borgia, most wordly of prelates, let his natural appetites reign and satisfied both his pleasure and his interests. Above all he looked on himself as a Renaissance prince, and permitted himself every licence and every luxury of that exalted state. The palace that he built in Rome, part of the present-day Palazzo Sforza-Cesarini, was acknowledged one of the grandest in Italy. He had purchased the ground, the site of the old mint, from his uncle Calixtus for 2000 ducats. In 1462, when the holy relic of the head of St Andrew came in solemn procession across Rome, Pope Pius likened Borgia's palace to the golden house of Nero. The entire processional route was expensively decorated, but Rodrigo's new palace 'outstripped all others in richness, effort and ingenuity'. The 'huge, towering edifice' was covered with tapestries and even the square in front was full of ingenious devices, so that 'the whole scene looked like a kind of park full of sweet sounds, or a great palace gleaming with gold, as they say Nero's palace was'. In 1484, Ascanio Sforza gave a more detailed description of the fabulous building. He mentioned the vast tapestries with hunting scenes, the carpets harmonized with the furniture, the canopied daybed of red satin, the chests laid out with a collection of gold and silver plate.

Luxury required money, and to balance the cardinal's public show and munificence there was a private venality which reminded Italians why Catalans had always been thought greedy. There was an infamous occasion when Count Jean d'Armagnac had asked the pope for a dispensation to marry his own sister. The shocked Pope Pius had ordered an investigation, which seemed to implicate Borgia. Armagnac claimed that he had asked Calixtus for a dispensation and the secretary Volterra had promised him one on condition that Borgia, the pope's nephew, received 3000 ducats in gold. The money had been sent to the secretary but the dispensation never arrived, and now Armagnac wanted the document he had paid for because, as he brazenly said, the union with his sister was already consummated. Enquiry revealed that Calixtus had indeed granted a dispensation to marry a relative of the fourth degree of consanguinity – a second cousin – but the scoundrel Volterra had altered 'fourth' to 'first': a sister. The principals in the disgraceful affair, Volterra and the French bishop of Lectoure, were gaoled, but the money had disappeared. Perhaps Volterra pocketed it, and it was never proved that Rodrigo had any part of the dealing. But the stain against him remained, a hint of the kind of thing that he might be prepared to do, as a member of a notoriously corrupt Curia. 'Forgiveness of sins can only be obtained by purchase,' Piccolomini had written in his former, witty days; as pope he was only too painfully aware of that truth: 'There is nothing to be obtained from the Roman Curia without money, for even ordination and the gifts of the Holy Ghost are sold.' How was the well-meaning Pius to govern this worship of mammon? Once, Estouteville had entertained pope and cardinals to an open-air banquet among the ancient ruins of Ostia. In the evening the prelates retired to the bishop's palace, while the host of servants bedded down in tents, or in boats moored in the Tiber. In the night a hurricane struck with such violent thunder and lightning that in the midst of the storm Rodrigo's terrified servants clamoured at the door, drenched and dazed. In amazement Pius saw Rodrigo beat them out into the storm again, his only concern being for his valuable gold and plate that the servants had left behind.

Despite his famous qualities – his intelligence, his subtlety, his tact, his vast experience of men and affairs – Pope Pius was as wearily entangled in Italian politics as any of his long-suffering predecessors. In the absence of the pope in Mantua and Siena, Rome had reverted to a state of banditry. Roman republicanism, the dangerous undercurrent of city life, which had at least shown a vestige of dignity in the hands of Stefano Porcari, degenerated under his successor Tiburzio into a lust for spoil and a thirst for revenge. Packs of youths, often 300-strong with many members from good families, imposed a terror upon the city, sacking houses, holding enemies to ransom, violating women and drowning young girls who resisted them. In the countryside outside Rome, the established clans – Savelli, Orsini, Colonna, Anguillara and several others – fanned old antagonisms, inciting the city bullies to new horrors and using that violence to cloak their dynastic ambitions. The kingdom of Naples was in ferment, with followers of the French house of Anjou trying to make good an old claim and wrest the throne from the grip of Ferrante, Alfonso's hated bastard. And breeding on the un-rest, the faithless opportunists Piccinino and Sigismondo Malatesta prowled, ready to take advantage of any weakness in the papal lands.

The ailing pope, who had been all his life a man of peace and con-ciliation, took up arms, accepting the uncomfortable role of warrior that the possession of the papal states forced upon all the fifteenth-century popes. His generals had good fortune. Pius saw Ferrante con-firmed in Naples, the *condottieri* subdued, and the papal lands extended and pacified. In May 1463, Pius sat on the peak of Monte Cavo, con-templating with satisfaction the wide sweep of his estates, from Terra-cina to Monte Argentario. But to accomplish all this, the civilized, urbane pope had been drawn down the same road of woe that con-founded his predecessors. The man who abhorred war had turned warrior. The reformer had stumbled against the impediment of his corrupt, wordly Curia. The man of affairs, who was too wise not to see the dangers of nepotism, scattered the rewards of his patronage on his nephews as keenly as Calixtus had ever done. And last of all, the Crusade, the matter closest to his heart, went unrealized while he plunged into wars and politics.

The plight of this sick and struggling pope seemed to touch Rodrigo Borgia's genial nature. Perhaps he remembered his own uncle's des-perate efforts to warn Europe of the Turkish danger. In any case, though Rodrigo was surely too shrewd to expect any success from a papal Crusade, he was the only cardinal to build and equip a galley at his own expense and present it to the pope. Pius determined to lead the Crusade himself and in June 1464, accompanied by members of the Sacred

College, left Rome for Ancona, on the Adriatic coast, where he expected to gather the crusading fleet. Pius wept on the banks of the Tiber as he took leave of Rome. Dying slowly, he was carried by boat and litter across Italy. His attendants drew the curtains of his carriage so that he should not see the pillage and violence of his crusaders. In Ancona, only two galleys rode in the harbour. After a wait of nearly a month, during which the pope was sinking fast, the doge brought twelve ships from Venice, but Pius was too ill to welcome them. On 14 August he summoned Borgia, Bessarion, Carvajal and a few other cardinals to his bedside, and begged their forgiveness if he had failed in the government of the Church. 'Who will look to my funeral?' he asked with tears, and died.

In Ancona the plague was now widespread, and the derisory little band of crusaders began to desert as quickly as possible. Rodrigo caught the plague, but survived. He had rented a country villa some distance from the city, and his survival may be put down to fresh air free from the contamination of the port. Even so it was a close thing. The Mantuan envoy reported that Borgia's life was despaired of, for the doctors considered his health to be undermined by sexual intercourse, and 'recently he had not been sleeping alone'.

The new pope, Paul II, was Rodrigo's old friend Pietro Barbo, the man who had helped Pedro Luis escape the anger of the Romans six years before. The Venetian Barbo was a handsome, indolent man whose love of luxury was only equalled by his personal vanity. As a cardinal he had built himself the splendid Palazzo Venezia and had stuffed it with treasure. His collection of jewels was a wonder of the age, his tiara alone being valued at 120,000 ducats. He wore so many rings that it was popularly believed that he died of a chill brought on by the icy weight of the gems. He had wished to take the name of Formosus – 'the Most Beautiful' – until persuaded that it was not appropriate for a pope. He rouged himself before public appearances. Though conceited and pleasure-loving, Paul was a courageous, strong-minded man. The cardinals at the conclave, in the usual manner, had tried to bind him to their will. On election, Paul asserted his supreme authority with contemptuous ease. He set about a reform of papal administration and did not mind what hornets he stirred up. For many years it had been the practice to fill the administration with a crowd of favourite humanists

Loggias of the courtyard of Palazzo Venezia, the first great Renaissance palace of Rome, built by Pope Paul II.

and writers who carried out the tasks of 'scriptors' and 'abbreviators' – secretaries and clerks. These posts, profitable sources of income, were much coveted and were bought and sold for as much as 1000 ducats. Formerly, they had worked in the Chancellery under Vice-Chancellor Borgia and were a valuable part of his patronage. But Pius had given the abbreviators their own constitution and removed them from Borgia's jurisdiction. Now Pope Paul, the friend of Rodrigo, cancelled their rights, cleared out many from their posts, and put the rest back under the Vice-Chancellor. The humanists complained, for many had only recently paid for their positions, and their leader Platina sent Paul a strong, impudent letter. That was no way to deal with such a self-willed pope. He immediately suspected a plot among the *letterati* of the Roman Academy, so he clapped Platina and some others into gaol at Castel Sant'Angelo. Platina took his revenge by writing a history of Paul II, and the humanists in general hurled some brickbats at Cardinal Borgia as well, who perhaps instigated the whole affair.

Having favoured Rodrigo by preserving his ecclesiastical empire, Paul began a reign of bread and games which also pleased the self-indulgent Spanish cardinal. The ancient festivities of the Roman carnival were extended and popularized. From the loggia of his palace by San Marco, the pope presided at the finishing post of races that began at the Arch of Domitian. On one day Jews would compete, then young men, then the middle aged, and finally the elderly. Another day, there would be horse races, also races with asses and buffaloes. At the end of the games, Paul gave a large banquet in front of his palace, appearing at his window like some painted deity, 'with form more august than man', throwing coins to the appreciative crowd. Although he was a lover of Roman festivities, Paul was no friend to Roman republicanism and disorder. The effete pope was a bold politician, and the drift of his policy followed the traditional aims of the Renaissance papacy: to establish an authoritarian Roman pontiff, supreme in all matters of the faith, with a temporal power based on secure possession of Rome and the papal states. He suspected the humanists, since their scholarship and classical reading very often made them critics of Church authority. 'If God spares me for the task,' he said, 'I shall forbid the study of absurd histories and foolish poems, for they are full of heresy and evil spells.' Nor did he love the Roman patricians whose feuding brought such danger to the city and the surrounding country. To curb them, he brought in several new city ordinances, and tried to outlaw the vendetta together with the freelance thugs – the *bravi* and *brigosi* – who operated it on behalf of noble families. Paul was no warmonger, but when driven to it acted swiftly and forcefully. His generals, in particular Federigo of Urbino and the well-named Cardinal Forteguerra, were the equal of most opposition. When, in July 1471, Pope Paul died suddenly of an apoplexy, though he had done little for the well-being of Europe or the Church and had debased the spiritual realm by his frivolity and luxury, he left nonetheless a strong, prosperous papal monarchy.

In 1471 Rodrigo Borgia had been cardinal and Vice-Chancellor for fifteen years and was, without a doubt, a power in the land. In the conclave that followed Paul's death, Borgia was a popemaker, combining with Orsini and Bessarion to ensure the election of Francesco della Rovere as Pope Sixtus IV. Della Rovere came from a poor family: his father was said to have been a Ligurian fisherman; he had joined the Franciscan order and had shown great brilliance as a scholar and polemicist. He was a virtuous, unpretentious man of simple faith and sound morals, and the Romans, who expected a pontificate of unparalleled austerity, greeted him without enthusiasm. They pelted the papal litter with stones on its way to the Lateran. On 25 August 1471, Sixtus was crowned with the tiara by Rodrigo Borgia, and with the characteristic energy of the good friar began the work of Church government. For his part as popemaker, Borgia received the abbey of Subiaco *in commendam*, and was also designated to be papal legate in his native Spain. Sixtus had quickly taken up the international role of the Church which Paul had neglected, and wanted to pursue the war against the Turks. An examination of the papal treasure left in the Castel Sant'Angelo by Paul had revealed a lucky windfall – gold, plate and jewels to the value of $1\frac{1}{2}$ million ducats – and to build on this good fortune Sixtus sent his legates to France, Germany and Spain.

It was many years since Rodrigo had been in his native land. He had left it an impecunious youth seeking advancement; he returned in 1472 in the full dignity of a prince of the Church and bearer of the papal commission. His preparations were worthy of his state. Three bishops accompanied him, and he took also two Italian artists to decorate the cathedral of Rodrigo's bishopric at Valencia. At the Porta San Paolo, according to custom, the cardinals took leave of the legate. At the port of Ostia two Neapolitan ships waited to carry the legation to Spain. Reaching Valencia in mid-June, Rodrigo found that the city's welcome for its Cardinal-Archbishop was not quite ready, so with genial tact he idled up the coast, landing at Puig on 20 June. There he spent the night in vigil before the image of the Virgin, and on the 21st set out for Valencia. Outside the city, at the ancient crossroads to Murviedro, the

'The Adoration of the Virgin' with Ferdinand of Aragon and Isabella of Castile as donors. On his visit to Spain in 1472, Rodrigo Borgia made an impression on the Catholic monarchs which was to have a lasting impact on papal-Spanish relations for the rest of the century.

city fathers led by the auxiliary bishop met the cardinal. Rodrigo advanced under a canopy with stately pomp, and to the sound of trumpet and kettledrum went in procession through the crimson-hung gate of Valencia. It was an impressive homecoming.

Rodrigo's legation had several ends in view. It was, at the simplest level, a diocesan visit by the cardinal to his episcopal see. It was intended by the pope to promote, and to raise money for, a war against the Turks. And lastly, it was a papal embassy to the Spanish kingdoms of Aragon and Castile, about to be joined together in the persons of Ferdinand and Isabella. Their marriage had already taken place, but because of consanguinity it required a papal dispensation before it could be sanctioned by canon law. Rodrigo had the dispensation in his pocket and Sixtus had given him discretion to grant it if he thought the union was in the best interests of Spain and the Church. This was the kind of delicate diplomacy in which the Borgias were so expert. Alfons de Borja had been a masterly negotiator, and his nephew Rodrigo showed the same sympathetic qualities of understanding and judgment. He quickly decided that the union should be allowed, for he saw that Ferdinand and Isabella radiated intelligence and strength. Rodrigo then had the task of helping to reconcile Spanish opinion to the match. He spent Christmas in Castile, at the court of King Enrique. He won over Archbishop Mendoza with the promise of a cardinal's hat, and placated the Castilian nobles who had no love for Aragon. Rodrigo then left for Barcelona, to work the same spell with the quarrelsome barons of King Juan of Aragon. Throwing all the authority of his papal warrant behind the king, Rodrigo helped to bring an end to an obstinate civil war, and in doing so won the invaluable respect and friendship of the future King Ferdinand. The influence of Ferdinand, at the head of a powerful, unified and resurgent Spain, was the greatest help to the Borgia family for the rest of the fifteenth century.

For Rodrigo, the return to Spain was also something of a sentimental journey, a chance to refresh himself at the family source and to remind himself that his roots lay in the province of Valencia. It was wise to cultivate those roots against the day – always possible and even likely – when the flourishing Borgia fortunes might wither in the hothouse of Italian politics. So in July and August 1473, Rodrigo was resident in his see of Valencia. He visited Játiva and pointed out with pride the house of his birth. Only one sister, Joana, remained of his immediate family. She had married well, her husband being the blue-blooded Pere-Guillem Lanzol de Romani. Among the children of this couple were two sons, Jofré and Juan – later known as Juan Borgia Lanzol the elder – and a daughter, Isabel Lucrezia, who had married Rodrigo's second cousin Juan de Mila. The family was thus tight-bound and Rodrigo, who shared the well-known Borgia family exclusiveness, saw a lot of his sister and her children. Perhaps it occurred to him at this time that here was a place of safety where his own bastard son Pedro Luis could grow up free from the dangers of Rome. In September 1473 Rodrigo added a codicil to his will, leaving his nephew Jofré a large sum of money. That was insurance for the uncertain future.

ABOVE Palazzo della Cancellaria, Rome, monument to nepotism originally built by Rodrigo Borgia who sold the palace to Raffaele Riario, nephew of Pope Sixtus IV.

OPPOSITE ABOVE Leonora of Aragon, the Neapolitan princess for whom Cardinal Pietro Riario gave an extravagant feast as she passed through Rome on her way to marry Ercole d'Este of Ferrara (BELOW).

After fifteen months in Spain that had been in all respects a triumph for Cardinal Borgia, but not wholly so for the Church – the matter of the Crusade once more went by the board – the legate made a return to Rome that was as eventful as the outward journey had been quiet. Off the coast of Tuscany a violent storm broke out, overwhelming one boat which sank with all hands, and driving the other, with Rodrigo aboard, on to the beach near Pisa. Three bishops were drowned and the possessions of the whole party, valued at 3000 ducats, lost. The envoys of Lorenzo de' Medici hurried to Pisa to console Rodrigo. And in their frantic efforts to recover property lost to the sea, the envoys did not know which to lament the more, their loss or the cardinal's danger.

Cardinal Borgia returned to a Rome much changed, but with features that the nephew of Calixtus would recognize very well. Sixtus, the unworldly monk, was a surprise. He had very soon abandoned the war against the Turks and the wider aspirations of a universal pontiff, and had dragged the papacy back into the shameful labyrinth of Italian domestic struggles. He took up the familiar tools of war and nepotism, but wielded them with such a fierce, wholehearted energy that he amazed his contemporaries. Rome had not seen such power hunger, such simony, such favouritism for many generations. A rapacious band of della Rovere relatives descended on the city like locusts, making the nepotism of Calixtus III – only fifteen years before – look mild by comparison. In 1471 Sixtus appointed Pietro Riario and Giuliano della Rovere, two of his nephews, to the Sacred College. Riario, the younger and the favourite, was heaped with such profitable honours that his income amounted to 60,000 gold florins. Plucked from the cloister in his twenties, this poor young monk was transformed into a wild sensualist whose unbridled career of luxury, irreligion and unbalanced conceit blazed out in a mere two years. When Rodrigo returned to Rome in October 1473, the whole city was still talking of the entertainment given by Cardinal Riario for the Neapolitan princess Leonora of Aragon, passing through Rome on her way to marry Ercole d'Este of Ferrara. Riario built her a temporary palace next to his own, and there he gave an extravagant feast. The menu served fills two of the chronicler's pages: there were rabbits, hares, goats, fish, stags, pheasants, storks and cranes; boars were roasted in their hides, peacocks in their feathers, and a bear in its skin. Mythological heroes and events were shown life-

size on silver dishes. A man emerged, reciting verses, from a confec-
tionary mountain, and ships sailed by delivering cargoes of sugared
almonds. Within a year of the feast Pietro Riario was dead of excess,
though Machiavelli claimed that the Florentines had justly poisoned
him. He had run through an uncounted fortune and left debts of 60,000
ducats; even the slippers of his mistress were embroidered with pearls.

Sixtus IV, weeping at the death of his favourite, transferred his affec-
tions to Girolamo Riario, the dead man's brother. Pietro, not content
to have debauched the papal court, had schemed to possess the papacy.
He would help Galeazzo Maria Sforza to become king of Lombardy
and then the Milanese would win him the papacy, apparently with the
connivance of Sixtus. And when the pope bought Imola for Girolamo,
it was clear that Sixtus did indeed want a kingdom for his kinsman.
Soon the whole of Italy was thrown into an uproar by the pope's tyrannical effrontery on behalf of his relatives. The sinister figure of Ferrante
of Naples began plotting with Sixtus and the republic of Florence, in
particular, took fright. To rid himself of this opposition, Sixtus personally encouraged the conspiracy of the Pazzi against the famous Florentine house of Medici. And when Giuliano de' Medici was murdered,
and Lorenzo wounded, before the high altar of Florence Cathedral, the
pope was implicated. Sixtus excommunicated Florence and waged war
against the republic. Pressed by implacable enemies – Ferrante and
Sixtus – Lorenzo de' Medici saved his city only by an act of debonair
courage. Preferring to deal with the bestial Ferrante rather than the
treacherous pope, Lorenzo travelled to Naples with a few friends,
placing himself at the mercy of the king; yet he argued his case with
such wit and conviction that at the end of three months he emerged, to
universal amazement, not only alive but with Ferrante as his ally.

After the lapse of centuries the judgment on Sixtus may not be so
severe. He was the type of energetic tyrant who struck out both ways,
for good and bad. He was a capable, hard-working administrator and
began a valuable reform of laws and institutions within the Church.
He encouraged agriculture and commerce within the papal states. He
was a scholar and a friend to scholars, and a very great patron of the
arts. The magnificent Sistine Chapel in the Vatican bears his name, and
he had the taste to employ Botticelli, Perugino, Ghirlandaio and several
other famous painters. But against these virtues were placed his vices.

Pope Pius II's Congress at Mantua. Soon after his election Pius II left Rome for Mantua, accompanied by Rodrigo Borgia. The purpose of the congress was to spur the crowned heads of Europe to a new crusade against the Turks, but they came and went, leaving non-committal promises to support the crusade. It was while they were returning to Rome from Mantua that Pius received reports of Rodrigo's scandalous behaviour in Siena.

ELOQVII SACRI DOCTOR PARISINVS ET ING[
GEMIGNANIACI FAMA DECVSQVE SOLI
HOC PROPRIO SVMPTV DOMINICVS ILLE SACEL[
INSIGNEM IVSSIT PINGERE BENOTIVM · M·CCCC[

No opposition or argument would divert him from his plans to aggrandize his family and found a papal dynasty. His darling Girolamo, already lord of Imola and Forlì, turned greedy eyes on the other cities of the Romagna, and pulled Venice and Ferrara into the struggle. Naples and Milan were in arms. By 1482 the whole of Italy was consumed with wars, jealousies, plots, alliances and treacheries. As ever, in the midst of troubles, the Roman factions took the chance to settle old debts. The Orsini combined with Sixtus against the Colonna, and the family of the pope hunted down Lorenzo Colonna with mad hatred. When Lorenzo was executed and his remains delivered to his mother, she surveyed the scars of torture on the body, then held up the severed head by the hair, crying 'Behold, such is the faith of the pope!' But the feverish plotting of Sixtus for his family evaporated into nothing. Murder and dishonour marked down the family. Girolamo was assassinated by his own subjects in Forlì. Only the commanding figure of Cardinal Giuliano della Rovere survived to write his own stern pages to the history of the papacy at a later date. When Sixtus IV died suddenly, in August 1484, the Master of the Palace found the pope's body, abandoned naked on a table, while officials and servants plundered the papal apartments.

In these terrible years, Cardinal Rodrigo Borgia quietly consolidated his already considerable power. He stayed apart from the worst plots and treacheries of Sixtus' pontificate. Rodrigo was by nature a diplomat, not a fighting man, and he advocated a need to keep a careful balance between the greater Italian states. He himself maintained good relations with Naples – a Spanish kingdom – and also with the Medici in Florence. That alone must have limited his influence with the virulently anti-Florentine pope. But Rodrigo moved from one small, sure gain to another. He relentlessly amassed benefices, which not only added to his wealth, but also gave him control of strategic places. He possessed strong castles at Nepi, Soriano and Civita Castellana, to the north of Rome. To the south, the *commenda* of the abbey at Fossanuova put him in charge of a portion of the Via Appia, on route to Naples. The abbey at Subiaco, another *commenda*, became his favourite family retreat from the politics or the summer heat of Rome. And the neighbourhood around Subiaco had the profit from his talent for administration and patronage. He set out rules for markets and festivals, restored

t Augustine leaves Rome
or Milan, Benozzo
Gozzoli's fresco painted
n about 1463, the year
hat Pius II began his
onstruction work on St
eter's Basilica. The
decorative landscape is
n idealized view of the
Borgo and the Vatican,
nclosed by the Aurelian
alls, with the huge mass
f Castel Sant'Angelo
ominating the city.

Palazzo Vescovile, Pienz
built by Rossellino for
Cardinal Rodrigo Borgi
Pius II transformed his
birthplace of Corsignanc
into a papal summer
resort. Many cardinals
were invited to participa
and Rodrigo Borgia wa
among the first to build
a palace there.

the buildings of the monastery, and built the impressive Torre Borgiana
in the town. The worldly current of life at the papal court suited
Rodrigo very well, and allowed him to express himself freely as a
Renaissance prince. In company he was affable and easy, and he became
something of an official papal entertainer, feasting ambassadors and
dignitaries. He enjoyed his riches. We know from Ascanio Sforza that
the Borgia palace in Rome was rich enough to satisfy the most refined
taste for luxury. When Pius II was transforming his little birthplace of
Corsignano into the papal town of Pienza, Rodrigo added to the ele-
gance of the town by commissioning a palace from the architect Bernardo Rossellino. But as a practical, ambitious prelate, he did not
neglect castles and fortifications either, especially at Nepi and Subiaco.

In one other respect, Rodrigo fitted easily into his time. The preva-
lent Italian morality made his amours nothing extraordinary, even for
a churchman. When he returned from Spain in 1473 and met Vanozza
dei Catanei, she settled into a life of affectionate domesticity and he
became the fond, indulgent lover. Rodrigo had discovered Vanozza
already married to the respectable lawyer Domenico da Rignano, but

LEFT Portrait of a woman, presumed to be the young Vanozza dei Catanei, who became Rodrigo Borgia's mistress in 1473. The only known authentic portrait of Vanozza (RIGHT) portrays her in middle age as the capable mother of Rodrigo's children: Cesare, Juan, Lucrezia and Jofré.

living poorly in a little house on the Via del Pellegrino, near the Borgia palace. The couple already had a child who outlived all Vanozza's children by Rodrigo. Around 1474 Vanozza became Rodrigo's mistress, but still maintained a succession of three complacent husbands who seemed willing, and even proud, to be cuckolded by the notoriously licentious cardinal, perhaps for the sake of the benefits that flowed their way. The four children born to Rodrigo and Vanozza, between 1475 and 1482, never neglected their mother, not even Cesare in the blackest days of his black life. She was a sensible, prudent woman who, foreseeing the inevitable cooling off of the cardinal's ardour, invested her money in inns. When her liaison with Rodrigo came to an end, about the year 1482, she blossomed into a prosperous hotelkeeper, the owner of the Vacca, the Biscione and the Albergo del Sole, in the fashionable quarters of Rome.

Rodrigo was, by all accounts, a solicitous but discreet father. He felt the natural Borgia desire to look after his own. The children of great men were, at that time, weapons in a political armoury, so Rodrigo looked after his offspring with the care of a father and the calculation of a general. The eldest son Pedro Luis, born in 1462 of an unknown mother, went at an early age to Spain, marked out for military duty. And because of the friendship between Borgia and King Ferdinand, Pedro Luis quickly did well in the royal service. His prospects, however, depended directly on the state of relations between king and cardinal. When Rodrigo was invited, in 1478, to be godfather to the son of the Catholic monarchs, the way forward looked clear. But then Rodrigo claimed for himself the see of Seville, a benefice that Ferdinand wanted for his bastard son Alfonso, and the king grew angry. He plucked Pedro Luis from the Aragon army at Granada and imprisoned him; he also confiscated all the Borgia estates. Then king and cardinal came together once more in support of Ferrante of Naples. Pedro Luis was released in 1485, fought well at the siege of Ronda, and was allowed to buy the estates of Gandia. He was created a duke and betrothed to the king's cousin. As the girl was still under age, Rodrigo hastily recalled his son to Rome where he could sit out the time without tempting the king to further rage. Pedro Luis died in 1488, leaving his duchy to his half-brother Juan, and a handsome dowry to his half-sister Lucrezia. Isabella and Girolama, the two Borgia girls from the early years before the advent of Vanozza, both married into noble Roman families. Girolama was wed at a very early age to Gianandrea Cesarini, making a sound political alliance for Rodrigo with a famous patrician clan; but both bride and groom died soon after. Isabella was married to Pietro Matuzzi, a minor aristocrat who spent a lifetime in the Roman city administration. Isabella died at the age of eighty, a well-respected Roman matron. If Rodrigo's first brood left little mark on the world, that was certainly not the case with the offspring of Vanozza. These four children inherited as much from their capable mother as from their calculating, sensual father, and the stamp they put on history bears signs of two traditions, the Spanish and the Italian struggling together in strange antipathies.

In the conclave that followed the death of Sixtus in 1484, Rodrigo Borgia, at fifty-three one of the senior and most experienced cardinals, seemed a likely candidate for the papal chair. But all the Spanish cardinals did not attend, and the warlike della Rovere, who in the reign of his uncle Sixtus had been opposed by the smoothly diplomatic Borgia, marshalled Italian support against the Spanish candidate.

'Borgia has the reputation of being so proud and false', the Florentine envoy reported, 'that there is no danger of him being elected.' The envoy was right. Della Rovere forced through the undistinguished Giovanni Battista Cibo, who became Pope Innocent VIII.

Cibo was a tall man of impressive bearing, open-hearted and good-humoured. Beyond that, he was a man without qualities. He was not wealthy, or clever, or brave; he was described as being 'not well read, but not entirely ignorant'. He had numerous children from an early stage of his career, and his gentle heart doted on them. His favourite son, Franceschetto, passed off as his nephew. Giuliano della Rovere had made him pope, and in general he was malleable in the cardinal's strong hands. Yet there had hardly been a time when the papacy was in such need of strong direction. The turmoil and hatreds roused by Sixtus persisted into the new pontificate. The struggle between Orsini and Colonna went on. War between Naples and the papal states recommenced. Innocent could find no policy but to follow the disastrous precedents of his forerunners. The pope's family, advanced to positions of power, bought and sold justice quite openly. Franceschetto had an arrangement whereby all fines over 150 ducats came to him and not the Apostolic Camera. Every vice and every crime could be redeemed for a price. 'God wills not the death of a sinner,' the Vice-Chamberlain is reported to have said, 'but that he should live and pay.' Rome was once more a city of horrors, pilgrims robbed at every gate, and the morning light revealing murdered bodies in the street. Both nobles and cardinals lived among armed servants in the security of fortified palaces. The little empires of the wordly prelates functioned independent of papal control. Innocent was liable to be insulted roundly if he dared to come out of the safety of the Vatican and advance into the cardinals' business. Seeing the spoils of the Church falling into the many, greedy hands of the Cibo family, the rulers of the Italian states clamoured for a share of the plunder. Even Lorenzo de' Medici, *il Magnifico*, agreed to a match between his daughter Maddalena and the wretched Franceschetto Cibo. Disorder increased throughout the land. Brigandage, which the ferocity of Sixtus had at least restrained, burst out again. Maximilian, who was heir to the Holy Roman Empire and boasted the traditional title of King of the Romans, had his envoys stripped of their clothes outside the city, and many an ambassador was forced to turn back within sight of Rome.

The three soldiers in Pinturicchio's 'Resurrection' are believed to be the pope's sons, Cesare, Juan and Jofré.

The eight years of Innocent's pontificate were critical for Rodrigo. He was growing old and felt that the next election must be his last chance to become pope. The excesses and sorry incapacity of Innocent day by day lessened the prospects of Cardinal della Rovere and his faction. There was little that Rodrigo could do except wait quietly and cultivate important allies. He had powerful Spanish backing. Ferdinand of Spain supported him, and nearer home Rodrigo was careful to keep on good terms with Ferrante of Naples and with his son Alfonso, Duke of Calabria. At the other end of Italy, Rodrigo allied himself with the Sforzas of Milan. He used every chance to spin a web of influence. For some years Rodrigo's cousin Adriana de Mila had acted as governess to his younger children. Adriana was a widow but not unattractive, so Rodrigo wove her into the loom of his destiny. She was married to Ludovico Orsini, a widower and a junior member of the great Roman family. And the skein was stretched still further. Adriana's new stepson, Orso Orsini, a moody boy who had lost an eye, was betrothed to Giulia Farnese. The marriage took place, in May 1489, in 'the room of the stars' at the Borgia palace. The bride was fourteen and so beautiful that the Romans called her Giulia Bella. Though the union was not a success, Rodrigo was 'like a father' to the young couple; and when Orso wandered off on pilgrimage, Rodrigo progressed from paternal affection to a lover's passion. Giulia, most scandalously for one so young, became his mistress and the love of his late years.

In 1490 Innocent fell ill. Forebodings shook Rome. All Italy seemed under a despondence; prophets predicted doom and the end to priestly power. Even Ferrante of Naples condemned the corruption of the pope and the flaunting of his children, and called on Maximilian to force through a reformation of the Church. Savonarola began his frantic denunciations in Florence. Then, in the first six months of 1492, there was a sudden fitful blaze of lights, illuminating the almost universal darkness. On 2 January, Granada, the last stronghold of the Moors in Spain, fell to the army of the Catholic kings, Ferdinand and Isabella. The good news coincided with the Roman carnival, and the Romans put all their pagan vitality into the rejoicings. Rodrigo and his son Cesare devised an entertainment in the Spanish mode and gave the citizens their first experience of a bullfight. Then in March, amid great feasting, young Giovanni de' Medici arrived triumphantly in Rome to receive his cardinal's hat. Two months later there came from the Turkish Sultan Bajazet II the gift of the Holy Lance, believed to be the one that pierced Christ's side on the Cross. Cardinal della Rovere accepted the Lance at the Porta Flaminia and carried it, enclosed in a crystal casket, through Rome. Then Borgia, the Vice-Chancellor, standing beside the pope, took the relic and held it aloft for all Rome to see.

In July 1492 Innocent was sinking; he died on the 25th. Cardinal Rodrigo Borgia had of late been much in the public eye. Over many years of careful diplomacy he had secured his position, amassed riches, fostered powerful allies, been discreet about his vices, and at last had even won some popularity among the games-loving Romans. Now all must be put to the test. Rodrigo was a robust, florid man of sixty-one and ready for the last gamble.

CHAPTER FOUR
POPE ALEXANDER VI

N THE LARGE TRAGEDY OF THE FIFTEENTH-CENTURY popes, the period up to the death of Paul II was the prologue. The pontificate of Sixtus IV began the sharp slide into the abyss. Two impulses towards dominion and grandeur, which in their proper place constituted noble ideals, drove the governors of the Church down. And nowhere were the elements of the tragedy better exemplified than in the person of Rodrigo Borgia. He had the energy, intelligence, ambition, political and administrative skill of a great ruler; he also had the charm, love of ease, taste for art and luxury, and the self-indulgence of the hedonist Renaissance prince. He was the worldly man *par excellence* projected by a sad accident of birth and time into the spiritual realm. And as men like Borgia possessed more and more the upper ranks of the Church hierarchy, so the spiritual foundation of the Church was weakened and corrupted, not so much by heresy or un-belief but by the drive to secular power and the capitulation to selfish appetites. The infection at the head spread throughout the limbs. 'In the primitive Church', said the famous preacher Savonarola, 'the chalices were of wood, the prelates of gold; in these days the Church has chalices of gold and prelates of wood.' And another despairing re-former cried out: 'The very men whom Christ has set apart have fallen away. The vineyard of the Lord is laid waste. If they did but go alone to destruction, it is an evil that might be borne; but as they are spread all over Christendom, like veins through the body, their iniquity must bring with it the ruin of the world.'

There seemed no way out of the maze. Every aspect and peculiarity of Italian life encouraged the worst tendencies of the papacy. 'I used to think', said one well-meaning prelate, 'that it would be as well to sepa-rate the temporal and spiritual powers entirely. But I have learned that

Pope Alexander VI adoring the risen Christ, painting by Bernardino Pinturicchio in the Borgia Apartment.

virtue without force is ludicrous. The pope of Rome, without the hereditary possessions of the Church, is only the servant of kings and princes.' Lorenzo de' Medici, accounted the wisest man in Italy, advised Pope Innocent VIII to set aside 'decorum and modesty' and stir himself in the interests of his power and his clan, among whom was now numbered Maddalena de' Medici, the pope's daughter-in-law. Lorenzo was voicing not only his own self-interest but also the general Italian opinion when he wrote:

> Your Holiness is now excused in the sight of God and man, and perhaps men may even censure your reserved behaviour and ascribe it to other motives. My zeal and duty make it a matter of conscience with me to remind you that no man is immortal. A pope has no importance other than what he can get for himself. He cannot make his dignity hereditary. The honours and benefits that he gives to those belonging to him are all that he can call his own.

The pope was merely another ruler in search of power and possessions. Yet, as Lorenzo himself noted, the result of playing at princes was to become the plaything of princes. A monarch, said Lorenzo, might promise anything; 'but rather than having to fulfil his promise, he will experience the indulgence that all popes have had for all kings'. Lorenzo de' Medici obeyed the pope only so far as it pleased him to do so.

So the election of a new pope was a working out of old themes, a pursuit of political aims according to party loyalties. 'In regard to these intrigues,' wrote the Florentine envoy on the death of Innocent, 'I will not attempt to enter into details which would only bewilder you and myself, for they are innumerable and change every hour.' Some things, however, were clear. Cardinal della Rovere, the *nipote* of Sixtus and the power behind Innocent, was a dangerous force, either as a candidate or popemaker. It was reported that Charles VIII of France had paid 200,000 ducats, and the republic of Genoa 100,000, to support della Rovere. He had perhaps nine cardinals attached to his cause. The chief opposition came from a group of cardinals marshalled by Ascanio Sforza in the interests of the duchy of Milan. Rodrigo Borgia, who rated only an outside chance because he was a Spaniard, was counted within the party of his friend Sforza. Nonetheless, the Bishop of Modena commented on Borgia's wealth, his many benefices, his Vice-

The strong profile of Cardinal Giuliano della Rovere, nephew of Pope Sixtus IV and Rodrigo's chief rival in a long struggle for power.

Chancellorship, and wondered what advantage that might give him. When the conclave began, the mood swung immediately against della Rovere, who was hated for his manipulation of the last pope and for his intrigues with the French. And when, after the third ballot, Cardinal Sforza saw his own chances disappear, he listened to the rich promises of his friend Borgia and threw his vote and his influence behind the Spanish cardinal. Rodrigo, as the Bishop of Modena had foreseen, reached into his deep sack of benefices and began to scatter rewards profusely. On the fourth day, one more vote would make Borgia pope. But the lines seemed drawn; those who could be bribed were satisfied, and the enemies of Rodrigo were immovable. The last hope was the venerable Venetian patriarch Gherardo, and finally the partisans of Borgia managed to penetrate the fogs that obscured the mind of the ninety-six-year-old prelate. On the dawn of the fifth day, the hall of the conclave was opened and the name of Rodrigo Borgia, Pope Alexander VI, proclaimed. The meagre crowd hurried away, as was the custom, to pillage the house of the new pope, while in St Peter's the giant Cardinal Sanseverino lifted Rodrigo bodily and placed him on the Apostle's Chair.

It was held against Alexander that he won his election by simony, by wholesale bribery and sale of offices. Stefano Infessura, the anti-papal Roman chronicler, had a picturesque story of four mules laden with silver passing on the last night of the conclave from the palace of Borgia to that of Ascanio Sforza. Such a blatant transfer was not necessary. The Vice-Chancellorship and the benefices that Borgia promised Ascanio were worth far more than four loads of silver. For many conclaves past, there had been an element of bribery and coercion in all papal elections, but the man chosen on past occasions had usually been a compromise candidate, deliberately selected to forestall the ambitions of the wealthiest cardinals. Alexander was perhaps the first who quite clearly bought the papacy for himself, and it was a measure of the times that this could happen. There were, even then, many laments that the Vicar of Christ had been elected in a wholly shameful manner, but the general reaction to the new pope was favourable. The Roman populace, torn as always between needing the pope and not liking him, at first feared for the future. The foremost city propagandist bewailed Italy's shame in permitting a Catalan to command the barque of St Peter, for the new pope

Cardinal Ascanio Sforza was to play a key role in the election of Rodrigo as Pope Alexander. After the election, it was said that four mules loaded with silver were seen going from Rodrigo's palace to that of Ascanio.

would surely sail away to Spain and take with him the Roman court and Roman prosperity. But soon, remembering Borgia's long residence in Rome and the rich ostentation of his life as cardinal, the city warmed to Pope Alexander, and on 12 August some 800 Roman notables went in horseback procession with lighted torches to the Vatican to welcome the pope, and the city blazed with bonfires.

The envoys and the ambassadors observing the conclave were also quite enthusiastic. Cardinal Borgia had been known as a talented man of affairs. He was just the right age, wrote one experienced official, 'about sixty, which is the age, as Aristotle says, when men are wisest'. The new pope was robust and dignified, understood etiquette thoroughly and shone in conversation; he also 'knew how to handle money matters very well'. He was a dominating figure: 'He is tall, neither fair nor dark in complexion. His eyes are black, his mouth rather full. His health is excellent, and he endures all fatigue marvellously. He is very eloquent in speech, and has a natural, graceful manner which never forsakes him.' But even that famous endurance was stretched to the limit by the coronation festivities, on 26 August 1492. The day was sullenly hot and the celebrations were prolonged with a magnificence beyond the usual. Great salvoes of artillery, of which Rodrigo was particularly fond, re-sounded across the city. Effigies, triumphal arches, altars stood in the streets. The Borgia arms, a bull on a golden ground, blazed from the roofs. The panegyrics, in that city of excess, went beyond all decency: Julius Caesar had been but a mortal, but Pope Alexander was a god. And everywhere there was the pressure of the crowd. 'You can imagine', wrote the Mantuan envoy, 'what it was to ride eight to ten miles at a stretch in that mob.' At the Lateran, the pope fell unconscious and had to be supported into the basilica by two cardinals. Seated at the altar in the papal chair, he fainted again and his head fell on the shoulder of Cardinal Riario. The incident was a salutary warning for one pious witness: 'it forcibly reminded me of the instability of all human things.'

The princes were reassured by Alexander. The usurping tyrant in Milan, Ludovico Sforza, known as 'il Moro', was more than pleased. His brother, Cardinal Ascanio Sforza, had made the pope and expected to benefit accordingly. In Florence there were public demonstrations of joy. The Knights of St John had high hopes that Alexander would sweep the Turks from the Mediterranean. Even Ferrante of Naples,

Ludovico Sforza of Milan, known as 'il Moro' from his emblem, the mulberry. Guicciardini described him as 'the guide and director of all the French dealings with the Italians'.

who had campaigned hard against Borgia, made some politic overtures, assuring the pope of his devotion 'as a good and obedient son'. Only the Venetians were actively hostile, muttering about simony and warning that the French king, for one, would never stand for such a fraudulent election. Outside Italy, comment was generally flattering. The by unknown women

Pedro Luis (1462?–88) First Duke of Gandia, 1485 (betrothed to Maria Enriquez)	Isabella (1467?–1541) **m.** Pietro Matuzzi	Girolama (1469?–83) **m.** Gianandrea Cesarini	Giovanni (1498–1548?) INFANS ROMANUS Duke of Camerino and Nepi | (possible offspring of Lucrezia or Cesare)	Rodrigo (born 1503)

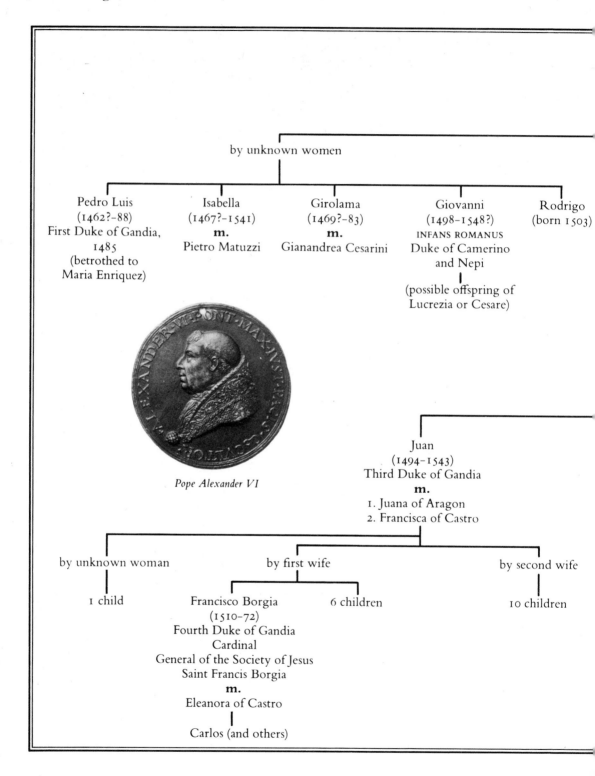

Pope Alexander VI

Juan
(1494–1543)
Third Duke of Gandia
m.
1. Juana of Aragon
2. Francisca of Castro

by unknown woman	by first wife	by second wife
1 child	Francisco Borgia (1510–72) Fourth Duke of Gandia Cardinal General of the Society of Jesus Saint Francis Borgia **m.** Eleanora of Castro | Carlos (and others) 6 children	10 children

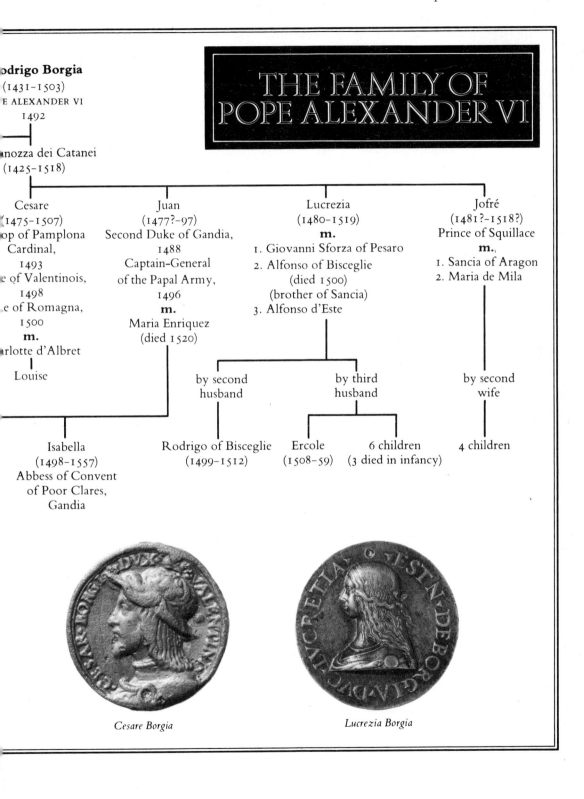

THE FAMILY OF POPE ALEXANDER VI

odrigo Borgia
(1431–1503)
E ALEXANDER VI
1492

nozza dei Catanei
(1425–1518)

Cesare
(1475–1507)
op of Pamplona
Cardinal,
1493
e of Valentinois,
1498
e of Romagna,
1500
m.
rlotte d'Albret

Louise

Isabella
(1498–1557)
Abbess of Convent
of Poor Clares,
Gandia

Juan
(1477?–97)
Second Duke of Gandia,
1488
Captain-General
of the Papal Army,
1496
m.
Maria Enriquez
(died 1520)

Lucrezia
(1480–1519)
m.
1. Giovanni Sforza of Pesaro
2. Alfonso of Bisceglie
   (died 1500)
   (brother of Sancia)
3. Alfonso d'Este

by second
husband

Rodrigo of Bisceglie
(1499–1512)

by third
husband

Ercole
(1508–59)

6 children
(3 died in infancy)

Jofré
(1481?–1518?)
Prince of Squillace
m.,
1. Sancia of Aragon
2. Maria de Mila

by second
wife

4 children

Cesare Borgia

Lucrezia Borgia

German chronicler Hartmann Schedel went into raptures about 'this large-minded man, gifted with great prudence, foresight, and knowledge of the world'. And Alexander's first acts seemed to confirm the high estimates of his character. He immediately took hold of Rome and imposed order on the city in which there had been 220 murders in the short interval between Innocent's last illness and Alexander's coronation. He set up commissions to look into grievances, and set aside his own Tuesdays to hear petitioners. He drew up rules for the papal household of exemplary austerity, extraordinary for a Borgia, his expenditure being only 20 to 30 ducats a day. At dinner he permitted only one dish, though he required it to be of good quality. The cardinals, and even the pope's sons Cesare and Juan, used to the abundance of former days, began to avoid invitations to this frugal table. Alexander also had bold and well-intentioned plans for the government of the Church. He was determined, he told the envoy of Milan, to bring peace to Italy and unite all Christendom against the Turks, following the example of his uncle Calixtus. His greatest desire, he told the Florentines, was to be father to all men without distinction. And the envoy of Ferrara reported that the pope had in mind the reform of the papal court and changes in the administration of the Curia; he also promised to keep his children at a distance.

The preferment of the Borgia children had begun long before. Cesare, destined for the Church as a younger son, had been proclaimed elegible for Holy Orders at the age of six, though his father was a cardinal and his mother a married woman. Innocent had made him Bishop of Pamplona before he was out of his teens and still a student at Pisa. For a while it looked as if Alexander would keep his initial promise. Cesare was ordered to stay away from Rome. But all too soon the inevitable pull of family tore apart the good intentions. In his first consistory, within a month of the election, Alexander granted Cesare the see of Valencia – Borgia property for more than fifty years – with its income of 16,000 ducats. At the same time the pope gave his nephew Juan Borgia Lanzol a cardinal's hat. Soon an avaricious horde of Borgia relatives advanced upon the indulgent pope. One document of the time numbers more than thirty Borgias in high positions of Church and state. 'Ten papacies', wrote an envoy sourly, 'would not be enough to satisfy this swarm of relatives.' Two Borgias were captains in the Palatine

Alexander VI saying mass. Like his uncle Calixtus, Alexander loved the holy theatre of the liturgy, enjoyed strict observation of feasts and fasts and demanded church attendance from the cardinals.

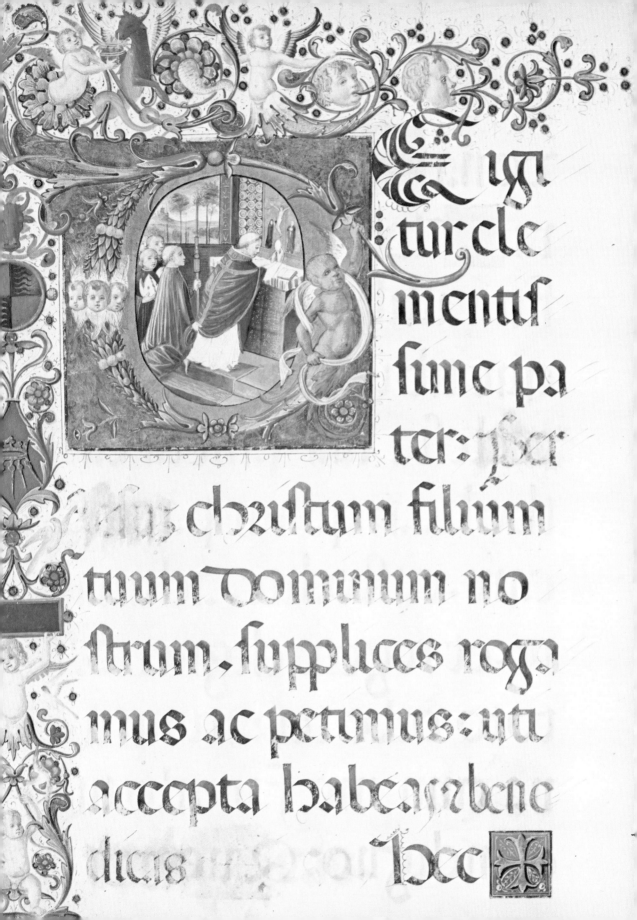

tur cle
mentus
sunc pa
ter: jsa
chustum filium
tuum dominum no
strum. supplices roge
mus ac petmus: ut
accepta habeas bene
dicas

Guard; another was castellan of the important town of Tivoli; another was the pope's equerry. In the course of his pontificate Alexander raised five members of his family to the College of Cardinals. His son Cesare became a cardinal in September 1493.

Papal nepotism was an old scandal; Alexander added a further disgrace to his high office in the person of the pope's mistress. Many previous popes had advanced their relatives, and Innocent VIII had made a shocking display of his children. But Alexander was the first not only to favour relatives, but also to honour his children, and to parade a mistress – a shameful trinity of vices. The position of Giulia Farnese was no secret to Romans. She lived, together with the pope's daughter Lucrezia, in the household of her mother-in-law Adriana de Mila. Cardinal Zeno had given them his newly built palace of Santa Maria in Portico, which, like the Vatican Palace, had a private door into St Peter's. Alexander had only to walk across the basilica to visit both his daughter and his mistress.

Trapped into the old ways of nepotism, Alexander was no more successful than his predecessors in avoiding the meshes of Italian politics. He had inherited from the incompetent Innocent a most precarious balance. The papal states were in uproar, as happened so often when the pope took his eye off them. Perugia had slipped under the unofficial lordship of the Baglione family, and other cities were on the verge of falling to local despots. Ludovico il Moro of Milan was intriguing with Charles VIII of France, and Alexander was being drawn towards them by his debt to Ascanio Sforza. Ferrante of Naples was thoroughly alarmed, for he had a niece married to the young duke of Milan whom Ludovico set out to depose, and moreover the French king was taking up the claim of the house of Anjou to the throne of Naples. So to frustrate the scheming of the pope and the Sforzas, Ferrante provided help for Virginio Orsini, the commander of the Neapolitan army, to buy and occupy Cerveteri and Anguillara, two dominating towns to the north of Rome, and thus threaten the city on behalf of Naples. In the Sacred College, Giuliano della Rovere and Ascanio Sforza were implacable enemies. Della Rovere, whose star was temporarily in eclipse, retired to Ostia and never ventured out without a strong escort. Ferdinand of Spain, who was naturally anxious that a Spanish pope and a Spanish king of Naples should not come to blows, attempted to act as

ncesco Gonzaga, in
nour, kneels in grati-
le on one side of the
rgin's throne. He
mmissioned Andrea
antegna to paint 'The
adonna of Victories' in
filment of a vow made
ring the battle of
rnovo and to celebrate
victory against
arles VIII in 1495 and
subsequent award of
Golden Rose.

peacemaker, but received from Ferrante a broadside of accusations against Alexander.

> The pope [he wrote] has no respect for the holy Chair, and leads such a life that people turn away in horror. By fair means or foul he seeks nothing but the aggrandizement of his children. What he wants is war, and has persecuted me without cease since the first day of his pontificate. There are more soldiers than priests in Rome. The pope desires war and rapine, and his cousins the Sforzas drive him on, seeking to tyrannize over the papacy and make Rome a Milanese camp.

These were partisan complaints, but they show the agitation in Italy, and a general recognition of the pope's immorality.

Events, in truth, began to frighten Alexander. His usual instinct had always been to buy time and to preserve a balance through negotiation and alliances. But the intrigues of the conclave had thrown him firmly into the arms of Milan, and the presence of the truculent Orsini waving the Neapolitan sword just outside Rome rattled him. In something of a panic he had solicited help from all the European powers, an appeal that France, for her own motives, would gladly answer later on. But the panic soon passed and Alexander seemed to be making headway by peaceful means. In April 1493 he joined with Milan and Venice in the League of St Mark, to which Siena, Mantua and Ferrara also assented. The pact was cemented, two months later, by the marriage of Lucrezia Borgia – only twelve years old – to Giovanni Sforza of Pesaro. The wedding feast was celebrated in the Vatican with inimitable Borgia theatricality and pomp. The pope and his mistress, the dazzling Giulia Bella, were in stately attendance. Juan Borgia, the Duke of Gandia, set a new fashion, dressed in the Turkish style in a robe of gold brocade embroidered with rubies and pearls. After the marriage ceremony, there was first a pastoral eclogue, and then a performance of Plautus' *Menaechmi*, which bored the pope greatly. In the evening, there was dancing and feasting, a 'worthy comedy' and much uproarious behaviour. Confetti was thrown into the low-cut bodices of the ladies' dresses, and handfuls of expensive sweetmeats were scattered from the windows on to the applauding crowd, much to the distress of that worthy German Johann Burchard, the pope's Master of Ceremonies. On account of the bride's extreme youth, the usual inspection of the

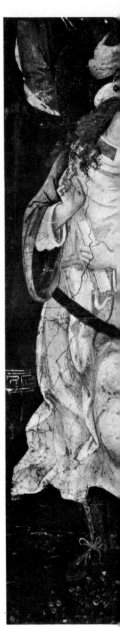

In 1493 the pope's son Jofré was betrothed to Sancia, Princess of Squillace, the illegitima[te] daughter of Alfonso of Calabria, to strengthen Alexander's alliance wi[th]

couple in the marriage bed was forgone, and instead the festivities went on all through the night. 'The ladies danced', wrote the envoy Gian-andrea Boccaccio, 'and as an interlude we had an excellent play with much singing and music. The pope and all the others were there. What more can I say? My letter would never end if I described it all. Thus we spent the whole night, whether ill or well, I leave your highness to judge.'

With Milan and Venice bound to the papacy by the League of St Mark, Alexander could now consider peace with Naples, and his thoughts were turned in that direction by the arrival of Don Diego Lopez de Haro, ambassador from Ferdinand of Spain. Ferdinand was worried by the pope's rift with Ferrante, but his ambassador also brought a great matter which urged Alexander to act once more the role of Universal Pastor, an office almost forgotten by fifteenth-century popes, immersed as they were in parochial Italian business. The discoveries of Columbus had within the last year pointed the way to the New World, and now the navigators of Spain and Portugal were in hot competition for those rich lands. Alexander was asked to arbitrate, and in the Bull *Inter Caetera* he divided the world very much in favour of his native Spain. By this act, however, he asserted the right of the papacy to have a voice in the new discoveries and paved the way for the vast Christianizing enterprise that the missioners of Spain and Portugal carried out on the heels of the conquistadors.

From the grandeur of the world view, Don Diego's tactful reminders brought Alexander back to the nagging question of Ferrante. The king of Naples was anxious to reach an accommodation, for he knew that a French envoy was due in Rome to seek the investiture of Naples for the French king. Alexander was open to persuasion, and went about the problem in his usual way by a series of strategic alliances. His much-loved son Juan, Duke of Gandia, was sent off to Spain to marry a member of the Spanish royal house, and his youngest son, Jofré, was betrothed to Sancia, the illegitimate daughter of Ferrante's son. Thus with two bold strokes of Borgia policy, Alexander formed important alliances and advanced his children into royal households at the same time. He also allowed himself to be reconciled, for a price, to both Cardinal della Rovere and Virginio Orsini. With masterly diplomacy, Alexander seemed to have disarmed all opponents and brought the fractious states of Italy back into equilibrium. The Milanese envoy wrote admiringly:

> Does this look like a pope who has lost his head? As far as I can see just the contrary is the case. He has negotiated a League which made the king of Naples groan; he has contrived to marry his daughter to a Sforza who, besides his pension from Milan, has a yearly income of 12,000 ducats; he has humbled Virginio Orsini and obliged him to pay; and he has brought King Ferrante into a family connection with himself. Does this look like a man whose intellect is decaying? Alexander intends to enjoy his power in peace and quietude.

This was the high point of Alexander's achievement. Yet peace and quiet were not granted him, nor was his power safe to enjoy. As a foremost temporal prince he played the pope's accustomed part in Italian polity with great skill, but that scheme of things, a fragile mosaic made by conscious art, was shattered by the force of its own contradictions, and then ground into dust by the brutal force of European nationalism. The historian Francesco Guicciardini, writing some forty years after the time, looked back on the few years around 1490 as the apogee in the history of the Italian states.

> In peaceful quiet, cultivated no less in the rough mountains than in the fertile plains, knowing no other rule than that of its own people, Italy was not only rich in population, merchandise and wealth, but also adorned to the highest degree by the magnificence of many princes, by the splendour of innumerable noble cities, by the throne and majesty of religion. She was full of men most able in public affairs, and of noble minds learned in every branch of study and versed in every worthy art and skill. Nor did she lack military glory, according to the standards of those times. And being so richly endowed, she deservedly enjoyed a most brilliant reputation among all other nations.

The patriot made a most affecting case for the triumphs of the Italian Renaissance, but he did not mention the quagmire on which this glorious edifice rested. The political artifices of wars, leagues, plots, alliances, treacheries, which the Italian rulers claimed to treat with such an objective certainty, were in time multiplied crazily in a pursuit of power which lost touch with morality, legitimacy, all settled and established order, and therefore lost touch in the end with outside reality.

Campaigns were pursued to mad ends, wretched villages of no value besieged for months at a time, and battles joined in which one man would be killed, smothered by the weight of his own armour. Peasant fields were trampled again and again by the mercenary armies of the *condottieri*, hurrying from one paymaster to the next. Italians were largely free from feudal ties, but they were subject to arbitary taxation very often to support tyrannical ruling houses of no legitimacy whatsoever. So the general populace, far from applauding that golden age of Guicciardini's memories, fostered another dream and, like Dante who sighed for the Holy Roman Emperor to impose order on this perilous land, prayed that the strong king of France would put an end to this age of mutability and woe. And when the French armies of Charles VIII did cross the Alps in 1494, many ordinary Italians greeted them, Philippe de Commines noted in amazement, 'like saints'.

The dire prophesies of the Dominican fanatic and reformer Savonarola were in part fulfilled. They were the last maledictions on the old order. When Lorenzo de' Medici, 'il Magnifico', died in April 1492 at the untimely age of forty-three, the great pilot of the Italian shoals went under. It was he, Machiavelli wrote, who had 'put a stop to the internal wars of Italy, and by his wisdom and authority established peace'. The heavens themselves seemed to give auguries of an approaching doom; in Florence, the pinnacle of the church of Santa Reparata was struck by lightning and crashed down before the frightened citizens. Machiavelli said that all the princes of Italy mourned Lorenzo, 'and the justness of their grief was shortly after apparent; for being deprived of his counsel, his survivors were unable to satisfy or restrain the ambition of Ludovico Sforza of Milan; and hence, soon after the death of Lorenzo, those evil plants began to germinate, which in a little time ruined Italy.'

In his Lenten sermons of 1494, Savonarola preached so powerfully on the text 'Behold, I shall bring a great flood upon the earth' that the listening Angelo Poliziano felt his hair stand on end, and the Florentines at first sobbed and then went about in a ghostly silence. The signs of a coming catastrophe had been multiplying. In the previous year, at the marriage of the pope's daughter Lucrezia, the envoy of Ferrara had noted that the presence of the French ambassador and his friendship with Milan had caused other states to boycott the wedding. The pope's children, necessary links in the papal chain of alliances, were becoming a cause of worry. Juan Borgia, the youthful Duke of Gandia, instead of binding Rome and Spain had earned the displeasure of King Ferdinand. When Juan had set out to marry Ferdinand's cousin, in August 1493, Alexander had given his profligate son a warning, in his own hand-writing, against gambling and womanizing. A bishop and two of the pope's most trusted servants accompanied the young duke to keep him out of trouble. By Christmas, Alexander heard with great consternation that Juan was gambling heavily, and that he spent his nights in the brothels of Barcelona or Valencia, roistering with street gallants, molesting honest citizens and killing dogs and cats for sport. Worst of all, Juan had not consummated his marriage. This insult to the Spanish royal family could hardly bear contemplation. In fury, both his father and his elder brother Cesare wrote to Juan that 'nothing could upset a woman more' than failure to consummate; hastily the pope wrote to his agents begging them to tell him 'the pure and simple truth' about his son's behaviour 'to our dear daughter the duchess'. Juan protested that the marriage had been consummated not once but many times, and at last the pope was reassured when the glad news of the duchess's pregnancy arrived. The marriage between Lucrezia and Giovanni Sforza was also unconsummated and a cause of trouble. Giovanni, impoverished by the demands that Rome made on his purse, had returned to Pesaro to try to recoup some of his debts, and from there he was forced to beg the pope for an advance on his bride's dowry, which was usually withheld until after consummation. Alexander was willing to pay the money but, having parted with his favourite son Juan, would not let his daughter join her husband. Nor was Giovanni anxious to come back to Rome. The division between the couple was a potential source of friction between Alexander and his allies the Sforzas.

It was now apparent that Alexander, increasingly beset by problems, needed his intimate household more and more. But the frivolity of his domestic circle exerted an influence that a pope in these baleful times could well have done without. In the Palazzo di Santa Maria in Portico, Adriana de Mila still presided over the joint households of the pope's daughter and the pope's mistress, and to the palace there came an un-ending stream of visitors in search of favours or intrigue. Gianandrea Boccaccio, the envoy from Ferrara, attended the papal ladies assidu-ously and has left several intimate pictures of the domestic scene. He was

there on the occasion when the question of a cardinal's hat for young
Ippolito d'Este was being discussed, and the matter was casually disposed of by Adriana de Mila. 'I've talked to the pope several times,' she
said, 'we'll make him a cardinal.' In the private apartments, Lucrezia
and Giulia, both married though not yet twenty, played the coquette
for handsome visitors. Lorenzo Pucci, calling on his relative Giulia,
watched her drying her hair before the fire, then gathering up the
tresses which hung to her feet, she dressed them in a gold net so that her
head 'looked like the sun'. Giulia's daughter Laura was brought in, and

though the child was only two, Pucci thought she resembled Pope Alexander, who was said to be the father. Indeed, the child was the real object of Pucci's attention, for a bastard of a pope, though still a baby, was already a candidate for a political marriage alliance. Neither boudoir nor nursery could escape the games of power.

Throughout the last months of 1493 Alexander maintained an uneasy peace with Ferrante. In his declining days, the king of Naples feared for the future of his Spanish kingdom in Italy, built up with such pain and bloodshed. He poured out letters of complaint against the pope, in angry protest against the French influence at the papal court. He feared also the power of Milan where Ludovico il Moro, going from strength to strength, had recently arranged a marriage between his daughter Bianca and the Emperor Maximilian. With the extinction of his own line much in his mind, Ferrante died in January 1494. Alexander could no longer temporize over Naples. Alfonso II, Ferrante's heir, clamoured for papal recognition of his right to the throne. Charles VIII, intent upon the same end, was known to be gathering a large army in France with the purpose, so it was said, of conquering Naples and then using southern Italy as the springboard for a magnificent crusade. Alexander sternly warned France against an attack on a fellow Christian kingdom, but softened the message by the gift of the Golden Rose. But the pope's mind was made up. Although he had dallied with France for the sake of a temporary advantage against Ferrante, Alexander could not allow the French king to dominate Italy. The papacy remembered only too well the 'Babylonian captivity' in Avignon. Seventy years of toil, intelligence and plotting had gone into the establishment of an independent Roman papacy, and no pope could bear to see the Supreme Apostolate fall under the ominous, selfish power of French nationalism.

Having decided in favour of Alfonso, Alexander drove a typical hard bargain on behalf of his children. Juan and Jofré received Neapolitan principalities, and Cesare got several benefices. Juan, though now resident in Spain, was also offered 33,000 ducats a year as a *condottiere* in the Neapolitan army. It was agreed that the projected marriage between Jofré and Alfonso's daughter Sancia should be brought forward immediately, and that the pope's nephew, Cardinal Juan Borgia Lanzol, should crown the new king in Naples. On the day of the coronation Burchard, the papal Master of Ceremonies, was at the cathedral before

Alfonso II, Duke of Calabria, was crowned King of Naples by Cardinal Juan Borgia Lanzol on 8 May 1494. In the same week Jofré and Sancia were married.

dawn to supervise the arrangements for the complicated ritual. The day
was 8 May, Ascension Day, chosen by the superstitious king because it
coincided with the full moon. During the ceremony, Burchard noted
that the orb was attached to the king's hand by silken cords and a small
chain, for if it fell it would presage disaster. In the same week Jofré and
Sancia were married, and the pope's son became Prince of Squillace
with a yearly income of 40,000 ducats.

The die was now most firmly cast. Charles VIII was outraged and
threatened to withdraw his obedience. The College of Cardinals was
split. Giuliano della Rovere had retreated once more to the safety of
Ostia and began secret negotiations with France. At the end of April he
fled to the French, leaving Ostia garrisoned to hold out against the pope.
The port, which was the key to the Tiber and to sea communications
with Rome, was essential to Alexander, but luckily the defence was
half-hearted and it capitulated before long. That, however, was not an
end to the danger. Cardinal Ascanio Sforza was alienated from the pope
by the Neapolitan alliance, which went against the interests of Milan.
He reported that Alexander was frightened by the efforts of della
Rovere and the French to call a Church Council, which might very well
want to depose Alexander on the grounds of his simoniacal election. So
when the French envoys came to Rome in May to demand for their
master the investiture of Naples, the pope gave them soft answers and
the charming courtesy for which he was renowned. But the French
were not deceived. They began to suborn prelates from the pope's side
and finance unrest in the papal states. A French invasion seemed inevitable. Alexander, said an official in the Curia who was a keen observer
of these events, could expect help from no one but Alfonso; the papal
army was insignificant; the loyalty of cities within the papal states was
suspect. In desperation, Alexander even solicited money from the
Sultan Bajazet, whom Charles was threatening with a crusade. But all
in vain. There was nothing left but to meet Alfonso and try to devise
a plan of defence. They met at Vicovaro in July and decided to send
their joint forces, under Alfonso's eldest son Ferrantino, into Romagna
to hold the Lombardy border; meanwhile the king's brother, Federigo
of Aragon, would take the fleet and try to capture Genoa.

There was also another serious embarrassment in the pope's family.
Giovanni Sforza, Lucrezia's husband, was in the difficult position of

being a *condottiere* of Milan by virtue of his name and birth, and a *condottiere* of Naples by virtue of marriage to the pope's child. The poor young man did not know what to do, and Alexander, waving aside such moralistic quibbles, curtly told him to suit himself. Giovanni's instincts were all in favour of his Sforza clan, but he was afraid to lose Pesaro, which was a papal fief. In an agony of indecision he wrote to his cousin Ludovico il Moro, protesting his loyalty to the Sforza cause, saying that he would have eaten the straw of his mattress rather than become a papal *condottiere*, had he but known where that would lead him. He decided to retreat with his wife to Pesaro, where he would be safe from Rome and closer to his Milanese roots. Alexander, reluctant as ever to let his children go, was persuaded by an outbreak of plague in Rome to release Lucrezia, and gave her permission to stay in Pesaro for two months. On 31 May, Giovanni and Lucrezia left Rome, accompanied by Adriana de Mila, Giulia Farnese and a bevy of maids-in-waiting, all carefully shepherded by the pope's confidential agent Francesco Gaçet, who had strict orders to have the whole party back in Rome by the end of July.

Giovanni Sforza, lord of Pesaro and one of the papal vicars of the Romagna. His marriage to Lucrezia Borgia in 1493 sealed papal adherence to the League of St Mark.

Released from the oppressive fears of Rome and the dominating figure of Pope Alexander, the girls – Lucrezia was fourteen and Giulia five years older – were in good spirits. They thought chiefly of balls and entertainments, singing and dancing; they dressed with a fine disregard for expense, 'as if we had despoiled Florence of brocade'. They wrote dutiful letters to the pope, showing an affectionate solicitude for him amid his trials. 'We hear that things are going badly in Rome', Lucrezia wrote, 'and I implore your Holiness to leave, but if that is not practical to take the greatest possible care.' Alexander was satisfied by frequent letters, but when the round of pleasures interrupted the flow of the correspondence he grew testy. He complained of the dangerous decisions forced on him 'when the French are coming by land and sea' and played the jealous lover, scolding Giulia for her frivolity and heartlessness. Giulia replied with meek submission: 'As your Holiness, upon whom all my well-being and happiness depends, is not here, it is impossible for me to enjoy these pleasures, because where my treasure is there my heart is also.' The protestations were not very convincing; above all the young women were not anxious to return to Rome. They were mistresses of a small, admiring society, full of gallantry and play-

Lucrezia Borgia, Alexander VI's beloved daughter. She was described as being 'of middle height and graceful in form. Her face is rather long, the nose well cut, the hair golden'.

fulness, and had no wish to suffer under the weight of Roman despondency. Giovanni also had good reason to avoid the pope. Pressed by Alexander to put his *condotta* under the command of Naples, Giovanni had decided to play a double game, joining the Neapolitan forces but acting as a spy for his Sforza relatives.

In early July, when Giulia heard that her eldest brother was dying, nothing could stop her from hurrying to him, so Adriana and Gaçet escorted her across the mountains, through a land made dangerous

Charles VIII, the hideous
young King of France,
crossed the Alps into
Italy in 1494, threatening
the papal states, the
Italian balance of power
and even the position
of the pope.

The young Alessandro Farnese, brother of the Pope's mistress Giulia Farnese, was elevated to the Sacred College by Alexander to balance the power held by the Orsini and the Colonna families.

by the preparations for war, to the Farnese family home at Capodimonte on Lake Bolsena. Alexander returned to Rome after his meeting with King Alfonso, worried by the absence of Giulia, but apparently content that she should remain at Capodimonte. Then he heard that Giulia's long-forgotten husband, the one-eyed Orso Orsini, had reappeared and was at Bassanello, not thirty miles from Capodimonte, neglecting his military duties and calling for his wife to join him. Alexander was furious. He sent peremptory orders for Giulia to stay away from her husband and to return to Rome; and when Giulia did not return he struck out with the jealousy of a wounded lover against the 'thankless and treacherous Giulia', against her brother Cardinal Alessandro Farnese, universally known as 'the petticoat cardinal', and particularly against the governess Adriana de Mila, who had failed in her trust and had 'finally laid bare the malignity and evil of her soul'. In his rage, in a tragi-comic perversion of his spiritual power, he threatened his mistress with excommunication.

On 2 September 1494 the French army crossed the Alps and pressed on down the leg of Italy. In November the pope's ladies were still at Capodimonte. They had avoided Bassanello, and now that Orso had joined his troops, having first wrung some money out of the pope, Alexander, with so many great matters on his mind, forgot his lover's quarrel. In late November the ladies set out to join Cardinal Farnese in Viterbo. But they had misjudged the speed of the French advance. On the Via Cassia they encountered a French detachment and were taken prisoner. The captain, on learning their identities, courteously escorted them to Montefiascone and demanded the customary ransom. At once the pope dispatched 3000 ducats. On 1 December, accompanied by a large troop of French soldiers, the ladies were brought to the gate of Rome, and there a striking figure came forward to meet them, a tall, portly man of sixty-three, 'arrayed in a black doublet edged with gold brocade, belted in the Spanish fashion with sword and dagger; he wore also Spanish boots and a velvet biretta.' Pope Alexander had come to play the gallant to his mistress while Church and state tumbled down; and that night Giulia slept in the apostolic palace.

Both the warnings of the wise and the ranting of fanatics were now realized. Charles VIII, the hideous young king with the lacklustre eyes, the hooked nose, the stuttering, blubbery lips, and hands convulsively

twitching, led a national army of about 40,000 men. With the megalomania of the simple, against the advice of his counsellors, he intended to conquer Naples, extend an imperial rule throughout Italy, subject the papacy once again to France, and make himself the master of Europe. The French invasion was the first incursion of a strong national army into the Italian realm of mercenary warfare, and the results horrified the Italians. War, in the Italian way, had been reduced to art, and the elegant manoeuvres of the *condottieri* were aimed at the possession of territory and the capture of prisoners for ransom rather than the slaughter of the enemy. Italian soldiers had become the scholars, not the practitioners, of war; no one in Europe knew more about the theory of fortifications, of artillery, of offensive and defensive strategies, yet hardly anyone fought with less heart, or with more determination to keep the whole murderous business within human bounds and thereby save one's own skin. Battles before 1494, said Guicciardini, were protracted but largely bloodless, and artillery, although in general use, 'was managed with such want of skill that it caused little hurt'. The general attitude sympathized with Paolo Vitelli who, it was said, put out the eyes and cut off the hands of captured artillerymen, indignant that a knight could be slain at long distance by a mere lackey behind a gun. But the French had cannon hauled by horses, not oxen, firing cannon balls not of stone, but of unshatterable iron, and with this 'diabolical rather than human instrument' they intimidated castles and played havoc with armies. The Swiss infantry employed by the French advanced steadily without breaking rank, more arrogant and more bestial, wrote the Ferrarese envoy, than any soldier he had ever seen.

At first the French met no opposition. Their march was more like a triumphal procession. Charles was welcomed by pantomime and festivities, by children with banners bearing the French arms. At Asti, his Italian allies Ludovico Sforza, Giuliano della Rovere and Ercole d'Este greeted him. Here the king went down with smallpox and the expedition was delayed while he recovered. The Neapolitan fleet was defeated at Rapallo, and the French turned the flank of the papal army in the Romagna. Accompanied by frightening reports of French brutality and bloodlust, Charles's army strode down the peninsula. The Florentine fortress of Sarzana capitulated at the first shot. The closer the French came to Rome the more panic and disorder there was in the city and

arles VIII and his army
de down the Italian
insula, while Alex-
der prepared to defend
me.

among the pope's allies. In September, Ascanio Sforza instigated a revolt among the Colonna, who treacherously occupied Ostia and hoisted
the French flag. French ships began to appear in the mouth of the Tiber.
Alexander was at his wit's end. The Neapolitan resistance was crumbling
away and the pope's traditional friends were deserting. When Orsini
changed sides and placed the huge castle of Bracciano in French hands,
Alexander knew that the defence of Rome was impossible. On Christmas Day he ordered Ferrantino to take his troops back to Naples. The
city fathers, with the pope's approval, surrendered the city to Charles
at Bracciano, and Alexander retired to the security of the Castel
Sant'Angelo to await developments. On the last day of 1494, the French
army marched through the Porta del Popolo and took possession of
Rome. 'The French', said Alexander, 'came in with wooden spears and
found they had nothing to do but the quartermaster's work of marking
the doors with chalk.'

The pope's first instinct had been to flee. Then he considered that his armies and his allies were his weakness and that his strength lay in his own subtlety and in the majesty of his position. He did not take the cowardly step, but decided to match the cunning of a Supreme Pontiff, long-experienced in the ways of the world, against the wit of a twenty-two-year-old king who showed every sign of instability. Charles entered Rome to cries of *Viva Francia*, but taking no chances he massed his artillery in front of his residence at the Palazzo Venezia and had every bit of food and drink tasted in his presence. Romans, as the world knew, had a reputation as poisoners. Locked within the Castel Sant' Angelo, Alexander began to set nets to catch the unwary king. Before long, the French popularity had worn thin. Charles was offensively ugly; he came to table in clogs and dined with boorish gluttony. The French 'barbarians' were sacking the houses of prelates, strangling Jews in the ghetto, and hanging Romans on the Campo dei Fiori. Even Vanozza, the mother of the pope's children, had her palace ransacked. Time was on the side of Alexander. Della Rovere and the cardinals of France pressed for a Church Council to depose this simoniacal pontiff, but Alexander's negotiators quietly insinuated into the king's ear that, if his ambition was the conquest and investiture of Naples, he might be better off dealing with a pope who not only had the papacy actually in his possession, but also was generally recognized as having it by right. 'The king was young', Philippe de Commines sagely remarked, 'and his surroundings did not fit him for so great a work as the reform of the Church.' The king was impatient to move on to Naples, and the pope was anxious to get rid of him now that his own safety was no longer secure; for on the night of 10 January a portion of the wall of Sant' Angelo had collapsed of its own accord. On the 15th terms were agreed. The French would have free passage across the papal states and Cesare Borgia would accompany them as papal legate – in reality as hostage. The Turkish Prince Jem, who had been a papal prisoner since 1489, with the connivance of the sultan who paid a yearly sum to keep his brother out of the way, would be handed over to Charles for use in his crusade. Several cities and castles would have French governors, and prelates who had gone over to France were to be granted an amnesty. In return, the pope could keep the Castel Sant'Angelo and the departing French would hand back the keys of the city. Charles promised to offer obedi-

The Turkish Prince Jem handed over to King Charles by Alexander to pay for a relaxation of French pressure. Jem died soon after leaving Rome in French custody.

ence to Alexander, leave him master of the pontiff's spiritual and temporal realms, and protect him against all enemies.

The terms were hard but not ruinous, and Alexander thought it was now time to emerge from isolation. He invited Charles to stay at the Vatican and overwhelmed the young king with the wiles of a sophisticated charmer. In the matter of kissing of hands, doffing of hats, bending of knees, allowing precedence before doors, no one was so capable as Alexander in fostering a sense of inferiority in an inexperienced youth. The pope, wrote the Mantuan envoy, 'gratifies the French in every way; favours of all sorts are bestowed on them.' But every time the hard question of the Neapolitan investiture came up, Alexander wriggled free. On 28 January Charles left Rome with little for his pains but the agreement of the 15th, and the nomination of two new cardinals. Alexander, on the other hand, had heard from the royal lips – those loose, stuttering lips – the profession of the king's obedience. It was a remarkable triumph of papal wit; Rome was free of the French and the pope's tenure of the Sacred Chair was secure.

In fine weather Charles marched towards Naples, and although he met with some mixed fortune that might have deterred a more prudent man, the signs were generally good. In Velletri the ambassadors of Ferdinand the Catholic protested vigorously in the name of Spain against the treatment of the pope, against the French occupation of papal towns, and most vehemently against the attack on Naples, the brother kingdom of Aragon. Charles felt strong enough to ignore these protests, but another unpleasant surprise also awaited him. Cesare Borgia, the hostage, had escaped. Better news, however, was that King Alfonso II had abdicated in terror and fled to Sicily, leaving a desperate inheritance to his son Ferrantino. The road was clear to Naples. Rumours of French brutality were enough to make resistance melt away. At the end of February, in unusually good weather with the spring flowers already showing, Charles entered Naples to a tumultuous welcome. 'In the short space of a few weeks', a chronicler wrote, 'the French conquered, as by a miracle, a whole kingdom, almost without striking a blow.'

While Charles dallied in Naples, seduced, as all conquerors have been by the drowsy humours of that fickle, enticing city, the rest of the world awoke at last to the dangers of the invasion. Italian opposition, formerly

udovico il Moro, Duke
f Milan, and his family
s donors before the
Madonna and Child
nthroned. Fearing that
Charles VIII would put
orward an old claim to
he duchy of Milan,
udovico regretted his
nvitation to the King of
rance to claim the
ingdom of Naples.

a placid beast that Charles drove with hardly a touch of the whip, now became a tiger. Alexander steadily refused to invest Charles with the conquered realm, though the king tempted the pope with enormous bribes. Ludovico il Moro, having helped the French to come, now prayed for them to go, fearing that the French crown was going to put forward an old claim to the duchy of Milan. The Venetians, worried about trade, showed a traditional disquiet at the imbalance of power and the likely disturbance of the Mediterranean sea routes. Spain had already indicated that she would not be idle while France took one Spanish kingdom in Italy and threatened another in Sicily. The famous Spanish general Gonzalo de Córdoba was sent to Sicily. And lastly, Emperor Maximilian, who had some pretension to be the foremost Christian prince, could not sit by while France swept over Italy, the foremost Christian land. On 31 March 1495, all the enemies of the French came together in Venice and formed a Holy League, ostensibly for the defeat of the Turks, but in reality to defend Italy and to preserve the rights of the papacy and the Holy Roman Empire. On Palm Sunday Alexander ordered the solemn proclamation of the League throughout his territories. The great European monarchies were now engaged in Italy, and the papacy was caught between these mighty grindstones.

CHAPTER FIVE
ALEXANDER AND CESARE

THE OPPOSITION OF THE HOLY LEAGUE, WHICH threatened to cut the lines of communication and isolate Charles in southern Italy, forced him to retreat from Naples. He left a viceroy and half his army, then burdened with 20,000 mule loads of Neapolitan spoils he retraced his steps to the Alps. Rome, which had celebrated his departure but three months before, shuddered at his reappearance. 'People are in terror,' an envoy wrote in May; 'Rome has never been so entirely cleared of silver and valuables. Not one of the cardinals has enough plate left to serve six persons. The very houses are being dismantled.' And among these canny Romans fleeing with their goods was the florid figure of the pope. Alexander had no wish to be caught by the French king, so he took himself to Orvieto, and when that seemed uncomfortably near to the French line of retreat, he went on to Perugia. With the Milanese and Venetians massing in the north, Charles could not afford to delay. He abandoned all attempts to force recognition from the pope, and in doing so effectively lost the possession of, if not the claim to, the kingdom of Naples. It was clear that Charles had failed. He had failed France as a conqueror; and he had failed Italy as a reformer. At Poggibonsi, in June, Savonarola assumed his prophetic mantle and as the conscience of an age invoked the wrath of God against the king who had promised so much for Italy and religion, and had done so little. Charles had no time for homilies; shepherding his mule train of treasure, he hurried on towards the Alpine passes. At the Taro the army of the Holy League, under Francesco Gonzaga, blocked his path. On 6 July 1495, at Fornovo, the tired and depleted French army was forced to give battle. The engagement was short but fierce, and both sides could claim a victory. The outnumbered French were only allowed to escape through the indiscipline of the Italian allies.

Charles reached his own kingdom safely but the Italians had the spoils which, besides hundreds of chests of treasure, included the sword and helmet of Charles, his gold seal, and a book with the portraits of his female conquests.

The Battle of Fornovo, 1495 where Francesco Gonzaga and the army the Holy League routed Charles VIII's troops.

Alexander was back in Rome by the end of June and within a short time had reason to congratulate himself on a comprehensive victory over France. Ferrantino returned to Calabria with the Spanish general Gonzalo de Córdoba, and they quickly harried the remaining French into submission. The city of Naples was recaptured in July; in little over a year the viceroy surrendered at Atella. Those soldiers who could escape took ship back to France, but the majority found a grave in the baked lands of southern Italy.

The triumph, however, was unreal. The French invasion had sown the seeds of future calamities. France, Spain and the German Empire

had all declared an interest in Italian territory. The uneasy coalition of the Holy League began to break up even before its task was done. Before he was made to quit Italian soil, Charles had already detached Ludovico il Moro from the alliance. The essential work of reform, which was the only true basis for the well-being of the papacy and the Church, had been forgotten once more while Alexander played politics and gathered armies. The conduct of the French had introduced a new, murderous spirit into Italian warfare. A country at war suffered the inevitable aftermath of dearth and plague, and in Naples the French left behind the legacy of syphilis as a physical manifestation of moral corruption. Rome, in a single year once abused and twice threatened by invading forces, ended 1495 with the worst floods in memory. Two and a half days of incessant rain at the beginning of December broke the banks of the Tiber and turned the low-lying parts of the city into a dangerous sea. The cardinals coming out of a consistory were very nearly swept away and just struggled to the bridge of Sant'Angelo in time. In places the floodwater was ten feet deep. Houses were carried away, men drowned by the score, and horses by the hundred. The flourmills by the river were destroyed and there was no bread throughout the city. The damage was estimated at 300,000 ducats. Many of the best men talked of 'a judgment of God', and more fevered imaginations saw signs and portents: monsters in hideous forms – a woman's body, ears of an ass, an old man's face, a tail like a snake, or flesh covered with fish-scales.

> O Italy! [cried Savonarola's despairing voice] trouble after trouble shall overwhelm you; troubles of war after famine, pestilence after war. There shall be rumour upon rumour: barbarians on this side, barbarians on that. The law of the priesthood shall perish and priests shall be stripped of their place. Princes shall wear hair-cloth, the people be crushed by tribulation. All men will lose courage, and as they have judged, so shall they themselves be judged.

In the face of the French invasion Pope Alexander had shown many impressive qualities. His political skills had not deserted him. He had schemed with courage and success for an independent papacy, no matter how impure his motives. Neither threats, nor bribes, nor the chance for a temporary advantage over old enemies had obscured his clear view of the French danger, and he worked tenaciously to put together the

Italian alliance. He knew very well that Florence was plotting for the
return of the French, that the old antagonists in Naples and Milan could
not be stalled together in the same stable for very long. The providen-
tial intervention of Spain had ensured the defeat of the French in Naples,
and as a Spaniard Alexander felt entitled to further support from King
Ferdinand. In the summer of 1496 the pope thought he was strong
enough to take on the most intractable local problem of the Roman
papacy; he intended to move against the Roman barons of the Campagna and the Patrimony whose double-dealing perpetually threatened
the pope's security in Rome. And Alexander felt particularly vengeful
against the Orsini, whose recent desertion to the French had been most
sudden and most damaging. The time was ripe for a crushing blow.
Virginio Orsini, who was still fighting with the besieged French remnant in Naples, was proclaimed a rebel, excommunicated, and his possessions declared forfeit.

But by now, long confirmed in the practice of nepotism and with
thoughts of mortality strong in a mind now growing old, Alexander
could undertake no action without a consideration for his children. In
his flight to Perugia, he had thought first of his daughter Lucrezia and
had summoned her from Pesaro to join in the celebration of his relief,
and it was thought nothing strange when the incestuous couple of
Perugia, Gianpaolo Baglione and his sister Pentesalia, sat down to feast
with a pope and his daughter. So when the campaign against the Orsini
was planned, Alexander decided to entrust the command of his army
to his son Juan, Duke of Gandia. After three years in Spain, Juan was
now twenty, a young man of proven licentiousness but of unknown
military capacity. His reputation in Spain was not good. 'A very mean
young man,' said one account, 'full of false ideas of grandeur and bad
thoughts, haughty, cruel and unreasonable.' His conduct did not please
Ferdinand and Isabella, and as he had done his duty, providing his wife
with a son and heir, the Catholic monarchs made no objection when
the pope recalled his son from Spain. Juan made his entry into Rome in
August 1496. He was dressed in velvet encrusted with pearls and pre-
cious stones, and the harness of his bay charger was covered with little
silver bells that jingled merrily as he rode to meet his doting father.

The campaign began fortunately. In August the last French garrison
had surrendered at Atella and Virginio Orsini was taken prisoner. By

order of the pope he was locked up in Naples where he soon died, perhaps from illness though some said by poison. In October the pope invested Juan Borgia with standard and baton as Captain-General of the
Papal Army. The soldiers summoned to assist him were Guidobaldo da
Montefeltro, Duke of Urbino, and young Fabrizio Colonna. Fabrizio,
who later made a great name as a soldier, could be relied on to do as
much hurt as possible to his hereditary Orsini enemies. The Duke of
Urbino, who was the real commander of the campaign, came from a
famous family of *condottieri*, but he was only a reluctant soldier, being
driven to it by family tradition and by the need for money, though his
brilliant qualities had marked him out as a most generous ruler and
patron in Urbino. At first the papal armies seemed invincible; within
two months five Orsini castles had opened their gates to the attackers,
and four others had been taken by force. Only the two lakeside strongholds of Trevignano and Bracciano remained.

Both these castles were impressively sited, on strong natural features overlooking the blue waters of Lake Bracciano. Trevignano was a medieval fortress of rather antiquated design, but Bracciano was a massive structure embodying the most recent improvements in fortification. The two places were able to communicate by boat across the lake and the defenders, when the papal army began the siege, were in good heart. The French flag flew from the battlements and the garrisons rallied to the cry *Francia*! Montefeltro tried to command the lake by transporting a small ship overland from the Tiber, but the general of Bracciano intercepted and burned it. Montefeltro was wounded and the inexperienced Duke of Gandia took over. The winter weather turned bad and the attackers, lying in open country, suffered more than the defenders. The besieged made several sorties and even appeared under the walls of Rome, where the Orsini faction was growing turbulent. As the days passed and the castles still held out, the pope fell ill with vexation and worry. Trevignano was at last reduced by artillery borrowed from Naples, but in the new year Bracciano still stood firm. In the meantime, Carlo Orsini had been using French money to gather troops in Umbria and Tuscany. He was joined by the untrustworthy Baglione of Perugia and by Giuliano della Rovere, the pope's fiercest opponent, and the combined army marched towards Bracciano, forcing Gandia to raise the siege. On 24 January 1497 the armies met at Soriano, in the difficult hill country to the north of the lake, and the papal forces were defeated. Montefeltro was captured and the Duke of Gandia wounded. Contemporary chroniclers, who had no love for the Borgias, took a particular delight in humiliating Juan, whose flamboyance, arrogance and loose morals made him a despised member of a hated family. But the defeat at Soriano was not his disgrace alone. The reliable Sigismondo de' Conti thought it a very close-fought battle, and the impetuosity of young Fabrizio Colonna was the chief cause of defeat. Romans, however, made no such distinction, and graffiti on the walls told passers-by if they saw a 'certain army belonging to the Church, please bring it back to the Duke of Gandia'.

Once again the Orsini controlled the lands in the Patrimony of St Peter, so Alexander hurriedly made peace with them, allowing them to buy back all their captured castles except for Anguillara and Cerveteri. The Orsini, on their part, were glad to stop the war, for the pope had

Anguillara (LEFT) and Cerveteri, the castles sold without the pope's consent to Virginio Orsini soon after Alexander's election. In 1497, as part of a campaign to reduce the lands of the Orsini to papal obedience, the castles were taken but, after the defeat of papal troops at Soriano, the pope restored all the Orsini castles, except for the strategic castles of Anguillara and Cerveteri.

summoned Gonzalo de Córdoba from Naples, and the Spanish general was a far more fearsome opponent than any Italian *condottiere*. The papal forces, still under the Duke of Gandia, joined Gonzalo and began the only task remaining, the reduction of the French garrison at Ostia. In March 1497 the fortress at Ostia fell to Italian bombardment and Spanish infantry assault, though the French commander complained later of noxious fumes used to devilish effect, and produced by throwing certain chemicals on bonfires set up to the windward of the castle. Juan Borgia returned to Rome as a conqueror, and received such favours from his father that the foolish young man strutted like an emperor. Gonzalo was so outraged at the precedence claimed by Juan, and permitted by Alexander, that he refused, on Palm Sunday, to take the palm from the pope's hand and quit his place in St Peter's to sulk on a bench below the altar steps.

It seemed that in Rome there was no way of avoiding the importunity and conceit of the Borgia children. Lucrezia and her husband Giovanni Sforza were again living in the palace of Santa Maria in Portico. Fifteen-year-old Jofré Borgia had brought his seventeen-year-old wife Sancia to Rome from his Neapolitan principality at Squillace. Already, in the two short years of this marriage, the pope had found it necessary to reproach the couple for extravagance. Jofré alone had seventy-three personal servants. Sancia, an illegitimate child, was a wild, headstrong beauty, brought up in the most pagan court in Europe, and there were persistent rumours of her immorality. She was about the same age as Lucrezia and though the two young women were different types – Sancia dark and fiery, Lucrezia more placid – they joined together, determined to make the Vatican a playground of fashion. Burchard, the stuffy Master of Ceremonies, thought their conduct 'a disgrace', and soon more censorious critics had worse things to say about Sancia's sexual habits. It was said, most scandalously, that the Borgia brothers, Juan and Cesare, were competing for the favours of their sister-in-law. Juan was a known womanizer; that Cardinal Cesare was one also would be no surprise to the papal court, used to the excesses of cardinals in general and to the morals of Borgias in particular. Nor would the interest of the two men in their sister-in-law raise many eyebrows in Italy where inbred relationships were common currency. Cardinal Cesare, a churchman in name only, was a handsome catch. He had the dash and presence of his father as a young man, but with far better looks; Boccaccio, the Ferrarese envoy, pictured him ready for the hunt,

> in a costume altogether worldly, that is to say in silk, and armed. He has only the first tonsure like a simple priest. He possesses marked genius and a charming personality and he bears himself like a great prince; he is especially lively and fond of society. Being more discreet, he presents a better and more distinguished appearance than his brother, the Duke of Gandia.

Whether Cesare was the lover of Sancia or not, there was nothing implausible about such an affair.

Everywhere trouble gathered around the Borgia family. Since Alexander had switched his alliance from Milan to Naples, Giovanni Sforza was a spent asset. He was twice the age of Lucrezia; the marriage was merely a political arrangement. Lucrezia had grown bored with the life of his petty court in Pesaro, and now that Rome was at peace it offered a far grander setting for the display of her spendthrift talents. Alexander censured Giovanni for neglecting his military duties – he was supposed to be a *condottiere* – and hinted contemptuously that he had information about Giovanni's spying for the Sforzas. Existing miserably in Lucrezia's shadow, Giovanni felt that he was on slippery ground. He knew too much of Italian politics to expect any special consideration from the Borgias. In April 1496 he joined the Neapolitan army in the south and performed with the utter lack of distinction that he had shown in all military enterprises. When the campaign was over he hurried straight to Pesaro. In his absence from Rome there were reports of something seriously wrong. 'The lord of Pesaro', the Mantuan envoy wrote, 'seems to be sheltering something under his roof that others do not suspect.' He returned to Rome in January 1497. He had one blazing row with the arrogant Duke of Gandia, yet the rest of the Borgia clan were forbearing and Lucrezia was affectionate – a man in his nervous state might well have interpreted these as ominous signs. On the morning of Good Friday, Giovanni came to his wife's chamber and told her that he was going to confession either at a church in Trastevere or on the Janiculum, and that afterwards he would make the traditional pilgrimage of the Seven Churches, an expedition that would

The seven churches of Rome, since time immemorial one of the chief objects of pilgrimage in the city.

take most of the day. But when he did not return at nightfall it was evident that something had happened. Giovanni, in fact, was in flight, riding to Pesaro as fast as his Arab horse could take him.

The flight had been well prepared. He left behind two messages, one asking Lucrezia to join him in Pesaro, the other informing the Milanese envoy that he had fled out of 'dissatisfaction with the pope'. The envoy, who had heard rumours, was not convinced and later wrote to Ludovico Sforza that the real reason was Lucrezia's 'lack of modesty, which had already put the lord of Pesaro into great discontent'. History has not discovered the truth of the various allegations made against Lucrezia, but the anti-Borgia chroniclers were soon ready with several embroidered tales of fanciful outrage. The worst of the accusations was that Giovanni had learned of an incestuous relation between the pope and his daughter, and he feared that the pope would demand a divorce in order to keep Lucrezia for himself. Giovanni may well have believed this, and there is evidence that he told Cardinal Ascanio Sforza some such story, but it was certain, once Giovanni had fled, that Alexander would begin divorce proceedings, and then Giovanni stood to lose not only his wife and her money, but also his town of Pesaro which he held as a fief from the pope. Soon an emissary arrived from the pope with an ultimatum: Giovanni had the option of an annulment either on the grounds of invalidity, or of non-consummation. In desperation the poor man turned to the Sforza cousins whom he had served so faithfully, swearing that the marriage had been consummated more than a thousand times, but his politic cousins had struck him off just as surely as Alexander had done. Since the charge of invalidity would not have stood up in an ecclesiastical court, the divorce had to be on the grounds of non-consummation. With calculated cruelty Alexander urged his daughter to petition on these grounds, and intimidated Giovanni to acknowledge his impotence. Giovanni, who was not very brave, not very intelligent, and certainly rather greedy, held out at least for the remainder of his wife's dowry. When 31,000 ducats were granted him and when Ludovico il Moro threatened to withdraw Milanese protection from Pesaro, he at last gave way. 'If his Holiness', he told his cousin, 'wishes to establish his own kind of justice, I cannot gainsay him.' He signed the confession of his impotence in November 1497. 'It seems he must needs be impotent,' wrote one envoy cynically, 'for otherwise a sentence of divorce cannot be granted, yet he says he wrote it in obedience to the Duke of Milan.'

Giovanni Sforza was a weak reed easily broken by a man of Alexander's authority and sense of purpose. But the episode had another victim, a rather unexpected one in the person of the seventeen-year-old Lucrezia. In June, at the height of the humiliating negotiations, Lucrezia had stopped her horse at the door of the Dominican convent of San Sisto and disappeared within; and to the surprise of everyone she remained within. 'Some say Madonna Lucrezia will turn nun,' a correspondent told Cardinal d'Este, 'while others say things I cannot entrust to a letter.' The pope at first explained away her absence as a retreat while her husband made up his mind about the divorce, but when she still did not reappear he sent the sheriff of Rome to fetch her out. That official was completely routed by the formidable abbess, and Alexander had to be reconciled to this state of affairs and wait until the tedium and discipline of convent life should drive her back into the world. Even if Lucrezia had no true desire to become a nun, there was much that was shameful for her to avoid. No doubt she knew she was lawfully married to Giovanni and that there were no grounds for an annulment. She was being made, after three years of marriage, to sign a statement of non-consummation, and realized that this would mean the possibility of an inspection by a midwife to see if she were *virgo intacta*. Worst of all, this ecclesiastical fraud was being perpetrated by the pope himself – her father, the supreme head of the Church, who did not care what injury was being done to his daughter, her husband, or religion just so long as an inconvenient puppet was put out of the way.

But the presence of his favourite Juan more than compensated the pope for the loss of Lucrezia. All honours and all treasuries were plundered for Juan's advancement; and what was left the pope shared between his other children and his Spanish supporters. The Sacred College had been packed with a further influx of Spanish cardinals. The restive Romans voiced their grievances against these oppressive Spaniards. The Colonna had not been paid for their part in the war against the Orsini, while the Orsini groaned at the heavy price asked of them for the return of their castles. The Duke of Urbino, captured while fighting for the pope, was still in prison at Soriano, trying to raise by himself the ransom that Alexander refused to pay. In the meantime the Borgia relatives grew fat on honours. In May 1497 Cardinal Borgia Lanzol became legate to Perugia. A month later the honour of crowning King Federigo, who succeeded Ferrantino on the throne of Naples, was given to Cardinal Cesare Borgia. But these favours were as nothing compared to those intended for Juan, the Duke of Gandia. There is little doubt that, had Alexander been victorious, he would have given his son the spoils of the Orsini war. Frustrated in that, the pope called a secret consistory in June 1497 to grant Juan and his heirs in perpetuity the papal cities of Benevento and Terracina. In the cowed and venal College of Cardinals only Piccolomini spoke out against this alienation of two important, strategic papal fiefs, but no less a power than Ferdinand of Spain tried to prevent this move, which he saw as an injury to the Church and to Christendom.

The transfer never took place. On 14 June Vanozza dei Catanei gave a family party for the Borgias in a vineyard by San Pietro in Vincoli. Vanozza and the pope had been separated for many years, but Alexander respected her, and her children were fond of her. She was now married to Carlo Canale, an official in the Grand Penitentiary who boasted openly of his wife's connections. She was, indeed, a substantial Roman citizen, a woman of business and the owner of valuable city property. On this occasion she was giving the banquet for her son Cesare Borgia who was about to depart for Naples to crown King Federigo. Among the other guests were the Duke of Gandia and his cousin Cardinal Juan Borgia Lanzol. When the party broke up, late in the evening, the three highly placed Borgias mounted their mules and set out together towards the Vatican Palace. At the Palazzo Cesarini the duke said good night and started for the ghetto attended by only one groom and by an unknown masked man who had been at the banquet and had visited Gandia daily for the last month. Cesare and Lanzol advised their relative to take more servants, as the way was dangerous, but they knew his reputation for nocturnal amours so they let him go with a few ribaldries. In the deserted gloom of the Piazza degli Ebrei, Juan told his groom to wait for an hour and, if he had not returned, to go home. Then the masked man got up behind the duke on the mule and the two disappeared into the night. The groom maintained his lonely vigil, but before the hour was up masked men attacked him and left him for dead.

The grim palace near Sa Pietro in Vincoli. Vanozza dei Catanei's family party in June 149 in honour of her son Cesare Borgia, is though to have taken place in th palace garden.

e old ghetto of Rome,
se to where Juan
rgia was murdered.

Next morning, Alexander was extremely perturbed when he heard that neither Gandia nor the groom had returned. But he knew his son's reputation and consoled himself that Juan was delayed by some discreet affair. When night came and still Juan was missing, the pope ordered a search of the city, from top to bottom. Rome was seized by panic and dismay; shops were locked and doors barred, for who knew what the enemies of Borgia might be planning? The Roman factions put their armed followers on the alert. The groom was found, severely wounded and hardly able to speak; then Juan's mule was caught, with the harness showing marks of a struggle. On the 16th a Slav boatman who had been keeping watch over a cargo of timber near the church of San Girolamo degli Schiavoni admitted that he had seen, at about 2 o'clock on the Thursday morning, a body brought dangling over a white horse to the river bank, and then hurled into the stream at the point where the city refuse entered the Tiber. Four men and a horseman had done the deed, and the rider had ordered his companions to throw stones to sink the dead man's cloak. When the Slav was asked why he had not told the authorities, he replied: 'In the course of my life I've seen more than a hundred bodies thrown into the Tiber from that spot, and I never heard of anyone troubling his head about even one of them.'

Immediately, men were set to drag the river, and about midday a body was found near a garden belonging to Ascanio Sforza. It was the Duke of Gandia with his throat cut and with nine deep wounds in his body, but fully dressed, with a dagger in his belt and money in his purse. The corpse was taken to Sant'Angelo to be washed, robed and laid out in state. 'When Alexander heard that the duke had been murdered', Burchard noted in his diary, 'and his body thrown like carrion into the Tiber, he was perfectly overcome; he shut himself in his room overwhelmed with grief and wept bitterly.' The crime, so brutally executed, had been planned by someone who knew the habits of the victim. Robbery was not the motive, for the money and the rich clothes had been left. The severity of the attack spoke of a violent hatred; there were wounds in the head, throat, body and legs. That night, 120 torchbearers escorted the corpse in procession to the church of Santa Maria del Popolo and there it was buried. The Castel Sant'Angelo was in darkness when the procession left and above the wailing of the mourners Alexander's voice was heard calling his son's name from an upper window.

The Duke of Gandia was twenty when he died, a youth already far gone in debauchery and pride.

The authorities made no progress with their investigation. Two days in the river had obliterated any clues and the groom, who might have told them something, died of his wounds. There were, however, plenty of suspects. Cardinal Ascanio Sforza, by whose property the body was found, was known to have quarrelled violently with Juan. The duke had insulted a guest in Ascanio's palace, whereupon the guest had called Juan a bastard to his face. This tale was reported to Alexander who straightaway sent a posse of soldiers to force an entry and hang the offending guest on the spot. Ascanio made himself scarce after the murder, yet the Spanish ambassador vouched for him. The Milanese cardinal, moreover, was far too wise and experienced to execute such a raw act of vengeance, particularly when so many of the signs pointed to him. Besides Ascanio, a host of other names fell under suspicion: men, great and small, whom Juan had cuckolded; those who hated him personally for his insolence and ambition; and those who saw in him the most dangerous of the younger Borgias, the dynast being prepared by Alexander to carry on the grasping policy of the family.

> The uncertainty has given rise to many conjectures [Ascanio wrote to his brother Ludovico]. Some think it had to do with a love affair; the Duke of Urbino, the Orsini, and Cardinal Sanseverino have also been suspected. Again, it is said that my people may have done it, on account of a recent quarrel with the duke. Finally, some think that either Giovanni Sforza of Pesaro or his brother Galeazzo is the murderer.

Juan's young brother Jofré, husband of the loose-living Sancia, was also suspect, though the pope, who hinted that he could make a shrewd guess at the killer, explicitly exonerated Jofré, Giovanni Sforza and the Duke of Urbino. It was, as all agreed, a puzzling case of a villain with *denti lunghi* – a powerful man with a long arm for vengeance.

In the search for the murderer the name of Cesare Borgia was not mentioned at the time. But later such a weight of whispers and innuendo gathered around him that, within a few years, chroniclers could confidently state his guilt as certain. Cesare had little reason to love his brother Juan. When their elder half-brother Pedro Luis had died in 1488, his duchy of Gandia had passed over Cesare and settled on the younger

Juan. And although Cesare advanced very rapidly in the Church, he was an unwilling ecclesiastic and perhaps he coveted the more spectacular titles and estates of Juan. The two brothers shared the same pleasure-loving appetites and the same drive to satisfy grandiose ambitions, though Cesare had more charm, more subtlety and more intelligence; they were also, according to popular report, rivals in pursuit of their sister-in-law Sancia. As a cap to his bitterness, Cesare saw that Juan was the darling of Alexander. Considering all this, and knowing what murderous havoc Cesare was later to spread in the lands of the papal states, the chroniclers had no hesitation in condemning him with hindsight. But if he was condemned, it was done without any evidence. In the weeks after the murder he stayed quietly in Rome, and amid accusation and counter-accusation not one breath of complicity touched him. The pope, who had hinted that he knew the truth, made Cesare executor of the Gandia estates and put into his hands the well-being of the duke's infant son.

The grief of the pope was plain for all to see. At a consistory held five days after the murder, and attended by all the important ambassadors and all the cardinals in Rome, except Ascanio Sforza, Alexander replied to their condolences:

> The blow that is fallen upon us is the heaviest that we could possibly have sustained. We loved the Duke of Gandia more than anyone else in the world. We would have given seven tiaras to be able to recall him to life. God has done this in punishment for our sins. We, on our part, are resolved to mend our own life and to reform the Church.

The shock spurred him to the kind of energetic action that the Borgias could always produce in time of crisis. An observer wrote:

> The pope is minded to change his life and become a different man. Yesterday, in the consistory, he promised both temporal and spiritual reform in the Church, and appointed a commission of cardinals and prelates for this purpose. Finally, he is going to equip forty squadrons, but will have no Roman barons among them. It is thought that he will give the command to Gonzalo de Córdoba, who is a truly able and worthy man. He has also promised many other excellent things, but time will soon show if he is in earnest.

The first signs were encouraging. In the sad summer of 1497, Alexander struggled hard with his nature. Jofré and Sancia were sent back,

The elaborate scabbard of Cesare Borgia's parade sword, used to crown King Federigo of Naples.

at least for the time being, to their estates at Squillace. From the end of July Cesare was in Naples for the coronation of Federigo. The pope, it was understood, would no longer give way to his children, and even Lucrezia was to be banished to Valencia. 'The reform commission sits every morning in the papal palace', the Florentine envoy wrote in some amazement. Pious men were truly hopeful that some good might come out of the pope's loss. The commission of cardinals, which included 'the best and most God-fearing' members of that questionable body, ranged widely over all the abuses of Church and Curia. Alexander himself, from thirty-five years experience as Vice-Chancellor, knew better than most what reforms were needed. By the end of July a comprehensive Bull of reformation had been drafted. In this, the pope and his officials received strict instructions as to their liturgical duties, their conduct and their morals. The pope was forbidden to alienate Church property, and regulations were put forward to govern custodians and vicars of papal fiefs, and to watch over the dealings between pope and secular princes. In the Sacred College it was decreed that no cardinal should possess more than one bishopric, nor have an annual revenue from benefices that exceeded 6000 ducats. Simony was anathema, and worldly lives must be put in order. Gaming and hunting were prohibited, as canon law required, and cardinals could not take part in tournaments, carnivals and pagan dramas. A cardinal's household was limited to eighty persons, nor should there be more than thirty horses. Conjurers, jugglers, comedians, troubadors, singers and musicians must remain outside the palace, boys should not be employed as valets or grooms of the chamber. No funeral should cost more than 1500 ducats.

All this, though a shameful indictment of the usual practice among cardinals, was but the beginning. The draft also acknowledged that the Curia was in the grip of corruption and extortion, that the laity in all countries was miserably exploited by Church administrators. The reform draft banned the sale of offices; a prescribed fee was set out for each transaction; bribery would be punished; the abuse of the *commenda* was regulated; rules for the collection of tithes and Church taxes were set; religious vows by children were declared invalid; priests must get rid of their concubines; abbeys and convents must put their houses in order. The draft also forbade wharf dues in Rome and tried to regulate the city's grain supply. However, this thoroughgoing Bull of reform never got beyond the drafting stage. The men who were supposed to carry out the reformation were the same unredeemed rogues against whom the reforms were directed. Too many of the cardinals and bishops could not rise from their worldly sloth; the hands of the officials were plunged far too deeply into the pockets of petitioners to be extracted with ease; the sullen lives of ignorant clergy could not be changed immediately by well-intentioned regulations. The commission, moreover, regarded a General Council of the Church as a precondition of reform, and the papacy had too recent and bitter an experience of Church councils to allow this to happen. As for Alexander himself, there is no reason to doubt that he wanted some kind of reform. He had a true regard for pure doctrine, hated heresy, wanted the religious orders cleansed, and asserted the dignity and rights of Church and papacy against any encroachment by princes. But he would not allow the Sacred College, under the guise of reform, to increase the power of the cardinals at the expense of the pope's own authority. And finally, he could not go against the inclinations of his own profligate nature. In September, Cesare was back in Rome.

In Naples, Cesare had brazenly pestered King Federigo for benefits and favours. He also had his eye on the king's daughter, Carlotta. 'It would not be surprising', an envoy wrote, 'if the poor king was driven into the arms of the Turks to escape from his tormentor.' At the first consistory after his return, Cesare was greeted distantly by his father; but the resolve did not last long and it was soon clear that Alexander intended Cesare to have the place and the favours formerly enjoyed by Juan. Cesare, a pre-eminently secular figure, at least had the honesty to deny the vocation that had been imposed on him at such a young age; he wished to resign his cardinalate and to marry. While the pope was trying to arrange this in as discreet a way as possible, he nonetheless gave Cesare benefices worth 12,000 ducats a year; he was also preparing, as a blessing on his son's new secular career, to give Cesare the towns of Cesena and Fano. Soon father and son were as thick as thieves, hunting together, in defiance of canon law, in the woods near Ostia. 'I will make no comment on these matters', the Venetian envoy wrote in September 1497, 'but it is certain that this pope permits himself things that are unexampled and unpardonable.'

Alexander, having struggled slightly to be free, was once more caught firmly in the meshes of family. The sinister Cesare, whose full power was yet to be revealed, cast a long shadow which began to eclipse the pope. His daughter, far from being banished to Valencia, was still living among the nuns of San Sisto, and now that her divorce from Giovanni was certain Alexander began, in the old way, to think of new marriages, new alliances. In the convent, Lucrezia still mourned her murdered brother. She was a good-hearted, affectionate girl, though rather heedless and extravagant, and Juan had been fond of her, sending her from Spain presents of jewelry, clothes, a leather harness for her horse, and even a sombrero. In her genuine grief and with her divorce pending, she saw no reason as yet to leave the haven of the convent. A young Spaniard, Pedro Calderon, or Perotto as he was familiarly called, acted as her go-between with the outside world. In December she emerged to appear before the ecclesiastical court in the Vatican to swear to the non-consummation of her marriage. She supported this indignity with such grace and such good Latin that the Milanese envoy compared her performance to a speech by Cicero. By Christmas the proceedings were completed and she was free from Giovanni Sforza. In the early months of 1498 rumours of her pregnancy spread around Rome. On 14 February Burchard noted that Perotto had been found in the Tiber, and added cautiously 'where he did not fall of his own volition'. Six days later another diarist wrote that 'a young woman of the retinue of Madonna Lucrezia was also found drowned in the river. The reasons for this are not known.' But by March there was further confusion. A correspondent wrote to Bologna that Perotto, far from being in the river, was now in prison for seducing the pope's daughter. Two weeks later another letter writer stated authoritatively: 'It is reported from Rome that the daughter of the pope gave birth to a child.'

Here was another mystery to add to the Borgia legend. Again, the truth of the allegations is not known. But the climate of evil gossip in which Lucrezia lived certainly helped to blacken her name. Was she the mother of Perotto's bastard? Was she, as her husband had implied, the incestuous plaything of Pope Alexander? Even more extravagant rumours were current. When the Prince of Salerno was asked if his son would marry Lucrezia, now that she was free, he replied: 'Do you think I would receive into my family a woman who, as everyone knows, has slept with both her brothers?' Later, the poet Jacopo Sannazaro added his biting wit to the familiar denigrations. He composed an epitaph for her: 'Here lies Lucrezia by name, but who was really a Thais, the daughter, wife, and daughter-in-law of Alexander.' But a pope's daughter, however black her reputation, did not lack suitors. A Riario, a Sanseverino, and an Orsini were considered in turn and discarded. Alexander was now inclined towards a strengthening of his Neapolitan alliance. Cesare, once free of his cardinal's robes, hoped to marry Princess Carlotta. Something less than a royal partner would do for Lucrezia, and at last a worthy groom was found. He was Don Alfonso of Bisceglie, illegitimate son of Alfonso II, nephew of King Federigo, and brother of Jofré's wife Sancia. This young man, although the son of the prince whom Commines called 'the cruellest, most vicious and lowest of men', was a gentle, unassuming seventeen year old of extraordinary good looks. His contemporaries did not neglect to remind him that, in marrying a Borgia, he was entering the most perilous den of lions. Recalling the first Spanish betrothed whom Lucrezia had been forced to give up for Giovanni, and the poor Giovanni who had been divorced for Alfonso, a Roman epigrammatist warned the young Neapolitan duke: 'The other husbands are not dead, Alfonso, they live. Two have been cheated of their hopes, and your punishment awaits you. It will profit you nothing to take your name from Parthenope, or to be of royal stock. You, too, will fall.'

Lucrezia married Alfonso in June 1498; she brought him a dowry of 41,000 ducats, but Alexander had enforced a condition that she should not have to go to Naples during his lifetime. The wedding took place quietly in the Vatican without any of the elaborate display that had advertised the earlier alliance between Borgia and Sforza. Times were hard, and perhaps the pope had lost some of his former confidence that he could work the world to the benefit of the papacy and his family. In any case the lines of advance were less clear, the need for duplicity and sleight-of-hand paramount. No alliance could endure long in changeable Italy. Alexander was now sixty-seven, still in good health but fretted by the trials of office and by the partial disappointment of his family plans. His eldest son, Pedro Luis, had gained a Spanish dukedom but died without issue. His successor, the murdered Juan, had indeed left an heir, but the mother Maria Enriquez absolutely refused to leave her child to the mercy of the pope and his venal children. The infant

Duke of Gandia would bear the Borgia name, but the Spanish inheritance was placed beyond the pope's reach. Alexander complained that
the heir to Gandia was 'closer to the king of Spain than to us'. Jofré, the
youngest son, was Prince of Squillace, but the pope had doubts about
his paternity and no faith in the future of this weakling. The Borgia
future, if there was to be one, must rest with Cesare, now in the course
of being metamorphosed from a prince of the Church to a prince of the
world.

In 1498 the Italian peace and the Borgia family fortune seemed to be
slipping away together. For the past year Charles VIII had been trying
to convoke a Church Council. He was aided by his Florentine ally
Savonarola whose hectic denunciations of the papacy – a stream of
abuse – only stopped when the exasperated Florentines burned their
prophet in May 1498. The unstable Holy League was falling apart.

First, Ludovico il Moro defected to France; then Florence made her French sympathies well known. Charles VIII steadily asserted his claim to Naples, though his troops had been driven out of the kingdom by Gonzalo de Córdoba. Matters did not improve when Charles died suddenly in April 1498 and his cousin Louis XII came to the French throne. As a member of the Orleans family, Louis already had a claim to the duchy of Milan; now a French king had an eye on both Milan and Naples, and he was supported by Venice, anxious as ever to hurt her old rival Milan. Around Rome the Orsini and the Colonna had been ferociously at war once again; yet when they made peace Alexander had every reason to suspect their intentions. A document was found nailed to the Vatican Library door, exhorting the Roman enemies to mend their quarrels and combine to throw the Borgia bull and his bull calves into the Tiber. The pope could expect little from Spain. The Catholic monarchs were severely critical of the scandalous papal court, and King Ferdinand had to bear complaints against the pope's family from his cousin, the Duchess of Gandia. Also, Spain now had on Italian soil, in the person of Gonzalo and his disciplined Spanish infantry, a body of troops capable of pursuing imperial ambitions every bit as dangerous to the papacy as the French. For the moment, Alexander put his hope in Naples, and he had tied the knots of that alliance firmly. Two of his children were married to illegitimate members of the reigning family, and the cold glance of Cesare had rested on the unattached Carlotta, though both the girl and her father objected most strongly to a man who was 'a priest and the son of a priest'. King Federigo of Naples was a peace-loving prince who ruled over a bankrupt realm and was at best only a reluctant supporter of Borgia plans.

In the first years of his pontificate, Alexander had shown, besides an all too obvious dynastic ambition, a certain rational plan to safeguard the rights of the papacy and to preserve the peace and well-being of Italy. As the years passed, and the course grew harder, the pope seemed to lose his way, making and unmaking alliances for no very clear reason other than the feeling of the moment and the desire to be on the side of the strong. In the end, the only certain Borgia policy appeared to be the aggrandizement of his family and Italy was abandoned to her fate, perhaps out of cynicism, perhaps out of a sense of hopelessness and misery at the chaos the pope had helped to bring about. Alexander had become

Louis XII, King of France. At his accession, Louis declared his claims to Milan and Naples, forcing Alexander to reshape Borgia policy.

what Federigo of Naples called him, '*il più carnale homo*'. So while Naples was wooed into marriage alliances, the pope was also secretly courting the French. Perhaps the integrity of Italy was beyond saving; it now seemed most important that the pope and his temporal lands should not be isolated between strong enemies. The accession of Louis XII in France dealt new cards into the pope's hand and he was determined to play them as cunningly as possible. Louis wished to get rid of his wife Jeanne and requested the pope for a dispensation to put aside this 'cripple, afflicted with scrofula, repellent in person and mind' on the usual grounds of non-consummation. The true reason for the divorce was not the unfortunate deformity of this saintly woman, canonized in 1950 as St Joan of Valois; Louis had a political reason in that he wished to marry his predecessor's widow, Anne of Brittany, and thus retain the large duchy of Brittany under the control of the French crown. Louis also wanted a cardinal's hat for his favourite minister Georges d'Amboise. Immediately, Alexander saw how to work these circumstances to the advantage of himself and his son Cesare. The French king would have to buy his privileges with friendship; he might also persuade Princess Carlotta, who was living in his kingdom, that Cesare Borgia was a suitable husband.

Throughout the early part of 1498, Cesare had worn his clerical robes less and less; sometimes he would appear in public as a French courtier, sometimes as a gallant fully armed for war or hunt, sometimes even in oriental dress. In August he came before a consistory and abandoned his cardinal's habit for ever. The cardinals unanimously agreed to this renunciation, and when the Spanish ambassador, who had a high idea of the sanctity of Holy Orders, protested, Alexander hotly declared that the change was necessary for his son's spiritual welfare. The renunciation of the cardinalate meant, of course, the loss of rich benefices, which amounted to about 35,000 ducats a year. But on the very day when Cesare gave up his Church wealth, the French envoy arrived in Rome with a draft treaty which would give the ex-cardinal compensating secular riches. By courtesy of Louis XII, the old Cardinal of Valencia was to become the new Duke of Valence, Knight of the Order of St Michael, with a guaranteed yearly income of 20,000 gold francs and a personal allowance of another 20,000. Louis promised to support the wooing of Carlotta, and further promised, after the conquest of Milan, to invest Cesare with the town of Asti, which the king had inherited, together with his claim to the whole of the duchy of Milan, from his Visconti grandmother. In return for these favours, the new duke – known in Italy as the Duke of Valentinois, or just as 'il Valentino' – would lead an embassy to France carrying with him the papal dispensation for Louis' divorce and the red hat for Georges d'Amboise. He also took an implied blessing for the French invasion of Milan and a guarded caveat against French interference in Naples, at least for the time being. 'We are sending your Majesty our heart,' Alexander wrote to Louis,

Cesare Borgia, the newly invested Duc de Valentinois, set sail for France in early October 1498. An observer wrote: 'The ruin of Italy is confirmed – observe the machinations of this father and son!'

'that is to say our beloved son, the Duc de Valentino, who is to us the dearest of all.' The pope was also delivering the death blow to the already expiring Holy League and marking the end of the Italian peace.

Cesare was now twenty-three, a handsome, virile man with many Borgia qualities – attractive to women, loose-living, luxurious, but also bold, energetic and intelligent. He added to this a restless, martial spirit and a quite ruthless willpower that had hardly been seen before within the family. Whether hunting or bullfighting, or in the softer pursuit of women, he drove on formidably through all obstacles. He was a magnificent specimen of Renaissance man, sleek, proud and ambiguous.

The preparations made for his departure were the wonder of Rome. The reports of the envoys entertained the disbelieving princes of Europe with examples of conspicuous excess: jewels to fill several chests, shirts that cost 50 francs each, horses from the famous Gonzaga stables and shod with silver, chamberpots also of silver, and a commode with a golden bowl covered by a golden cloth. A mule train carried his treasure, and he took with him the enormous sum of 200,000 ducats, provided by the pope and largely extorted from unwilling penitents. The aged Pedro de Aranda, master of the papal household, was accused of heresy and his confiscated estate was given to Cesare. Three hundred crypto-Christians, mainly Jews, were allowed to appear in the yellow garments of the penitent and commuted their sentences by the payment of heavy fines which went straight to Cesare. In early October 1498, Cesare Borgia set out from Rome dressed in a costume of white damask with gold edging, a mantle of black velvet in the French fashion, and on his head a biretta with plunging black plumes. His father watched from a window in the Vatican until his son disappeared from sight. At Civitavecchia two French ships waited to take him, his retinue of 200 servants, and his 50 mules to Marseilles.

From the port of Marseilles, Cesare began a leisurely, stately journey across France. The papal commission examining the question of Louis' divorce must have time to reach its verdict without unseemly haste. Cesare was welcomed at Avignon by Cardinal della Rovere, the archenemy of the Borgias, who provided a fitting banquet, though both men were suffering from syphilis and in low spirits. The procession went on to Valence, capital of Cesare's new duchy, then to Lyons, and finally to Chinon where the French court was in residence. The French nobility was surprised by the hauteur and the demands for precedence of this illegitimate son of a pope, and they looked with derision on his gaudy, parvenu display. It is said that Louis, concealed behind a window at Chinon, watched the arrival of the paragon from Italy – with his gold brocade studded with rubies, with his huge pendant of diamonds, with his boots and even his horse's tail covered with pearls – and commented on 'the vainglory and foolish bombast of this Duke of Valentinois'.

But in public the king was affable, fraternal. He courteously took Cesare to his private apartment and they talked far into the night. Next afternoon Louis, well-informed as to the tastes of his guest, arranged an

The Château of Blois where Cesare and Charlotte d'Albret were married in 1499. The bride was reputed to be one of the most beautiful princesses in France.

entertainment with fashionable courtesans. The serious negotiations could now commence, and they lasted throughout the winter. The divorce commission duly pronounced in the king's favour, and since it was common knowledge that Cesare had the dispensation with him, he was forced to hand it over. Georges d'Amboise got his cardinal's hat, but did not receive his second wish, which was to be papal legate in France. The slowness of the negotiations irked Cesare, especially as Louis could not prevail on Carlotta to accept the hand of a Borgia. She and King Federigo, who had reason to think that Alexander was now plotting with France against Naples, remained implacably hostile to Cesare; Carlotta was already betrothed to a Breton noble whom she later married. With Carlotta so adamant, Louis was forced to look elsewhere and found for his Italian guest a bride with royal connections. This was Charlotte d'Albret, the French king's cousin and the sister of the King of Navarre; the choice was satisfactory to both Cesare and the

pope. They were wed on 12 May 1499 and the next morning a messenger left for Rome with the glad news that the marriage had been
consummated; the Duc de Valentinois, said the letter, had given his
wife 'eight marks of his virility'. But the cynics of the French court,
where Cesare was never liked, told a different story. The apothecary,
so the story went, had been bribed to give the groom an aperient instead
of an aphrodisiac, with disastrous but comic results.

The fears of King Federigo had been well grounded. Even while
Cesare had been pursuing the Neapolitan princess into the middle of
France, the pope was secretly planning with Louis a future division of
the kingdom of Naples. When Carlotta was lost, and Cesare married a
French bride, all pretence was thrown off. The marriage contract between Borgia and Louis stated confidently that 'the Duc de Valentinois,
his house, his friends and allies would render great and noble services
to the French crown, particularly with regard to the conquest of Naples
and Milan.' In return Louis promised a small army to help Cesare
realize his own ambition in Italy, whatever that might be. Few in Italy
believed that Cesare had gone to France merely to find a bride. The
pope's rare talent for trickery was well known, so when the news came
that another French attack on Italy was imminent, the Italian rulers
reacted swiftly. Ascanio Sforza upbraided the pope and then left. Alexander dismissed him with a reminder that his brother Ludovico il Moro
had been the first to invite a French army into Italy. A few days later
Garcilasso, the Spanish ambassador, departed after a violent scene with
the pope. Alfonso di Bisceglie was the next to go, fleeing, like Giovanni
Sforza before him, on a fast horse. 'Madonna Lucrezia's husband', it was
noted, 'has secretly fled and gone to the Colonna in Genazzano. He has
deserted his wife who is six months with child, and she is constantly in
tears.' Alfonso wrote to her, asking her to join him, and Lucrezia who
loved her gentle eighteen-year-old husband would willingly have done
so. But papal soldiers intercepted the letter. Alexander then ordered
Alfonso's sister Sancia back to Naples, but had some trouble compelling
that reluctant and forthright girl to go. She was driven, protesting, from
Rome; in a fit of pique the pope refused to give her the funds for the
journey, though she was his own daughter-in-law. Alexander, however, could not afford to let his children join their spouses in Naples for
fear that they might be taken as hostages. He solved the problem in

typical ingenious fashion by making Lucrezia governor of the papal town of Spoleto, and sent her off to that relatively safe place in charge of young Jofré, from whom the pope seemed to expect nothing.

In September 1499 a French army marched once more into northern Italy. From the vantage point of Lyons, King Louis watched as city after city went down. The formidable coalition of France and Venice, with the blessing of the papacy, swept all before it. Ludovico il Moro, the tyrant whose treachery and double treachery over many years had caused so much Italian grief, fled over the Alps to Austria. The castellan of the Milan fortress sold his castle to the French; on 6 October, amid rejoicing, Louis entered Milan and was acclaimed as duke. By his side, among the gathering of his nobles, rode Cesare Borgia. After four months with his wife, Cesare had left her pregnant in Lyons. The Duchess of Valence never saw her husband again, and her child never knew its father. Cesare rode away to his destiny as scourge and terror in the land of his birth.

CHAPTER SIX
CESARE THE PRINCE

MANY WERE THE LAMENTS THROUGHOUT THE FIF-teenth century on the state of Italy. Yet in this land where wits were quickened to a degree unknown in the rest of Europe, and where the study of history had been ordered into the beginnings of science, wise men knew very well that the fault came from within, lying in the life and the people. 'In our change-loving Italy,' wrote Aeneas Sylvius Piccolomini, 'where nothing stands firm, where no ancient dynasty exists, a servant can easily become a king.' What Alexander VI and his son Cesare attempted was nothing more than the logical consequence of Italian political art. Their ends and their means were universally recognized, being in the tradition of Italian despotism. For several centuries the independent states of Italy had formed an arena in which any experiment was possible, and in which any man with talent, ruthlessness and an unquenchable thirst for fame could rise. As a result, Italian rulers had shown a sagacity, judgment, flexibility, and artistic impulse beyond the reach of any king or prince in the slovenly north; but all was allied to a cunning, faithlessness, cruelty and im-morality beyond the comprehension of colder, more conservative peoples. The great courts of the Italian tyrants had produced a life of unparalleled splendour; but at what cost in blood and guilt? The family of Este in Ferrara built a state so wealthy, so active in trade, so well-ordered as to the life and surroundings of the citizens that it was the envy of Italy and the pride of the populace. This was done by a ruling house that lived perpetually in the midst of violence and deceit. In 1425 a princess accused of adultery with a stepson was beheaded. Children of the house, legitimate and illegitimate, fled abroad pursued by assas-sins. A bastard of a bastard tried to steal the state from the lawful heir. In 1493, that lawful ruler, Duke Ercole, is said to have poisoned his wife

Duke Ercole and Alfons
d'Este, the ruling house
of Ferrara, prayed for
peace but lived in the
midst of violence and
deceit, pursuing a ruth-
less policy that denied tl
papacy temporal suppor

because he feared she might poison him. Thirteen years later, two
bastards rebelled against Duke Alfonso; one had his eyes put out by
another brother, Cardinal Ippolito, and both were imprisoned for life.

In Naples, King Ferrante, who had perhaps tried to poison his
brother-in-law Duke Ercole, was the most vindictive dissimulator of
his time. He governed his kingdom by profoundly secret manipulations
and by a despotism oriental in its all-embracing oppression. He liked
to have his enemies near him, either alive in his dungeons, or dead and
embalmed, and all Italy knew of these gruesome relics. He would invite
his victims to dine and seize them in the middle of the meal. No one was
safe with him, not even his most loyal servitor. In Milan, Filippo Maria
Visconti, a man of rare talent and with a greatness of spirit not seen in
Ferrante, still lived almost paralysed by fear. For years he never set foot
in his city, sequestered in his citadel and only emerging to make a tour
of his lands, from castle to castle. In the citadel no one was allowed to
stand at a window, for fear that he might be signalling to an enemy
without. Spies and informers were the normal residents of his household, and his *condottieri* and officials were encouraged to cross and
double-cross each other. He was so credulously superstitious that he
believed in magic and prophecies of all kinds, and prayed indiscriminately to any unseen power. Yet he handled complicated international

affairs with ease and carried on wars with a bold certainty. He was succeeded by his *condottiere* and stepson Francesco Sforza whose brilliant
career was still marred by the horror that always seemed to run with
Italian despotism. His wife killed his mistress out of jealousy. Some
good friends abandoned him for Naples, and another he hanged for
treason. He imprisoned a son for plotting against him, and his brother
invited the French to attack him. Of his children who ruled in Milan,
one thought so much of his beautiful hands and his mellifluous voice,
and lived so much for the satisfaction of his irrational cruelty, that his
citizens finally murdered him. So the way was paved for his brother
Ludovico il Moro, who usurped the duchy from his nephew and played
upon the keys of policy with such artfulness that he could boast, in 1496,
that the Emperor was his *condottiere*, Venice his chamberlain, the pope
his chaplain, and the king of France his courier. Yet from this supreme
display of political trickery there flowed the French invasion and the
disaster that afflicted all Italy.

Not even Florence, the wisest state, or Venice, the most stable and
circumspect, could avoid the prevailing alarm, capriciousness and terror.
Venice, indeed, went beyond others in making calculated terror an
effective instrument of government. And if these large entities were a
prey to demoralizing forces, there was no hope at all for the petty
princelings who dominated central Italy, specially in the lands where
the pope exercised his traditional rights of a suzerain. This was the
breeding ground for the *condottieri*, the soldiers of fortune who by luck
and force aimed to take some small territory, and then hold on to it,
occasionally by genius or enlightened rule, but more usually by a bloody
tyranny. Their task was made easy not only by the military weakness
of the pope, whose writ did not run far in his own lands, but also by
the system of papal administration which let out small fiefs to independent vicars, *condottieri* expected to govern and raise taxes on behalf of
the pope and also to fight his wars. The system was perfect for abuse;
and for every family like the Montefeltri, who, for all their faults, made
the court of Urbino one of the jewels of Renaissance culture, there were
many others who were little more than bandit chiefs, leading lives of
frightening instability, sucking the community of its lifeblood, and
perpetually denying the papacy the temporal support on which its
independence rested.

The Malatesta in Rimini, the Manfredi in Faenza, the Varani in Camerino, the Baglioni in Perugia, the Ordelaffi in Forlì, and many another family, led lives of savagery, decimating each other and their own families – they were as dangerous to themselves as to others – by atrocity after atrocity. Bernardo Varano murdered two of his brothers to add their property to his own. Pandolfo Malatesta, nephew of the monster Sigismondo, burned the convent into which the woman he wanted had been sent for safety. Another Pandolfo – Petrucci of Siena – rolled boulders down Monte Amiata for entertainment, without caring what damage he did to persons or property. In the course of the blood-stained feuds of the Baglioni, no less than four members of the family were murdered on the night of 15 July 1495. To maintain their grip on Perugia, the Baglioni turned the cathedral into a barracks; on one occasion they executed 130 would-be conspirators and hung their bodies in the Palazzo Comunale. When the French temporarily drove the Baglioni from the city in 1494, they fought so ferociously that every dwelling in the valley between Perugia and Assisi was razed and the bushes were laden with corpses rather than fruit.

Nor were the citizens ruled by the *condottiere* very different from the chief himself. A petty tyrant was a hostage to fortune and his only safety lay in success. There is an old story – they say it took place in Siena – that a certain soldier had delivered the town from foreigners, and the citizens got together to reward him. Since they could not agree, and decided besides that nothing they could offer, not even the lordship of the city, was enough, they resolved to kill the soldier and then worship him as a patron saint. And that is what they did. 'Nothing is cheaper here', Pontano wrote, 'than human life.' 'Shall I call the tyrant king and obey him loyally?' Boccaccio had said. 'No, for he is the enemy of the commonwealth. Against him I may use arms, conspiracies, spies, ambushes, and fraud. There is no more acceptable sacrifice than the blood of a tyrant.' And murder was but one type of the immorality that infected the whole of Italian life. Men and women were equally guilty. Overstating an evident truth with the licence of a novelist, Bandello condemned both sexes. 'Nowdays', he wrote, 'we see a woman poison her husband to gratify her lust. Another, fearing the discovery of an illicit affair, sends her lover to murder her husband. Then fathers, brothers, husbands wipe out the shame with poison, sword and other

gismondo Malatesta,
tron of the arts and
ler of Rimini. When
lexander found the lands
f the church reduced to
aos by such tyrants as
Malatesta, he resolved to
se fraud and violence to
al with them.

means, but still women follow their passions.' Men, too, are murderous
and far more tyrannical. 'Every day we hear that a man has murdered
his wife because he thought her unfaithful; that another has killed his
daughter who married secretly; that a third has put away a sister who
would not marry as he wished. If women do anything that displeases us
men, we are at them with cords and daggers and poison.'

Surrounded by a general infection, the Church and the clergy could
not avoid the taint. 'We Italians are irreligious and corrupt above
others,' Machiavelli said; and the reason was 'because the Church and
her representatives set us the worst example.' Another critic wrote: 'No
one passed for an accomplished man who did not have heretical opinions

about religion. At the court, the rules of the Church, and Holy Writ itself, were only spoken of in jest, and the mysteries of the faith were despised.' Church and society interacted; and who could say whether the Church was rotten because society had corrupted it, or society grew worse because the Church pandered to its evil? Priests were certainly as capable of crime as any layman. In August 1495, Niccolò de' Pelegati, a priest of Figarolo, was hung in an iron cage from the tower of San Giuliano in Ferrara. On the day of his first Mass he had committed murder but had been absolved by Rome. He was later known to have killed at least four others, and he had two wives. He became the head of a robber band, killing, violating women, waylaying travellers, extorting ransoms. The Church, with its extraordinary privileges, was sometimes a haven for criminals, and Massuccio knew a pirate in a Neapolitan monastery. Church buildings themselves, since a man did not take his bodyguard to Mass, often saw appalling scenes of violence. The citizens of Fabriano rose up at the words *Et incarnatus est* and slew members of the ruling Chiavistelli family. In Milan, a Visconti was killed at the church door, and a Sforza done to death before the altar by killers who prayed before the act and sat devoutly through the service. When the Pazzi conspired against the Medici, the professional assassin had refused to do the act in the cathedral, so they were forced to rely on some of the clergy 'who knew the sacred place, and thus had no fear'.

Conduct and morality in Italian Church and state were so intimately mixed, so tied to common experience and a common life, that what was possible in one was always possible in the other. Men knew very well what was moral and religious behaviour in churchmen, but because great prelates were great princes also, it was generally allowed that they should use the weapons of their kind. The historian Guicciardini expressed the paradox clearly:

> No man is more disgusted than I with the ambition, avarice and profligacy of priests, not only because these vices are hateful in themselves, but also because they are utterly repugnant in those who claim to have a special relation with God. Nonetheless, my position at the court of several popes forced me to desire their greatness for the sake of my own interest.

That was the kind of honesty and precision that Europe shuddered at and admired in Machiavelli. It was therefore a matter of little surprise to contemporaries that, when Alexander found the lands of the Church reduced to a terrible chaos by the likes of Malatesta and Baglione, he should decide to resolve the question in the manner of a Ferrante, a Sforza, or even a Pope Sixtus IV.

Alexander could be in no doubt about the deplorable condition of the papal states in the aftermath of the French invasion of 1494. In the summer of 1497 he sent his relative, Cardinal Borgia Lanzol the younger, to investigate the cities of Umbria. He went without troops, merely as papal legate, to test the extent of the pope's authority in a dangerous area. From Narni, on the first day, Lanzol wrote that he could do nothing without troops as the demons he faced were not frightened by holy water. But no troops were sent, and the legate was generally derided. The *condottiere* Bartolomeo d'Alviano seized and sacked a papal town before the cardinal's face, saying contemptuously that, as a mercenary, he would gladly help the pope keep the peace, but having taken the town he would rather destroy it than give it up. Throughout the district there was neither peace nor order. The citizens of Todi, left to the mercy of brigands, abandoned their town. In Perugia the legate caught a murderer and put him to death. The event caused a sensation, because murders in the territory of the Baglioni were two-a-penny but justice was as rare as gold. The cardinal boasted of his success and assured the pope that the country could only be pacified by measures of extreme rigour.

Alexander's reading of past and present pointed to the same conclusion. Surrounded by enemies and having to shift distrustfully between calculating allies, he knew that his safety depended on the skilful handling of his assets. He had, in particular, two chief assets: the moral and spiritual power of the Supreme Pontiff, and his children. With him, nepotism had become far more than a fault of the heart, a desire to enrich his children. It had become the core of his policy, the means by which he removed the independent and fractious vassals of the papal states and replaced them with one man who intimately represented his own person. No one could do this as well as a son. He must go on as he had started, using the means to hand, for as Guicciardini wisely said, sometimes fraud and violence are the only way to take and hold a state. In 1499, with Cesare poised in Milan supported by French troops, Alexander needed no further encouragement to authorize a campaign into the lands of the Romagna which stood to benefit the papacy, his own peace of mind, and the advancement of his son.

In September 1499 Alexander collected his family together at Nepi and outlined his design. He planned the creation of two strategic Borgia estates: one for Lucrezia and her progeny in Latium, formed at the expense of the troublesome Roman barons; and the other, of far greater extent and importance, a duchy for Cesare which would incorporate papal lands in the Romagna and extend gradually into the Marches, Umbria, and perhaps to territories beyond. In Latium, Alexander began with the Gaetani family, encircling them with a web of deceit until at last he had confiscated their estates, caused young Bernardino Gaetani to be murdered, and handed to Lucrezia the town of Sermoneta, for which she was supposed to pay the Camera Apostolica 80,000 ducats. In the Romagna, he announced the excommunication of the lords of the chief towns for non-payment of their annual dues to the Church, and he connived with the French and the Venetians that Cesare should set out on a path of conquest. In November, Cesare Borgia, a general of unknown quality, left Lombardy on his first campaign, leading an army of some 8000 soldiers supplied in the main by the French king, and including a strong body of Gascon and Swiss mercenaries. The money was provided by the papal treasury and by a loan of 45,000 ducats from Milan. Cesare was to proceed first against members of the Sforza family, the enemies of Louis XII, and with this in mind the army marched towards Imola where Caterina Sforza, the widow of Girolamo Riario, governed.

Caterina, who knew what was in store for her, had made preparations. She was a valiant, forceful woman but in her two towns of Imola and Forlì she was obeyed from fear rather than love. Remembering the destruction done by the invading French in 1494, the citizens had no heart for another war on behalf of a tyrannical ruling family. Caterina remained in Forlì and gave the defence of Imola to the *condottiere* Dionigi Naldi. This man was no more conscientious than most of his kind, so when the town immediately opened the gates to Cesare's army, Naldi, in the fortress, held out only until the artillery was brought up, then surrendered and offered to take service with Cesare. Two days later, the augmented army, strengthened by the acquisition of Naldi's infantry, marched to Forlì. Until Riario, the *nipote* of Sixtus IV, had

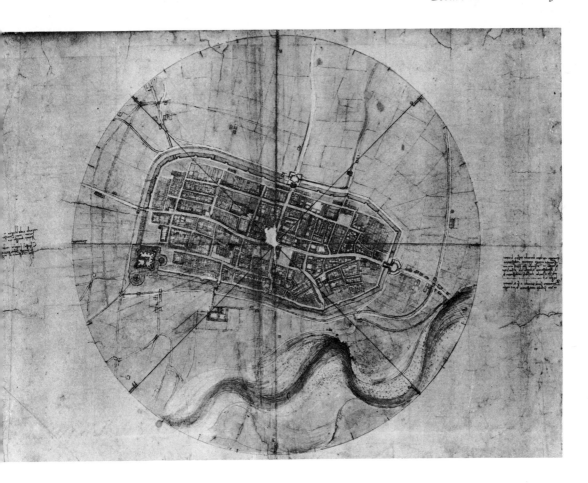

Leonardo da Vinci's map
Imola, the city
governed by Caterina
Sforza. The city and its
fortress (see colour plate,
facing page 157) at lower
left are surrounded by
moats. Leonardo's notes
on either side of the
circle refer to the
geography of Bologna
and other cities in which
Cesare Borgia had a
military interest.

taken the city, Forlì for 200 years belonged to the Ordelaffi family, the best-known member of which had murdered his mother, brother and two wives. Nonetheless, the citizens had conspired to assassinate Riario in an effort to reinstate their old, bloodstained masters, and now saw no reason to support Riario's widow. They also opened their gates. But the castle of the city, the forbidding Rocca di Ravaldino, was commanded by Caterina herself, and the fifteenth century limped out with Cesare still halted before this obstacle.

Cesare had covenanted with the inhabitants of Forlì not to let his French troops enter the city. But to attack Caterina in the citadel, he found it necessary to override this condition. The French marched in and the Gascons began a mercenary terror so that the city chronicler thought he had seen 'a glimpse through the gates of hell'. In the future, Cesare stamped out this kind of indiscipline, for he shrewdly judged that agreements of surrender were better honoured than broken. But he was still green in war, and his cause was not helped by the spirited resistance of Caterina, who bombarded the houses of the chief citizens of her own town. For three weeks she held out against the battering of the French artillery. And when at last a breach was made, she was at hand, a resplendent figure in armour, to put heart into the defenders. Even when the cause was lost, she was determined to go out in a blaze, and would have blown up the magazine and the castle had not a fuse failed.

Captured by French soldiers, Caterina was taken to their captain Yves d'Alègre. To Cesare she was a menace to be treated with the ruthless dispatch that Italians habitually used against enemies, men and women. But to the chivalrous French captain she was a figure of sentimental awe, a fiery amazon out of some medieval romance, and there were hard words before d'Alègre reluctantly gave her up, on payment of a ransom, and having extracted from Cesare a promise of good treatment. But now she was in Borgia hands she could expect nothing more than bare existence. Caterina Sforza was still a noble beauty at the age of thirty-six, and there were reports that Cesare assaulted and even raped her. It is also possible that Caterina, who could evaluate her own appeal well enough, made certain overtures to her keeper. Cesare's main interest, if she were not to be killed, was to have her well and truly locked up, and whatever may have happened between them at Forlì he made sure that she went to Rome for an extended period of imprisonment.

Now Cesare headed for Pesaro, the town of his ex-brother-in-law Giovanni Sforza. Sforza fled to Venice, and the march to Pesaro continued unhindered. So far the campaign had gone excellently. Imola and Forlì had fallen 'like harlots'. At once Cesare had shown the Borgia talent for administration and had set up a local government on sound principles. He had shown, also, the Borgia cunning, secretly drawing up and supporting a petition whereby the citizens asked the pope to grant them Cesare Borgia as their lawful ruler. He now styled himself 'Cesare Borgia of France, Duke of Valence, Count of Diois and Issoudun, Papal Vicar of Imola and Forlì'. But at Cesena, on the road to Pesaro, he received his first check. Ludovico Sforza was returning to Milan at the head of Swiss mercenaries, and therefore d'Alègre and the French troops would have to withdraw from the Romagna to defend

Caterina Sforza, the beautiful virago, captur at Forlì and taken as Cesare's hostage to Rome. She wrote of poisons as well as of prescriptions to maintai beauty in her *Experimen* and claimed to concoct *veleno attermine*, a poisor which gave 'perfect slee

French interests in Milan. He also heard that his cousin and colleague Cardinal-legate Juan Borgia Lanzol, the younger of the two cardinals of that name, had died of fever on the way from Urbino. The chronicles, such was the hatred of the Borgias, spread the familiar whispers that Cesare had poisoned his relative. But there were no grounds for thinking this; the two had worked well together, and Lanzol, in his capacity as legate, had been able to soothe the suspicions with which Florence and Venice viewed the campaign in the Romagna. Now Cesare was on his own. He no longer had the support of the legate, and the sudden withdrawal of the French warned him that he could not win a state with French arms. He was left with only a small force of about 1000 infantry and 500 cavalry, so he decided that before he went any further he must raise and command an army that owed loyalty to none but himself. He fell back on Cesena, left his Spanish captain Ramiro de Lorca as governor of the newly won territory, and returned to Rome in triumph.

On 26 February 1500 Cesare approached Rome in the guise of victorious general. His father, the old master of theatricality, had arranged a welcome that was part Renaissance carnival, part ancient Roman triumph. Cardinals Orsini and Farnese, as the pope's personal representatives, met Cesare on the road and led him solemnly to the Porta del Popolo, where the assembled ambassadors and cardinals awaited him bareheaded. Wagons of spoil, covered with black cloth, led the procession, followed by two heralds, one wearing the French fleur-de-lis and the other the Borgia bull. Then came the Swiss pikemen, the horsemen, and the duke's bodyguard each with the word 'Caesar' embroidered in silver on his doublet. The *condottiere* Vitellozzo Vitelli led the gentlemen of the staff, and at last came the victor himself, severely dressed in a black satin surcoat with the French Order of St Michael about his neck. He had brought with him his prisoner Caterina Sforza whose majestic presence in her plight moved one tender-hearted observer to speak of 'another Zenobia, bound in golden chains'. The procession made its stately way through Rome towards the Vatican while the cannon of Sant'Angelo roared their salute and the bells rang out in every church. Crossing the bridge of Sant'Angelo, Cesare could see his feats proclaimed on vast standards which hung from the battlements of the fortress. In the audience chamber of the Vatican, Alexander and his son spoke in Spanish, the language of their private or emotional moments. Cesare knelt to kiss the pope's foot but his father, weeping and laughing at the same time, raised him up and embraced him.

In Rome, city and Church alike were celebrating the jubilee for the year 1500. On Christmas Eve of 1499 Alexander had gone with taper and silver hammer to knock on the door of St Peter's that was only opened in jubilee time. Masons unbricked the door and the pilgrims flowed in, approaching along the broad prospect of the Via Alessandrina which the pope had recently caused to be built, lancing through the old slums of the Vatican from the bridge of Sant'Angelo to the doors of St Peter's. Pious men rejoiced to see evidence of religious enthusiasm, even in the corrupted Roman heart of Christendom. Two hundred thousand pilgrims collected in the Piazza of St Peter for the pope's Easter blessing. The coffers of the Church began to fill up with their offerings. Since the

me: the papal blessing
he Piazza of St Peter.
o hundred thousand
rims attended Alex-
er's Easter blessing in
jubilee year.

DISEGNO DELA BENEDITIONE DEL PONTEFICE NELA PIAZA DE SANTO PIETRO ·

Turks were again advancing, threatening the eastern limits of Venetian territory, the pope in this year of rededication called to mind his pastoral duty to the whole of Christendom and announced preparations for a Crusade. In the spring he sent legates to preach throughout Europe and authorized the levy of the crusading tax. The efforts met the usual indifference of the European princes, and when the Bull of Crusade was promulgated on 1 July 1500 it had as little effect as the forlorn attempts of Calixtus III or Pius II. Nor was Rome in any way reformed by the fervour of the jubilee pilgrims. People who had come with such trial and expense from the ends of Europe to pray in the Basilica of St Peter, recrossed the bridge of Sant'Angelo and saw, hanging in rows, the criminals executed on the battlements of the fort. At one time there hung among them the members of a gang that had robbed and stripped the French envoy on his way to Rome; at another time, a notorious doctor from the hospital of San Giovanni in the Lateran who shot lone travellers in the dawn streets and robbed their bodies. This rogue also conspired with the hospital confessor to seek out wealthy invalids, poison them, and share the spoil.

As crime continued to thrive in Rome, so too did the Borgias, the great beneficiaries of a criminal papacy. Cesare ruled his father's heart, and in doing so seemed to rule the Church. Those seeking a nomination to the Sacred College begged for his good word. All new governors and castellans in the papal states had first to pass his scrutiny. The commander of the Castel Sant'Angelo was one of his men. On 9 March the pope invested Cesare as papal vicar of the Romagna. On the 29th he was confirmed as Captain-General of the Church, receiving from Alexander the insignia of Gonfalonier, and with it the decoration of the Golden Rose. In all the festivities, both sacred and profane, of the jubilee year, Cesare was a magnificent presence. The story of his revelry runs through the pages of Johann Burchard's diary: how the Duke of Valentinois set up a bullring in the Piazza of St Peter and from horseback slew five bulls with the lance and severed the neck of a sixth with one blow of his sword; how he wagered at a duel on Monte Testaccio between a Frenchman and a Burgundian; how, on a Sunday evening, he gave a banquet for his father and his sister at which fifty courtesans danced first clothed and then naked, and how the naked whores crawled among the feet of the diners gathering chestnuts from the floor; how races were

Alexander VI was never described as handsome – the nose and mouth were too heavy – but even at sixty he had those qualities that his tutor Gaspar da Verona had noted in the youthful Rodrigo: 'His attraction for beautiful women, and the manner in which he excites them – and they fall in love with him – i quite remarkable. He attracts them more powerfully than a magn does iron.'

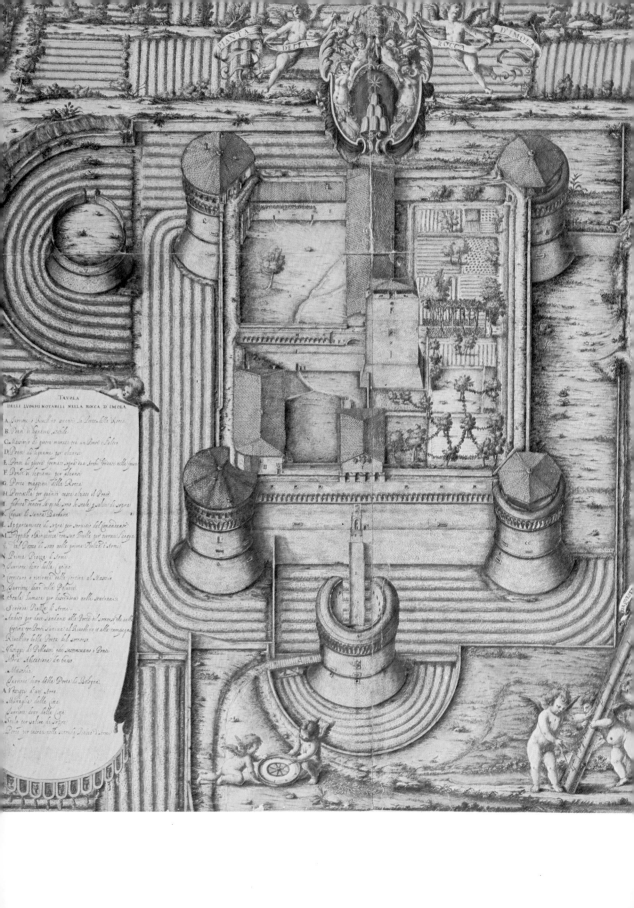

TAVOLA
DELLI LVOGHI NOTABILI NELLA ROCCA D'IMOLA

A Terrapieno e fianchi per auenti la Porta della Rocca
B Ponti di legname mobile
C Cataratta di graue messa tra un Ponte e l'altro
D Ponti di legname per alzarsi
E Ponte leuatore leuato sopra una Arco e ferrato nella sponda
F Ponte di legname per alzarsi
G Porta maggiore della Rocca
H Porticella per entrare mentre alzato il Ponte
I fabrica innanzi di quella, oue le scale se alzano di sopra
K Capella di Santa Barbara
L Appartamento di sopra per seruitio del commandante
M Coperto e banchina con un fiancho per cauar l'acqua
   del Pozzo li sono nelle prime Piazze d'armi
N Prima Piazza d'armi
O Saracino sotto della salita
P coperture e riparati nella fortezza di Maestri
Q Saracino sotto della Pittura
R Scale lumace per discendere nelle sauranea
S seconda Piazza d'armi
T Andare per discendenza alla Porta di Lorenzo che salda
   coglina per Ponti leuatori del Riuellino e alla campagna
V Riuellino della Porta dal sorriano
X Ntorzzo il Pellaccio che sostengono i Ponti
Y Altra Mitatione da basso
Z Mischia
& Saracino fuor della Porta di Bologna
A V terzza d'ari Arco
B Misaaglia della fine
C Saracino doue della saga
D Sala per salire di sopra
E Porta per entrare nella sortita Doppo il Arco

held in the city streets with boars, with prostitutes, with Barbary stallions, with Spanish ponies, with heavy warhorses, and how the rider of Don Cesare won the prize.

The pope looked on with parental indulgence. In the early part of the year Alexander had been severely ill with fever, a sickness welcomed by his many enemies: one of them portrayed the pope beseeching Death to let him expire in the arms of one of his concubines. He recovered, and though his health was generally robust he suffered from mysterious fainting fits which reminded his dependants that the pope was growing old. There was further evidence of his fallibility when, on 27 June, Alexander was the victim of a bizarre accident. As he was about to begin an audience in the Sala dei Pontefici a violent summer storm blew down a chimneystack which crashed through the roof and collapsed the floor above the pope's head. The Cardinal of Capua and a papal secretary only saved themselves by leaping into a deep window embrasure, and when they looked up they saw the papal chair completely covered with dust and rubble. At once the cry went out 'The pope is dead', and Rome was on the edge of panic. Men set to with shovels and after half an hour Alexander was extracted still sitting upright, unconscious, but only slightly hurt. The episode was worrying to a superstitious age. Only the previous day, the Mantuan envoy reported, the pope had just escaped the fall of a heavy iron chandelier. It was high time for papal favourites to consider the future. Soon after the accident, the Venetian ambassador Capello found himself taken aside familiarly by Cesare Borgia, who admitted in confidence that the injury to his father had opened his eyes to his own precarious position; he therefore wanted to offer his services to Venice as a *condottiere*. The ambassador, who had some experience of the Borgias, gave a noncommital answer. And soon, as the pope recovered, the matter was forgotten. Alexander gave thanks to God, to the Blessed Virgin, to the saints, and was his old genial self again. 'The pope is now seventy,' Capello wrote in September 1500, 'but he grows younger every day. He is always cheerful and never does anything he dislikes. The advancement of his children is his only care, nothing else troubles him.'

While Alexander was recovering from his wounds, a still worse tragedy struck at his house. Since the pope had changed his alliance from Naples to France, the two Neapolitan partners of his younger children

The Fortress of Imola. One of Cesare Borgia's first targets in his Romagna campaign of 1499–1500 brought him up against the Sforza family, the enemies of Louis XII. His attack on Imola (see Leonardo's map of Imola on page 151) governed by Caterina Sforza, lasted only a week. The *condottiere* Dionigi Naldi surrendered the fortress and offered his services to Cesare.

became something of an embarrassment. Driven from Rome in the previous year, Alfonso di Bisceglie and his sister Sancia returned to their spouses in 1500, but they lived uneasily in the midst of the Borgias. On the evening of 15 July, when Alfonso was leaving the Vatican after a visit to the pope's sick room, he was attacked in the Piazza, at the door of St Peter's, and deeply wounded in three places. His life was saved by the courage of two gentlemen who came to his aid, beat off the assailants and dragged the young duke back to the safety of the Vatican. Stabbed in the head, right arm and leg, Alfonso was carried into the papal apartments and placed in the room known as the Sala delle Sibille, where his wife Lucrezia and his sister Sancia came to care for him. At first he refused a doctor, saying he could trust no one in Rome; then he got word to his kinsman, the King of Naples, that his life was not safe, and Federigo sent his own doctor from Naples to look after him. Both the reason for the attack and the identity of his enemy were unknown. Some suspicion pointed to the Borgias, but the plotters were just as likely to be Orsini, for the young Neapolitan duke was a good friend of the Colonna; moreover his wife's estates were threatening to engulf Orsini lands. But no guilt could be fixed in the city of plot and terrorism. 'There are', wrote the Florentine envoy, 'in the Vatican so many causes of hatred, both old and new, so much envy and jealousy, both public and private, that scandals will always arise.'

For a month Alfonso recuperated, lovingly tended by his wife and his sister. His food was prepared separately and tasted for poison, and Alexander posted a guard on the door. At first the name of Cesare had not been mentioned in connection with the attack, but gradually Alfonso became convinced that his brother-in-law the Duke of Valentinois was the would-be assassin. Hazy and contradictory accounts related a swift progression to disaster. Cesare, said one report, visited the wounded man and told him ominously that 'what was not done at noon may be done by nightfall'. The pope, Lucrezia and Sancia were in despair, sure of some terrible impending fate. On 18 August the Venetian envoy wrote that Alfonso had seen Cesare walking in the garden below and, in a fit of anger, had loosed a crossbow at his enemy. That afternoon Michele Corella – Cesare's henchman Don Michelotto – forced his way in with armed men. His instructions from his master were to find the man who shot the arrow. Turning the protesting ladies from the room,

ta Maria delle Febbre,
me, where Alfonso di
ceglie was buried next
Lucrezia's great uncle
ixtus III.

Don Michelotto then strangled the Duke of Bisceglie. That same night
the corpse of the nineteen-year-old was buried without ceremony in
the church of Santa Maria delle Febbre. 'The physician of the dead
prince and a certain hunchback', Burchard noted, 'were brought to
Sant'Angelo. They were examined by the inquisitors but soon released,
since the man who had done this thing was well known, but went unpunished.' On the 23rd Alexander told the Venetian envoy that Alfonso
had tried to kill Cesare, implying that was sufficient cause for revenge.
Nothing more was said: it was prudent to let the matter lie. The pope,
the envoy wrote, was afraid of his son.

Alexander wanted no weeping faces to remind him of guilt and
terror. 'Madonna Lucrezia', Capello reported, 'was formerly in favour

with the pope, but now he does not love her and has sent her to Nepi.'
She called herself *La Infelicissima* and mourned in the black-hung halls
of the castle, fretting about her baby son Rodrigo and lamenting the
dangers of Rome where, it was openly said, il Valentino reigned supreme. 'This duke,' said the cold and knowledgeable Capello, 'if he
lives, will be one of the first captains of Italy.' Cesare now pressed ahead
with his plans for the conquest of the Romagna, and for this he needed
not only money but also the goodwill of Venice, the northern neighbour to the lands of the Romagna. The acquiescence of the republic was
purchased by Alexander who promised help against the Turks and supported Venetian interests in the College of Cardinals. Money for the
campaign was available, in large quantities, from the treasury of the
Church. No pope before Alexander had been so successful in turning
spiritual office into hard cash. His intercession in the troubled matri-
monial affairs of the European princes often resulted in an increase to
the papal treasury. King Ladislaus of Hungary, for example, was
allowed to cast off his wife for 25,000 ducats. A Greek princess in
Poland, who was reluctant to change from Orthodox to Catholic, was
threatened with the confiscation of all her goods. Alexander levied
double annates and double, sometimes triple, tithes. He was the first
pope to declare that indulgences released souls from purgatory. Two
kings of Portugal having died under sentence of excommunication
were posthumously granted absolution so long as Portugal discharged
their debts to the Church. And to deliver ordinary souls out of purgatory, neither contrition, nor confession, nor even Mass was necessary, but only payment. As a preparation for Cesare's wars, the pope
created twelve new cardinals in September 1500. Cesare entertained the
new prelates at a banquet, where they registered their loyalty and
settled their accounts. They provided his war chest with 120,000 ducats.

With money to hand, the way into the Romagna was clear; for the
political ground had been carefully prepared throughout the summer.
In August, the pope excommunicated Giovanni Sforza of Pesaro, Manfredi of Faenza and Malatesta of Rimini. In the same month the French
terms for participation in Cesare's *impresa* were negotiated. Machiavelli
later commented, from the French court at Blois, that Louis XII had
given way because he did not know how to withstand the pope's in-
sistence. But the Florentine was not privy to the secret plan between

Nepi Castle, a sombre
place overlooking a deep
ravine, bestowed upon
Lucrezia in 1498. Bur-
hard describes Lucrezia's
departure from Rome at
the end of August 1500
with her infant son
Rodrigo 'to ride to Nepi
and there seek consolation
and relief for her sadness
and grief at the death of
her husband'.

France and Spain to partition the kingdom of Naples, and to achieve that Louis needed the pope's help. The support of the pope's son was a small price to pay. So Louis agreed to give Cesare a body of French troops, once again under Yves d'Alègre. Cesare, however, had learned that he could not rely on French arms and was also forming a mercenary army based on Spanish infantry. He had bought, too, the services of several Italian *condottieri*, including Paolo Orsini, Gianpaolo Baglione and the noted artillery captain Vitellozzo Vitelli. In the tracks of the military there followed a group of papal clerks, secretaries, and the Sienese banker Alessandro Spannochi, for no one knew better than a Borgia the value of efficient administration in newly won territory. On 30 September, Cesare paraded the Spanish infantry for his father in front of St Peter's. Three days later he led his army into the Romagna.

Cesare intended to begin where he had left off in February, with an attack on Pesaro. On the way across Italy he heard that the city had risen against Giovanni Sforza, driving him to exile in Venice. At midnight on 27 October, amid general enthusiasm, Cesare entered the gate under heavy rain. In the previous year, at Imola, he had seen the necessity for good order, and Pandolfo Collenuccio commented on the discipline and restraint of the army. Collenuccio, an envoy from Ferrara, sent his master Ercole d'Este – a man who knew that Ferrara itself was not beyond the reach of Borgia ambition – a careful account of the Duke of Valentinois at work. At first Cesare was indisposed. He sent the envoy gifts of wine, grain, poultry, candles, and two boxes of sugared almonds, but he was suffering from the recurrent malady of syphilis and could not be disturbed. By the next night the duke had recovered, and in excellent humour received the envoy after dinner. Ferrara need have no fears, Cesare assured him; he hinted that plans were even now afoot to tie the widowed Lucrezia to a prince of the d'Este family. Collenuccio was impressed by the Borgia intelligence, though puzzled by the duke's eccentric way of life. Cesare liked to turn day into night, going to bed in the dawn hours and starting work in the early evening. He had a love for theatrical gestures, for mystery, for striking clothes, for disguise. But as to his ability, the envoy had no doubt:

> He is bold, vigorous and without prejudice. He respects honest men but according to many he is bitter in revenge. He has a vast spirit and pursues

Portrait sketches of Cesare by Leonardo da Vinci. After the fall of Milan and of his patron Ludovico il Moro, Leonardo found employment with Cesare as his chief engineer, his main tasks being to supervise fortifications.

greatness and fame, but he seems in a greater hurry to acquire states than to set them on a sound and orderly basis. Tomorrow he will go to Rimini. He must go slowly, he told me, because he cannot afford to be separated from his artillery.

Rimini capitulated at once, the hated Pandolfo Malatesta being one more fugitive to Venice, and Cesare entering yet another town unopposed. But Faenza refused to surrender and under the energetic young Astorre Manfredi resisted successfully. Manfredi was helped by Florence and Bologna, for both these cities had begun to fear for their own safety. As winter came on, and Faenza remained uncaptured, Cesare's captains started to quarrel, and soon unruly Baglione took his troops back to Perugia. Supplies were also difficult to obtain, so Cesare called off the campaign until the spring and retired to Cesena, which he made his administrative capital. Despite the setback at Faenza, it was clear to Italy that the Duke of Valentinois was a prince in the making, and he began to attract to Cesena those indispensable acolytes of the great Renaissance lord – scholars, artists, sculptors, craftsmen, and all those who laboured to enhance the temporal glory of great men. The duties of this prince were manifold; he had government to attend to, art to encourage, sport, hunting, carnival and bullfighting to entertain his leisure. He was also accused of abducting Dorotea da Crema, a young beauty brutally waylaid on the road from Urbino to Venice. In the spring Cesare set out for Faenza as a man refreshed and after a long bombardment the city agreed to terms of surrender which included a safe conduct for Astorre Manfredi. But however it came about, and there is no agreement as to what happened, young Manfredi, like Caterina Sforza before him, found himself a prisoner of Cesare. In June 1501, on the very day when Caterina was finally released from Sant' Angelo through the intercession of the French, the doors of the Roman prison closed on Astorre Manfredi. A year later, he and his younger brother were done to death. The strangled corpse of Astorre was found in the Tiber – yet more work for Don Michelotto. All Italy took the murder of the spirited Manfredi as an omen of coming terror. Everything that had formerly been whispered about Cesare, that he had killed his brother Gandia and his brother-in-law Bisceglie, was believed. Those who had good reason to fear his ambition now knew what they must expect.

With the fall of Faenza, the conquest of the Romagna was nearly done. An intimidatory march almost to the gates of Bologna warned Giovanni Bentivoglio to make peace for the good of his city. He ceded to Cesare the outlying fortress of Castel Bolognese, and then the Duke of Valentinois was the master of the whole territory and had gone as far as the pope's authorization allowed. Alexander gave his son the title of Duke of Romagna and ordered him back to Rome, where he was needed to assist in the plot to partition Naples. Cesare reluctantly obeyed, but bringing his victorious and restless army of mercenaries down the Via Flaminia he could not resist the chance to benefit on the way. Florence, which knew that some of the mercenaries with a grudge against the city were in touch with the exiled Medici, bought Cesare off with the offer of a *condotta* worth 36,000 ducats a year. Piombino was not so lucky. Cesare left his captain Vitellozzo Vitelli to drive out the petty despot Jacopo d'Appiano while he hurried on to Rome where the French army was already massing by the Milvian bridge, preparing for the attack on Naples.

In June 1501, Alexander welcomed his son to Rome 'as though he had conquered the lands of the infidel and not the devoted subjects of the Holy See'. Now that all preparations were made, the pope published a Bull assenting to the secret Treaty of Granada which France and

Spain had signed seven months before. By this agreement, Louis of France would become King of Naples, and Ferdinand of Spain would have the provinces of Apulia and Calabria with the title of Grand Duke, both monarchs to hold their lands in fief from the Church. The Supreme Pontiff congratulated himself on this master stroke accomplished by the Catholic King of Spain with the Most Christian King of France against an independent realm of Christendom. On St Peter's Day, Alexander stood at the loggia of Sant'Angelo and blessed the French army as it set out to seize Naples from the grandson of King Alfonso I, the man to whom all the Borgias owed their rise from obscurity. The army, complemented by Cesare's mercenaries, marched through Colonna territory, destroying towns at will. Capua, by the Volturno, which Hannibal had besieged for a year, was taken in eight days amid terrible slaughter. Burchard put the number killed at 6000, including priests, monks, nuns, women and girls: 'Whatever women they found they treated without mercy, cruelly raping the girls or taking them as booty.' The story grew, such was the willingness to blacken Cesare's name, that forty of the most beautiful girls were reserved for his pleasure alone. From Capua, the way was open to Naples, which surrendered on 4 August 1501. King Federigo, the last of the Aragonese line, was taken to a comfortable retirement in France, but his son the Duke of Calabria, who had the misfortune to fall into Spanish hands, spent thirty-eight years in the prisons of King Ferdinand.

The conquest of Naples resulted also in the temporary destruction of the Colonna, the ally of Naples. At the end of July the pope visited the captured castles in the Campagna to exult over the fall of an old enemy and to plan, in his usual way, a division of the territory among his family. In his absence from Rome, he left Lucrezia, to the scandal of the cardinals, as his regent in temporal affairs, a thing that had never been done before. Viewing the lands of the defeated Colonna, he decided to take the duchy of Sermoneta for Lucrezia's infant son Rodrigo, and the duchy of Nepi for another infant, the mysterious Giovanni Borgia aged about three, who may have been the child of Lucrezia, the child of Cesare, or most likely, the child of Alexander VI himself. For the first time in the history of the papal states, almost the entire area was in the hands of one family. Cesare had the Romagna, Lucrezia and the infant Borgias shared the hereditary estates of the Roman barons. Nor was that to be the end of Borgia expansion. Cesare was not content to stop at the borders of the Romagna; he had designs on the small pockets of independence left in Umbria and the Marches, and beyond these he had the greater ambition to control the ancient cities of Florence and Bologna. As a move towards this aim Alexander arranged, as the envoy Collenuccio had guessed, a marriage between Lucrezia and Alfonso d'Este, the heir to Ferrara. This alliance would protect Cesare at the northern edge of his domain. And despite the initial resistance of Alfonso himself, his father Ercole and the Emperor Maximilian. Alexander and Louis XII together forced the hand of Ferrara, so that Lucrezia and Alfonso were betrothed in September, and married on 30 December 1501.

Cesare was now poised for another predatory flight, and in the meantime seemed to rule his father with such sinister intent that Romans imagined their pope to be possessed by a succubus. Virulent pamphlets utterly damned Alexander and his offspring. 'These are the days of Antichrist,' his enemies proclaimed to the world; 'the bestiality and savagery of Nero and Caligula are surpassed. Rodrigo Borgia is an abyss of vice, a subverter of all justice, human or divine.' Alexander, who never lost his good-humoured composure, regarded these attacks with indifference. Not so Cesare. 'The duke', his father told the envoy of Ferrara, 'is a good-hearted man, but he cannot bear an injury. I have often told him that Rome is a free city, that everyone has a right to say what he pleases. Many things are said of me, but I take no notice. The duke replied, 'It may be that Romans can publish slanders, but I will teach them to repent.' The Borgia spies waited in shops and alleyways, in piazza and private house, and a word against the duke was high treason. A masked man railing too freely in the Borgo had a hand and his tongue cut off and fastened together. A pamphleteer who had the protection of the Venetian ambassador was still strangled and thrown into the Tiber. A friend wrote to Machiavelli concerning the death of Cardinal Lopez: 'If you ask what kind of death he suffered, it is commonly said to be by poison, since the great *Gonfaloniere* [Cesare Borgia] was not his friend, and such deaths are frequently heard of in Rome.' All this was looked on with complacency by Alexander, who played the role of the ancient tyrant Sulla: 'He takes one man's goods, another man's life, a third he drives into exile, a fourth he condemns to the gallows, a fifth he throws from his house for the sake of some Spanish heretic.' In the city of Rome and in the lands of the Church, men saw darkness, suspicion, terror and sudden death.

> The dead of night covered all things [said Egidio of Viterbo]. Besides domestic tragedies, never were sedition and bloodshed more widespread in the states of the Church; never were bandits more numerous, never more wickedness in the city; never were informers and assassins more used. Men were safe neither in their rooms, nor their houses, nor their castles. The laws of God and man were as nothing. Gold, violence and lust ruled undisputed.

This condition in Italy, appalling though it was, seemed in 1502 very favourable to Borgia designs. Siena and Florence, weakened by internal troubles, were ripe for attack. France was occupied in Naples and needed papal support. Ferrara was an ally, and Venice was already stretched to deal with the Turks. In February, the pope, Cesare and six cardinals travelled to Piombino to inspect Cesare's base camp and to admire the fortifications built for him by Leonardo da Vinci. On the

Drawings of war machines by Leonardo da Vinci. Like Cesare, Leonardo was fascinated by all the paraphernalia of war.

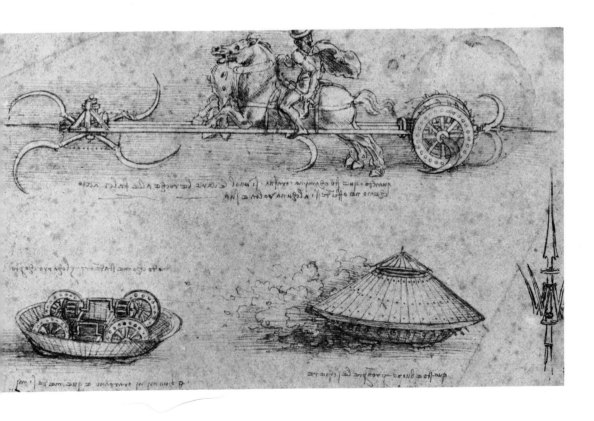

return journey, Alexander endured with complete calm a storm at sea which reduced the cardinals to weeping and had the sailors clinging to the rigging; Catalans and Valencians, he seemed to imply to effete land-bound Romans, were still famous mariners. At Piombino, Cesare prepared to advance. He withdrew large sums from the papal treasury and bought the artillery train of the deposed king of Naples. Several of his *condottieri* from former years rejoined him. He employed also some new men and among them was Oliverotto Eufreducci who had recently murdered his relatives in Fermo in order to present his home town to the pope. Cesare set out in June at the head of a seasoned mercenary force. No one was sure where it was going, said Sigismondo de' Conti, but everyone in the papal states trembled at the approach, for the soldiers behaved as if they were in enemy country.

One wing of the army went to Arezzo, to stir up strife against the Florentines. Cesare took the main body into the territory of Urbino, heading for the small Varano town of Camerino. Perhaps the Duke of Urbino thought he was safe. His family, the Montefeltri, had long been one of the most distinguished and generous of Italian ruling houses, and

Urbino, the Palazzo Ducale on the hill, annexed in a lightning raid by Cesare in 1502, the treacherous attack th impressed Machiavelli.

the present Duke Guidobaldo had served the pope with reasonable loyalty as vicar and *condottiere*. Such considerations meant little to Cesare. Hemmed in by converging bands of troops, Guidobaldo realized too late what Cesare intended. He barely had time to flee the city with his nephew, following peasants through the fields down to the coastal plain, and from there he made his way to the safety of the Gonzaga court at Mantua. His young nephew Francesco della Rovere, lord of Senigallia, was smuggled right across northern Italy to Savona where Cardinal della Rovere met him and led him to France. The cardinal was taking no chance with his young relative. He recalled only too well the fate of Astorre Manfredi, whose youthful body had been found in the Tiber hardly a month before. By the end of July Alexander heard that his son was master of Urbino and Camerino. 'He could not contain his joy at the news,' the Venetian envoy reported, 'but he must get up from his chair and go to the window, and there have the letter from his Duke of Valentinois read aloud.' However, the treacherous attack on Urbino both shocked and impressed other Italian rulers. Florence hurriedly sent Niccolò Machiavelli to Urbino to sound out the conqueror's future plans. The report that this coolest of political observers sent back had little comfort for the republic.

> This lord [he wrote] is very splendid and magnificent, and there is no war-like enterprise so great that it does not seem small to him. In pursuit of land and glory he knows neither fatigue nor danger. He arrives in one place before men know he has left another. He is liked by his soldiers and has collected the best men in Italy; for this reason he is victorious and formidable, and has added to that perpetual good fortune.

The Borgia success caused a general alarm, not only in the Italian states but also among Cesare's own *condottieri*. These mercenary captains were all lords of towns and owners of estates, and they saw what was happening to others of their kind; 'they were afraid', said one of them, 'that the dragon was preparing to swallow them one by one.' They began to plot against their master. Louis XII of France was also worried. He was being overwhelmed by complaints against Cesare, so he sent the duke a peremptory order to stop his offensive. Showing the bold decisiveness that Machiavelli had noted, Cesare decided to tackle the king face to face, and putting on a disguise he hurried in August to

Niccolò Machiavelli, Florentine statesman and political philosopher. Cesare Borgia became one of the examplars of *The Prince*, in which Machiavelli described the ruthless qualities of the successful ruler.

ovanni Bentivoglio of
logna, one of the
ders of an alliance
ainst Cesare known as
e diet of failures'.

the French camp in Milan, where he managed to persuade Louis to support him in return for a promise of help against the Spanish in Naples. France was scarcely placated when the *condottieri* broke out in open revolt, spurred on by Bentivoglio of Bologna and members of the Orsini clan. In October the conspirator Paolo Orsini, known to his soldiers as 'Madonna Paolo' for his effeminate ways, occupied Urbino, and Camerino was also lost. But the revolt was strangely lackadaisical and misdirected, as if the rebels mistrusted their own ability to exorcise the Borgia devil. Cesare, with the promise of French help, concentrated his loyal troops in the Romagna, quickly employed new *condottieri*, and spoke with contempt of 'the diet of failures' who opposed him. 'As regards the state of affairs here,' Machiavelli reported from the Borgia camp at Imola, 'the firm conviction is that the King of France will help the duke with men, and the pope with money; he had also been aided by the dilatoriness of his enemies. I judge that it is now too late to do him much harm.'

Machiavelli had judged right. As French troops appeared, and as the conspirators realized that they would have no help from the great princes, one by one they sued for forgiveness. Cesare seemed the soul of generosity. With charming dissimulation he concluded with each a separate agreement which put them all into his hands, except the old fox Baglione of Perugia. And though they went away satisfied, they should have known better. 'The nature of the duke', commented the Venetian envoy, 'is not one to pardon those who have injured him, nor to leave a vendetta to others.' But for the moment all was sweet concord. Urbino and Camerino reverted to Cesare, and preparations began to attack Senigallia. In December, Cesare ordered his *condottieri* to invest the town while he moved up in a leisurely way from Cesena. The captains might have wondered why such a large force was needed to reduce so small a town. It was said that Vitellozzo Vitelli, the best soldier of them all, arrived irritable and full of foreboding. On 30 December the commander of the fortress at Senigallia agreed to surrender, but would only hand the keys to Cesare himself. Next day, Cesare joined his captains before the gates, talking affably yet carefully surrounding them with soldiers of his own guard. In this way, they all entered the town and the gates closed quietly behind them. With the certainty of sleepwalkers the *condottieri* went with Cesare to the palace where, with many extravagant gestures of hospitality, he invited them in. On the threshold, the arresting officers laid hold of them. Vitellozzo, Oliverotto da Fermo, Paolo Orsini and the Duke of Gravina were seized; only Pandolfo Petrucci escaped. The fate of the two Orsini – Paolo and the Duke of Gravina – hung in the balance, dependent on certain decisions to be made in Rome regarding the whole Orsini family. Vitellozzo and Oliverotto were seated back to back and strangled, the latter in tears and the former begging to be allowed absolution from the pope, the father of his murderer.

To Italians there was nothing extraordinary in this action at Senigallia. Cesare made some perfunctory excuse to Machiavelli, but that was hardly necessary. In a land accustomed to tyrants, conspiracies were among the greatest evils that a prince could endure. 'There is nothing', Machiavelli himself wrote in a notorious chapter of his *Discourses*, 'more inimical to princes than a conspiracy.' And he recommended that rulers 'practise dissimulation as best they can'. Indeed, the excellence of the deceit at Senigallia, and the brilliant way it was carried through, enhanced Cesare's reputation as a forceful and politic prince and hastened the disintegration of his opponents. 'This lord', Machiavelli wrote admiringly, 'never speaks of his intentions until he puts them into practice, and he does that just at the proper moment.' With his revenge complete, Cesare was away with characteristic speed, heading for Perugia on the first day of the new year. He swept through Perugia, forcing out the Baglioni and bringing the city once more under papal control; then he drove on towards Siena, eager to settle his account with Petrucci and the Duke of Urbino. The fate of the captive Orsini was also sealed, for the Borgias had decided to make another attempt to eradicate Orsini power entirely. Cesare had Paolo and the Duke of Gravina quietly executed in Tuscany, while in Rome the pope arrested all the Orsini and their supporters he could reach. On 3 January 1503, Cardinal Orsini, the crafty head of the family, blind but still sportive, was cast into Sant'Angelo where he soon died. His palace and his property were confiscated by the pope, despite the intercession of the other cardinals. Unhappily for Alexander, whom the Orsini had successfully defied throughout his reign, Giulio Orsini escaped the net, and retiring to his castle at Ceri, ten miles from Rome, rallied the remnant of his clan into an energetic counter-offensive. They destroyed the alum

Cesare Borgia: 'his head is most beautiful', wrote the Venetian ambassador when he was twenty-five 'The pope loves and fears his son, who is . . . physically most beautiful; he is tall and well-made.'

mines at Tolfa, an important source of papal revenue, and chased weak young Jofré Borgia back to the safety of his father's skirts. The pope was so alarmed by these savage blows that he had the Vatican barricaded and advised the cardinals to fortify their palaces.

Throughout the first months of 1503 the castle of Ceri under Giulio Orsini, and the huge fortress of Bracciano under Giangiordano Orsini, easily repulsed the pope. Cesare was still busy with his dream of a grandiose kingdom in central Italy, but Alexander needed his son nearer home and threatened him, so it was said, with excommunication if he did not come and put down the Orsini. Cesare obeyed, but with caution. He knew the strength of Bracciano; he knew also that the Orsini had the protection of the French king. In late February, Cesare was rumoured to be in Rome, going about in disguise. In March, avoiding the almost impregnable Bracciano, he blockaded Ceri which, after a most terrific bombardment of some 6000 cannon balls, surrendered in April. Giulio was allowed to withdraw to France, but Alexander himself supervised the destruction of his castle, watching while the cisterns were smashed and steps cut into the precipitous cliff on which the castle stood. Soon Bracciano also surrendered. Louis XII persuaded Giangiordano to hand over the fort and join Giulio in the safety of France.

Once again, the good fortune that Machiavelli noted seemed to smile on Cesare Borgia. His father Alexander was in unassailable control of the Church, full of authority and rude health. In April, an envoy who heard him sing Mass in St Peter's 'so harmoniously and with such strength of body and voice' thought it could not be done better. The Roman barons, those damnable promoters of discord, seemed at last completely broken. The College of Cardinals acquiesced lamely in all Borgia plans. Cesare was master of the papal states and only held back from greater conquests for fear of France. But here, too, events began to run his way. The partition of Naples had not been a success. Two such aggressive predators as France and Spain could not be caged together in such a small region for very long. When fighting did break out, the brilliant Spanish general Gonzalo de Córdoba was far too strong for the French, and by the middle of May 1503 his army had occupied the city of Naples. The Borgias were not displeased, since their alliance with France had reached the limits of usefulness. Cesare's

e Palazzo Ducale,
bino, built by the
at soldier Federigo da
ntefeltro. After his
 on Urbino in 1502,
are occupied the
ntefeltro palace and
as here that he and
chiavelli first met.

ambition in the north of Italy was everywhere blocked by French interests. But with the success of Gonzalo, Alexander and Cesare felt
they had the measure of France. They could exact a price for further
support while at the same time inclining slightly towards Spain. The
pope permitted Gonzalo to raise mercenaries in Rome, and hinted to
Maximilian that the papacy and the Empire might join Spain against
France.

With the political current running so well for him, Cesare began to
refill his war chest. He and the pope once again used their well-tried
means of extortion. Don Michelotto and his gangsters raided the homes
of Jews and Marranos, then allowed them to purchase freedom for large
sums. A consistory in March decided to create eighty new places in the
Curia, at the price of 760 ducats each. 'I leave it to your highness', the
Venetian envoy reported, 'to count the profit to the pope.' Cesare personally supervised the exactions from rich cardinals, and the nomination of new members to the Sacred College. In April the very wealthy
Cardinal Michiel was poisoned and died after two days of violent
vomiting. The pope's favourite secretary unwisely complained that he
was not on the list of new cardinals. Cesare, who had drawn up the list
and who also suspected the secretary of complicity with France, had
him hunted down and strangled by Michelotto. Bishop Santa Croce,

an ally of Orsini, was executed and his property confiscated. In May, nine new cardinals were nominated. Five were Spaniards, in line with the drift of papal policy, bringing to sixteen the total of Spaniards in the Sacred College. Antonio Giustinian, the Venetian envoy, was not impressed by the quality of the candidates:

> Most are men of doubtful reputation; all have paid handsomely for their elevation – 20,000 ducats and more – so that something between 120,000 and 130,000 ducats has been collected. Add to this the 64,000 from the sale of offices plus what Cardinal Michiel left behind, and we have a fine sum. Alexander is proving to the world that his income is just as large as he chooses it to be.

In June 1503, Cesare was busy in his lands, joining the Romagna to the Marches and providing a firm administration and a rigorous justice for both. His speculative eye was now on Tuscany. His father was trying to persuade the Emperor Maximilian to invest Cesare with Siena, Pisa and Lucca. At the beginning of August he was back in Rome. The weather was sultry, excessively hot, and in the city there was an epidemic of malarial fever. On the 5th, the gross but efficient Cardinal Borgia Lanzol the elder died of fever. Two days later the Venetian ambassador found Alexander in low spirits, oppressed by the many deaths and alarmed by the approach of a French army bound for Naples. From a window he watched the funeral procession of his kinsman Juan Borgia Lanzol and remarked gloomily 'It is a bad month for fat people.' When an owl flew in at the window he muttered 'an omen, a bad omen'. On the day that Lanzol died, the pope and Cesare had been to dine with Cardinal Castellesi in the pleasant country air of Monte Mario. But malaria was rife in the Roman hills and within a few days both the pope and his son were ill. The eleventh of August was the anniversary of Alexander's election, but it was noticed that the pope, who had always loved grand liturgical occasions, did not celebrate in St Peter's with his usual gusto. Two days later the pope was bled, but was well enough to play cards. The fever returned on the 14th and Alexander was bled again, a dangerous procedure in a man of seventy-three. Cesare, a strong, fit young man, was holding out against the sickness. On Friday 18 August, Alexander made his confession and received communion seated, in the presence of five cardinals. In the evening his confessor

At the celebration of the anniversary of his election, many observers noted that Alexander sang Mass in St Peter's without his usual enthusiasm. The next day he was struck down by the fever.

administered extreme unction. About six o'clock Pope Alexander VI lost consciousness and died around the hour of vespers.

The solemnities of the laying-out and funeral were performed by Burchard, the Master of Ceremonies, with his usual meticulous attention. But no silks, no perfume, no art of man could keep corruption from the body in a hot August. The corpse lay between the railings of the high altar in the Sistine Chapel, blackened by the drip of wax candles and befouled by decay.

> The face had changed to the colour of mulberry and was covered with blue-black spots. The nose was swollen, the mouth distended where the tongue had doubled over, the lips seemed to fill everything. After five o'clock the body was carried to Santa Maria delle Febbre and put in its coffin in a corner by the altar. Six labourers cracked blasphemous jokes. The carpenters had made the coffin too small, so they put the pope's mitre by his side, rolled his body in an old carpet, and shoved and punched it into the coffin. There were no tapers nor any lights; neither a priest nor anyone else attended the body.

Such was the judgment of the commonalty on Pope Alexander VI. The dry sentence of Machiavelli voiced the more considered condemnation of the age. 'The soul of the glorious Alexander', he said, 'was now borne among the choir of the blessed. Dancing attendance were his three devoted handmaidens: Cruelty, Simony, and Lechery.'

PIVS III SENEÑ PII II NEP AÑ
M·D·III· SEPTEMBR·XXI·
APERT ELECTVS SVFFRAG·
VIII OCTOBR·CORONATVS EST

CHAPTER SEVEN

THE BORGIA ECLIPSE
AND THE GOOD DUCHESS

'I HAD FORESEEN MY FATHER'S DEATH', CESARE TOLD Machiavelli, 'and made every preparation for it, but I had not anticipated that I should be, at that moment, wrestling with death myself.' The time was critical. The cardinals preparing for the conclave amid the customary turmoil of the *sede vacante* feared war and the division of the Church. Francesco Gonzaga was approaching with a French army from the north, Gonzalo was advancing with Spaniards from the south. In Rome, the old rebellious factions were determined to throw off the Borgia yoke immediately. Cesare lay in bed, his skin peeling and his face suffused to a violet colour. His troops were within easy reach of Rome and had he called them in at the first moment he might have commanded the city. But such decisive action was beyond the sick man. The best he could do was to send Don Michelotto to threaten the papal treasurer and ransack Alexander's private riches. He took, according to Burchard, 100,000 ducats. But the first chance was gone, and nothing but extreme danger confronted Cesare. Orsini and Colonna hurried back to Rome in an exultant mood to reclaim their old lands and old rights. In Umbria, Gianpaolo Baglione and the Vitelli clan were in arms. Piombino, Urbino and Camerino revolted. The cities of the Romagna were on the edge of revolt, though their governors were able to hold them for Cesare for the time being. The little empire assembled by Cesare so swiftly and with such apparent good fortune seemed about to disintegrate in a moment.

But the key to the future was in Rome. As soon as he could collect himself, Cesare saw that he must try to dominate the conclave, to ensure the election of a pope devoted to his interests. To frighten the cardinals, he attempted to get possession of the Castel Sant'Angelo, but the commander resisted both his bribes and his threats. The Sacred College,

The coronation of Pope Pius III, elected on 16 September 1503. The new pope was old and sick and he died after a reign of only twenty-six days, leaving Cesare at the mercy of his enemies.

which knew and feared his intentions, resolved to hold the conclave in Sant'Angelo if il Valentino could not be persuaded to leave Rome. The moment for force had passed, so Cesare tried another tack, giving way to the cardinals with surprising submissiveness and sounding out an alliance with the Colonna. He was concentrating all his resources on negotiations with the cardinals. On 1 September 1503 he agreed to withdraw from Rome, and left the next day borne on a stretcher covered with crimson velvet. If not a defeat, at least the departure from Rome was an admission of waning power. The old Borgia enemy Cardinal Giuliano della Rovere had returned for the conclave, and his strong presence cast a longer shadow than Cesare. The duke took his artillery and the nucleus of his mercenary army to the Borgia town of Nepi. There he entered into an agreement with Louis XII to support the French as a good vassal, and in return Louis would help him recover the towns he had lost on Alexander's death. This agreement was merely a precautionary measure; much more depended on the conclave in Rome.

In early September the intrigue was extreme. The cardinals were 'buzzing like bees', the Mantuan envoy wrote, and he added that none of the great wealthy prelates – neither della Rovere, d'Amboise, Sforza, Caraffa, nor Riario – would be pope. Piccolomini, the well-respected nephew of Pius II, might do; 'but the common opinion is that the cardinals will not be able to agree'. The large Spanish contingent held the balance in the Sacred College. Following the Borgias, a Spanish pope was not possible; but no one was certain where the Spaniards would cast their vote. On the 16th the conclave met at last, and for five days the wily old politicians della Rovere and Ascanio Sforza struggled for supremacy. When they saw that neither could win, they came to terms; both proposed Piccolomini and, with the backing of the Spaniards, swept him triumphantly to the Chair of St Peter as Pope Pius III. The new pontiff was old and sick; he would not last long.

'The former life of the new pope,' wrote the Venetian envoy, 'marked by many deeds of kindness and charity, leads people to hope that his pontificate will be the exact opposite of Alexander's, and thus they are beside themselves with joy.' The new pope, who was universally admired as a learned, kindly, religious man, still had to come to terms with his evil inheritance in the person of Cesare Borgia. 'I wish no harm to the duke,' he said, 'but I foresee that he will come to a bad end by the judgment of God.' Although he was right, he might also have foreseen that he needed the greatest wit and caution when dealing with this God-forsaken prince. Cesare was deeply in trouble. The pope was certainly not of his party. The French army had marched to Naples, leaving him unprotected in Nepi. The fierce *condottiere* Alviano was on his way from Venice breathing fire and retribution. The Orsini and Savelli were gathering to attack. Cesare pleaded with the pope to be allowed back in Rome and Pius, pressed also by the Spanish cardinals, gave way. Cesare returned on 3 October, not so ill as he had pretended and as full of guile as ever. Pius apologized for his leniency. 'I have been deceived,' he explained; 'I am only a man and liable to err.' But Cesare was still by no means safe. His army was reduced to a fragment, numbering only 650 men. Yet even this was too much for the cardinals; della Rovere and Riario were threatening to arm their followers unless the pope forced Cesare to disband his troops entirely. Alviano and Baglione were in Rome, waiting for a moment of weakness. Orsini and Colonna had overcome their rivalry, such was their hatred of the duke, and formed a pact for his undoing. The pope, who might have protected Cesare out of a tender love for all humanity, was already dying. Cesare tried to escape, intending to join Michelotto in Orvieto; but many of his followers deserted and the Orsini turned back the remnant. Alviano was raging like a mad dog and posted guards at every gate. On 15 October Cesare took the two infant Borgia dukes and fled by secret passage to Sant'Angelo while the Orsini were storming his residence in the Borgo. In this desperate plight, utterly surrounded and with nowhere to go, he was saved by the death of Pius III.

A truce was declared while the process of the conclave began again. This time Cardinal Giuliano della Rovere intended to make no mistake. He quickly came to an agreement with Cesare, offering protection, and the duke would deliver in return the vote of the Spanish cardinals. When the conclave met on 31 October, the rest of the Sacred College saw how strongly the tide was running for della Rovere, and encouraged by some well-placed bribes, steered their own boats into that persuasive current. Next morning, Giuliano della Rovere was proclaimed Pope Julius II after one of the shortest conclaves on record. 'People here expect this reign', a correspondent wrote to Ferrara, 'to be glorious, peaceful, genial and free-handed. The Romans have left off their habitual plunder and are behaving so quietly that everyone is amazed. We have a pope who will be both loved and feared.'

In *The Prince*, Niccolò Machiavelli censured Cesare for supporting della Rovere and thus permitting his great enemy to become pope. But the duke had little choice. His power and authority had drained away so suddenly that his only thought was for survival. Borgia policy had always, and on the whole successfully, sought out the winner at all cost. But when Alexander manipulated alliances with such dexterity, he could always offer his control of the Church and the awe of his Sacred Office. Once Cesare had helped to deliver the Spanish vote in the conclave he had no further points to bargain with. He had gained a temporary respite, but his enemy held him in his power; and Julius was not known for a forgiving nature. The Venetian envoy reported:

> No one has any influence over him, and he consults few or none. It is almost impossible to describe how strong and violent and difficult he is to manage. In body and soul he has the nature of a giant. Everything about him is on a magnified scale, both his undertakings and his passions. He inspires fear rather than hatred, for there is nothing in him that is small or meanly selfish.

He was a stormy friend and a terrible enemy.

But the new pope had debts to pay. Cesare Borgia had helped him to the Apostle's Chair, and though Julius abominated the Borgias he knew he must tread carefully. Though it was not in his nature to temporize, Machiavelli noted that the pope must do just that, for he had no money, no army, and sterner opponents than Cesare were threatening him. Venice was the worst danger, where a matchless opportunism for which the republic was notorious had caused her already, in the fleeting reign of Pius III, to bite voraciously into the lands of the Romagna. If Julius did not intend to let Cesare keep those lands, he certainly did not mean Venice to possess them. 'I have always been a friend of Venice,' he told Cardinal Soderini, 'but if the Venetians persist in robbing the Church of her property I shall use the strongest measures and call all Christendom to help me.' And as usual the craggy, irascible pope impressed his listeners. 'Words fail me', the envoy warned Venice, 'to describe with what resolution he spoke, and not once, but again and again.' Julius wanted the states of the Church entire, but in the meantime Cesare Borgia was a safer and more temporary tenant of the Romagna than the Venetian republic. He reluctantly gave Cesare papal briefs to his Romagnol towns, and thus discharged his debt.

The news from those towns was very bad. Of all Cesare's conquests, only Forlì, Cesena and Bertinoro remained loyal to him. This and all the other hammer blows he had received since the death of his father unseated the duke. He was irresolute, puzzled by adversity. 'He has lost his head', said an old companion, 'and does not know himself what he wants to do.' He tried to arrange various Borgia dynastic marriages, but it seemed merely for the sake of form, going through the motions of a policy he had learned at his father's knee. But he was uncertain what to do next. He worried Machiavelli with his perplexities. In November the duke wrote to Florence begging for troops to help him reconquer the lost ground and offering his service to the city as a *condottiere*. He left Rome to try to complete this arrangement. But the Venetians were continuing their advance into the Romagna, declaring cynically that their only object was to drive out the Borgias. Faenza fell, then Rimini, so that Julius, in desperation at the ruin of his state, first ordered Cesare to give up his remaining castles to the Church, and when the duke refused the pope had him arrested and brought back to Rome. Cesare wept. He feared the instant execution that the pope's counsellors were advising. Julius, however, tempered his great irritability with sound political judgment, expecting to get more by leniency, and received Cesare with kindness. But when the Borgia governor in Cesena still would not hand over the keys to his fortress, the short-tempered pope veered round and clapped his guest into the close confines of the Torre Borgia in the Vatican. In December 1503 the friends of the Borgias, fearing the worst, fled from Rome. 'This duke of ours', commented Machiavelli, 'is slipping little by little into his grave.'

Then once more his conspicuous luck came to his rescue. On 28 December, Gonzalo de Córdoba crushed the French army at Garigliano, and by the new year the King of France had lost Naples. The large body of Spanish cardinals in the Sacred College assumed a new importance. Spain was in the ascendant and Spaniards must be placated. The pope began to renegotiate terms with Cesare. They agreed that the latter's castles must be handed over within forty days, and during that period Cesare would be placed in the custody of Cardinal Carvajal at

Ostia. He would be freed when the transfer was completed. The cardinal released him a little prematurely in April, when only Cesena and Bertinoro had surrendered. Cesare did not lose time but immediately took a ship to Naples, to the welcoming household of his uncle Cardinal Luis Borgia, and there Gonzalo greeted him formally but with respect. Within a short time Cesare was a man renewed. Forlì still held out in his name. Starting with this fortress, the duke would re-create his duchy in the Romagna, and Gonzalo seemed to fall in with his schemes, offering aid and arms: only the permission of the Spanish monarchs was lacking.

The Spanish general Gonzalo de Córdoba, E Gran Capitan. When Cesare was arrested by Gonzalo and imprisone in Castel Nuovo, he sai 'With me only has my lord Gonzalo dealt cruelly: to all other but me he has shown mercy

King Ferdinand, however, would have none of it. He prized the support of the pope far above the re-establishment of Borgia ambitions and wrote to Gonzalo ordering him to arrest Cesare. On 27 May 1504, going to take his leave of the Spanish general before departing to the Romagna, Cesare was arrested instead, and placed in the Castel Nuovo. For a further two and a half months Forlì defied the pope, awaiting the return of its Borgia master. But when it was clear that Cesare's cause was lost, the castellan struck the Borgia bull from the flagstaff and on 10 August marched his company out of the castle. Nothing was left of the little Borgia princedom in central Italy. The once-mighty Cesare was poverty-stricken, a man without bargaining counters, a beggar at the door of the great. He received the mercy usually accorded to his kind. On 20 August 1504 he was bound for Spain, a prisoner of King Ferdinand.

He landed at Valencia in September, an ironical first visit by the ex-archbishop to his former diocese. At first he was locked up at Chinchilla, a massive enough fortress, but soon considered unsafe for such a dangerous captive, so he was moved to the greater security of the royal palace-fortress at Medina del Campo, in the far reaches of Castile. He was confined in one tower room with one servant. His only recreation was

The Spanish royal palace-fortress at Medina del Campo. Cesare was imprisoned in the top room of the tower. After two years he made a daring escape, descending from his window by means of a rope.

a falcon, and the flights of this predator were the living emblem of the force he had once been. Though closely guarded, he could not avoid becoming an unwitting pawn in the politics of the Spanish royal family, in the old rivalry between Castile and Aragon. Helped by some disaffected Castilian nobles, Cesare escaped after two years. In October 1506 he appeared 'like the devil' in Pamplona, at the court of his brother-in-law the King of Navarre. The news of his escape was received with jubilation by his sister Lucrezia, with eager curiosity by his adherents in the Romagna, and with apprehension by Pope Julius and the Venetians. But Cesare was poor and far from the realms of his former influence. Louis XII had abandoned him, confiscating his French estates and leaving him without income. The large fortune that Cesare had seized on his father's death had been invested, in 1503, with Genoese bankers. But the long arm of Julius reached even into the banking halls of Genoa, and Cesare was left with nothing. Nor could he expect much help from the weak kingdom over which his brother-in-law reigned. Navarre was troubled by internal discords, so Cesare's first act towards the furtherance of his own career was to help the king put down his rebellious vassals. In the early months of 1507, once more the forceful *condottiere*, Cesare attacked Larraga, took it and immediately pressed on to Viana. On 11 March 1507, in a mêlée before the castle, Cesare outdistanced his troop in pursuit of the enemy. The fleeing enemy drew him into a deep ravine, then turned on the lone pursuer, unhorsed him, and killed him. He was thirty-one. His attackers took the expensive armour, the clothes, the harness and the horse, and left the body, hiding its nakedness beneath a large rock. When Cesare was recovered and recognized he was taken to Viana and laid out in the church of Santa Maria; in the same year a grandiose memorial tomb was erected over his remains. But in the seventeenth century the Bishop of Calahorra ordered the remains of Cesare Borgia to be scattered, the monument torn down, and the epitaph erased.

Owning neither grave nor monument, Cesare Borgia, the terror and wonder of his time, endures chiefly in the malignity of legend and as a figure of abuse. His contemporaries did not see him thus. Machiavelli, the observer least influenced by prejudice, sentiment or moral scruple, knew Cesare at several stages of his career and made him the object of critical attention. Il Valentino became one of the exemplars of *The Prince*, a failure perhaps, but a heroic figure who pursued a bold, rational and well-executed plan. He did brilliantly all that a politic prince could do in the circumstances, and his ultimate fall was brought about by events beyond his control. When Pope Alexander died so untimely,

> . . . he left the duke with the state of the Romagna alone consolidated, with all the rest in the air, and the duke sick almost to death, caught between two most powerful, hostile foreign armies. Yet the duke was so bold and able, and he knew so well how men are to be won or lost, and so firm were the foundations that he had laid in such a short time, that if he had not those armies on his back, or if he had been in good health, he would have overcome all difficulties.

And Machiavelli went on to give Cesare an extraordinary encomium, so carefully judged and yet so flattering:

> When all the actions of the duke are recalled, I know not how to blame him, but rather I think I ought to offer him for imitation to all those who, by fortune or force of arms, are raised to government. With a lofty spirit and far-reaching aims, the duke could not have regulated his conduct otherwise, and only the shortness of his father's life and his own sickness frustrated his designs. Therefore, he who wants to secure himself in a new principality, to win friends, to overcome either by force or fraud, to make himself loved or feared by the people, to be followed and revered by his soldiers, to exterminate those with power or reason to hurt him, to change the old order for the new, to be severe and gracious, magnanimous and liberal, to destroy disloyal captains and create new ones, to be friendly with kings and princes so that they must help him zealously and offend him with caution, cannot find a more lively example than the actions of this duke.

Nor did Italians in general, much as they hated the Borgias, dissent from this judgment. Cesare was, indeed, an illustration of Guicciardini's aphorism that 'he who esteems his own honour highly succeeds in all that he undertakes, since he fears neither trouble, danger nor expense'. Cesare was feared and respected, not so much because he was unusually tyrannical, but because he took pains to make his means – the common Italian means of murder, deceit, craft, cruelty and faithlessness – unusually effective. All the ways of murder and assassination were studied in Italy, but few studied them as keenly as Cesare. He had his strangler Don Michelotto, so also he had his chemist Sebastián Pinzón, reputed to be expert in poisons. Poisoning was an art much practised all over Italy. The mathematician and doctor Girolamo Cardano related that four members of his family had died by poison. Cesare's old enemy Caterina Sforza had written of poisons in her *Experiments* and claimed to concoct a *veleno attermine* that gave 'perfect sleep'. In Rome, it was not thought strange that cardinals should attend a banquet each with his own steward and his own wine, and this practice was done 'without insult to the host'. The science, however, was defective, and more was attempted than accomplished. The poisoned letter that Caterina sent to Pope Alexander certainly did him no harm. And nothing more could have been expected from the attempt of the *condottiere* Piccinino to smear poison on the litter of Pius II. When Cesare Borgia came to this part of the murderer's trade he looked into it with his usual sceptical thoroughness. During the first steps of his conquest he had addressed to Lorenz Behaim, the scientist of the papal court, ninety questions on scientific matters, thirteen of which were about poisons; he wished to know the ways of poisoning cups, perfumes, flowers, saddles and even stirrups, and the formula for the *veleno attermine*, the notorious white powder that killed with a delayed but sure effect. Lorenz Behaim, who found these enquiries quite normal, forwarded them to Willibald Pirkheimer of Nuremberg, a foremost European authority.

Legend portrays Cesare as an inveterate poisoner. No doubt he was interested, but the method was far too unsure for one who aimed to practise an efficient terror. The grip of Don Michelotto was more fatally certain than any *veleno attermine*. Of the great men whom the Borgias are supposed to have poisoned – these included the Cardinals Orsini, Ferrari, Lopez and Michiel – only the case of Michiel seems proved beyond a reasonable doubt. Cesare knew how to be subtle, but judged that the cause of terror was generally served best by a swift, straightforward act of brutality. He succeeded very well, as the words of the Venetian envoy testified in 1500: 'Every night four or five murdered men are discovered – bishops, prelates, and others – so that all Rome trembles for fear of being destroyed by the duke.' In this, as in all things, calculation, speed and a steely discipline lay at the heart of Cesare's technique. But he could withhold from vengeance as easily as he could pursue it. When he took Urbino so treacherously, he declared an amnesty and strictly maintained it, even in the case of his worst enemies. Yet those who had betrayed the Duke of Urbino to him, he arrested and punished; 'he hated the traitor,' wrote the chronicler, 'though he loved the treason.' When he decided, however, to make a sacrifice of a man, his way was truly terrible. At first, in the Romagna, finding the country full of lawlessness and bloodshed, he had appointed Don Ramiro de Lorca to be governor with the fullest powers. Ramiro, 'a swift and cruel man', did an excellent job with great barbarity. When peace was restored Cesare rightly considered that less oppression would win him more friends, so he set up courts under sound judges. And to transfer the odium of the past from master to servant, he decided to make an example of Ramiro de Lorca. Cesare caused him to be seized, hanged and quartered, and the next morning the citizens of Cesena viewed the remains of their governor exposed in the city square, with the block and the bloody axe beside the dismembered body.

A man of such dreadful capacity was universally feared and universally respected. But despite high ambition and ruthless purpose, Cesare suffered from one fatal flaw in his estate which precluded him from the achievement he had set his heart on. The sole basis of his power lay in his lineage, and without his father he was almost nothing. Without the support of Church and papacy he was merely an efficient adventurer, such as Italy had seen very often; with support from Church and pope he was a great Renaissance prince in the making. There were many contrasts between Alexander and his son. Whereas Cesare was secretive, violent, cold, unforgiving and excessively proud, Alexander was, on the surface, a more attractive personality. He was genial, always good-humoured, a lover of feasts and spectacle, often generous, and surprisingly tolerant. Several of his deepest enemies walked about in perfect safety. 'I could easily', he once told Cesare, 'have had Vice-Chancellor Sforza and Cardinal Giuliano della Rovere killed. But I did not wish to harm anyone, and I pardoned fourteen traitorous nobles in league with France.' But father and son made a formidable team. Schooled by the example of Popes Martin, Calixtus, Sixtus and Innocent, Alexander realized better than any of his predecessors the possibilities for papal rule latent in nepotism, and Cesare became his instrument. 'He was the first', wrote Machiavelli, 'who showed how much a pope with money and forces could make his power prevail.' For the accomplishment of their schemes, father and son were mutually dependent. To gain and hold territory, Alexander needed to use his son's iron will, his speed and determination, his ability to command men and armies. Perhaps he was afraid, indulgent satyr that he was, of Cesare's cold, cruel nature. He complained several times that he could not control his son. He told the Spanish ambassador that the duke was terrible, and that he would give a quarter of his lands to keep him out of Rome. It was commonly said that the son ruled the father, and Machiavelli advised Florence that an agent with the son in Cesena was more valuable than an ambassador with the father in Rome.

But Cesare was too wise to believe that he could go on without papal support, and however restive he might be under his father's command he always came to heel at last. The title to his lands was granted by the

papacy. His mercenary army was raised and maintained at the expense of the Church; his administrators and clerks were provided from the ranks of the Church. The historian Nardi told how, in the jubilee year of 1500, Cesare appeared in Florence demanding money for the jubilee coffers 'so that he could pay the soldiers who were plundering us, and it was no small sum that he wanted'. In the bad days after Alexander's death, Cesare claimed that he had not been responsible for his actions but had done them under compulsion from the pope. He knelt before the Duke of Urbino, a man whom he had grievously wronged, and begged forgiveness, blaming his youth and cursing the soul of the father whose evil influence had led him astray. That was a typical piece of calculated Borgia effrontery, but the complaint had an element of truth. 'Duke Valentino', said Machiavelli, 'acquired his state during the ascendancy of his father, and lost it when his father died, notwithstanding that he had taken every measure and done all that ought to be done by a wise and able man to fix his roots firmly in the lands which the arms and fortunes of others had given him.' The career of Cesare Borgia, though bold and glaring, was in a real sense only a reflection of the perverse genius of Rodrigo Borgia, Pope Alexander VI.

AS WITH THE SON, SO WITH THE DAUGHTER. Throughout her adolescence, Lucrezia Borgia had been the innocent victim of her father's wiles. At the age of eleven she had been betrothed to one Spanish noble, then that was broken off and she was engaged to another. He, too, was hastily cast aside when it became politic for her to marry into the powerful Sforza family. She was tied to a sullen, unbalanced man twice her age, and then forced into a shameful divorce. Her next husband, a young, attractive prince whom she loved, was murdered by order of her brother. Before her tears were dried, her father was chiding her grief and diligently searching for a new husband. A cousin of the French king was mooted; then the Duke of Gravina, a hardy suitor who had tried before, was considered and rejected. It was as well, for he too died by the hand of Cesare. At last Alexander hit on an appropriate man. Alfonso d'Este, heir to Ferrara, would be a valuable ally for the pope, and was a prospective groom who pleased Lucrezia.

Lucrezia was enthusiastic, and agents reported her to be a personable catch. She was warm-hearted, kindly and generous, though perhaps a

Lucrezia Borgia, Duchess of Ferrara, the innocent victim of her father's wiles.

little thoughtless, extravagant and self-indulgent. She was not a great beauty, but she had pleasant looks, an easy bearing and had inherited some of the Borgia charm. 'She is of middle height', wrote one observer, 'and delicate in form; her face is rather long, the nose long but well-cut, the hair golden, the eyes of no special colour; her mouth is rather large, the teeth brilliantly white; her neck is slender and fair, the bust well-proportioned. Her whole being radiates good-humour and gaiety.' But a generation of Italian writers had assiduously besmirched the name of Borgia and Lucrezia could not avoid that stain. Her reputation was bad; she was, besides, the daughter of Alexander and the sister of Cesare. Any prudent ruler would think very carefully before aligning himself with the Borgias. At first neither Alfonso nor his father Duke Ercole would consider the match. The illegitimate daughter of a Spanish priest was no bride for an Este. In February 1501, Ercole wrote to his ally Louis XII, asking the French king to prohibit the match, 'because to speak freely with your Majesty, we shall never consent to give Don Alfonso to Madonna Lucrezia, nor could Alfonso be induced to take her.' No help came from France, for at this moment Louis needed the pope more than he needed Ferrara. Since Cesare's conquests in the Romagna were endangering the borders of Ercole's lands, he judged it best to give way. But the duke was a man with a hard head and little sentiment, and he determined to wring from the marriage contract every possible advantage for Ferrara. It was, after all, a business proposition.

The terms that Duke Ercole proposed were heavy indeed. He asked for a dowry of 200,000 ducats, a reduction in the annual tribute due from Ferrara as a papal fief – from over 4000 ducats to a mere 100 – the transfer of two castles belonging to the Church to the duchy, and various benefices for his son Cardinal Ippolito. The pope countered with an offer of 100,000 ducats for the dowry, and other benefits to follow later. In August Ercole protested that he asked no more than what was right, and 'that we take more account of honour than money'. By the 26th a compromise was reached and the bargain struck. The dowry was reduced to 100,000 ducats, but Lucrezia was to have a further 75,000 for expenses, and the pope gave way to Ercole's other demands. He also made Ippolito d'Este arch-priest of St Peter's. On 1 September 1501, in the summer palace of Belfiore at Ferrara, the papal envoy concluded the contract. Three days later a courier arrived in Rome with the signed document, and the cannon of Sant'Angelo began a *feu de joie* that lasted into the night. Next day, Lucrezia went with escort and four bishops to the church of Santa Maria del Popolo, where her brother Juan of Gandia was buried and where the 'Adoration of the Child' by her favourite painter Pinturicchio stood over the altar. There she prayed in a golden robe, while the great bell tolled continuously from the tower of the Campidoglio and bonfires shot sparks into the evening sky.

September and October passed between business and pleasure. The cardinals in secret consistory reluctantly assented to the consignment of Church benefits and revenue to Ferrara. The agents of Ferrara pressed their master's demands so hard that Alexander accused Ercole of behaving 'like a tradesman'. But night after night there were the festivities, when Alexander led the gallants of the papal court in dance, so that even his daughter was fatigued. 'The illustrious lady', the envoy told Ercole, 'is somewhat ailing. At the Vatican Palace, the entire night till two or three is spent in play and dancing, which fatigues her greatly.' Alexander, who had an affectionate and genuine pride in his children, was not to be denied his triumph. The robust pope, in his seventy-first year, drove his enervated court into an excess of expensive, bawdy and profligate entertainment. Courtesans, the gossips said, were in the Vatican only too often. 'Everywhere in Rome,' the agent explained for the provincial innocents of Ferrara, 'from morning till night, one sees nothing but courtesans wearing masks, for after the clock strikes the 24th hour they are not permitted to show themselves abroad.' Crudity was no bar to enjoyment; the pope and his daughter looked on with a cheerful curiosity when mares and stallions were induced to couple in the Piazza of St Peter. In early December the Mantuan court, where Alfonso's sister was married to Francesco Gonzaga, was informed of Lucrezia's preparation:

> There will be silver plate to the value of 3000 ducats; jewels, fine linens, harness for horses and mules, together worth another 100,000 ducats. In her wardrobe she has a trimmed gown worth more than 15,000 ducats, and 200 dresses, many worth 100 ducats each; some have sleeves edged in gold at 30 ducats a sleeve.

She would also have an escort of a thousand men and horses, and 200 carriages, some – if there were time – made in France. On 9 December,

Cardinal Ippolito and two of his brothers came from Ferrara to collect the bride. After two weeks of weary, mud-splattered riding on winter roads, they entered Rome and were welcomed by Lucrezia with grave dignity, merely bowing to her brother-in-law the cardinal in the French manner. 'But this I know,' Duke Ercole's personal agent reported, 'that the eyes of Cardinal Ippolito sparkled.' The agent went on to reassure his master that Lucrezia was a devout, God-fearing Christian who went to church regularly, and that it was impossible to suspect anything 'sinister' in her character. Even to the last, Ercole and Alfonso d'Este were apprehensive. Under orders from Duke Ercole, the agent Castellini counted the 100,000 ducats of the dowry one by one.

On 30 December 1501, Lucrezia was married by procuration in the Vatican, with Don Ferrante standing in for his absent brother Alfonso. Cardinal Ippolito presented her with the Este jewels, but phrased the gift so that the jewels would return to the avaricious duke should Lucrezia deceive her husband or die in childbirth. After a further week of celebrations, she set out for Ferrara on 6 January 1502. Alexander said his farewell from the throne in the Sala del Pappagallo, then went from window to window to keep her in sight as she stepped out into light snow. For the first time she was bereft of help from her close-bound family. She was leaving behind her father Alexander, her mother Vanozza, her brother Cesare, and her little son Rodrigo, for it was not the custom that a widow should take her children to a new husband. Cesare, in his solicitude, had provided at his own expense a special escort of 200 gentlemen, with musicians and entertainers to lighten the road. She had besides a huge retinue, worthy of the greatest princess in Europe. The cardinals, the ambassadors and the city magistrates accompanied her to the Porta del Popolo and watched her set out, a trim figure in red silk and ermine riding on a white jennet.

Setting out on this journey, Lucrezia needed all the courage she could muster. She knew very well how strongly the Este family had resisted her. She knew also that she was joining a rugged, haughty, eccentric, violent clan. The family had ruled in Ferrara since the twelfth century, providing hard, stable government through many years of cruelty and splendour. For all their great achievement, the Estes were not attractive and not well-loved. Duke Ercole had the competence of his house; he was an astute politician, a patron of arts and letters, and an ostentatious

upholder of religion. He had a passion for music and theatre, maintained the best singers in Italy, honoured the composer Josquin des Prés, and was patron to the famous poets Matteo Maria Boiardo and Ludovico Ariosto. He was a careful observer of the outward forms of religion, 'because it is well always to keep on good terms with God.' He distributed alms every morning after Mass, and once a year collected food and clothing for the poor. But critics found him sly and mean-spirited, and thought his religious observance part humbug and part credulous superstition. Any mountebank or fanatic had the ear of the duke. The true state of his piety was revealed by his numerous illegitimate children, and by the career of his son, Cardinal Ippolito, tonsured at six, an archbishop at eight and a cardinal at fifteen. He became notoriously the suavest, most cynical and most licentious cardinal in the Sacred College.

Lucrezia's husband Alfonso, the duke's eldest son, was a blunt, uncouth man in his middle twenties. He had no use for the frivolities of the courtier but devoted himself to artillery and the casting of cannon. A restless, unemotional prince, he was not without talent, performed well on musical instruments and was quite at home at the potter's wheel. His manner was abrupt and his clothes rough. His first wife Anna Sforza, to whom he had shown little affection, died in childbirth. His contemporaries regarded him as eccentric to the point of lunacy, and there was a hint that this might have been as a result of the pox; for he was, like many of his house, a keen visitor to brothels and shared the French disease with his brothers Ferrante and Sigismondo. He had suffered a kind of palsy from his illness and his conduct was strange. Once, in the summer of 1497, he had been seen walking nude through the streets of Ferrara. He was not a husband from whom Lucrezia could expect much consideration.

And from the beginning Lucrezia faced resentment and opposition. The old duke treated her with a grudging respect, but was mean about her purse and objected to her large following of ladies, among whom Spaniards predominated. After performing his duty to his wife, Alfonso was merely absent for a large part of the time. But the most testing opposition came from her new sister-in-law, Isabella, Marchesa of Mantua. Isabella had a reputation for brilliance, and a pre-eminence in the north of Italy which she did not intend to share with the upstart from Rome. She, like others in her family, had been against the marriage. No doubt she recalled every detail of Lucrezia's notoriety: her broken betrothals, her unlucky marriage, her shameful divorce; Giovanni Sforza's accusation of incest, and the Roman gossip of Perotto's bastard; the terror of Gandia and Cesare, and the licentious influence of her father Alexander. Isabella was cool and censorious and did her best, throughout the extended celebrations in Ferrara, to make Lucrezia uncomfortable. 'The wedding was a very cold affair,' she wrote to her husband Gonzaga. 'It seems a thousand years until I shall be in Mantua again; I am anxious to get away from this place where I find absolutely no pleasure.' Lucrezia endured these trials with a dignified patience that won her eventually the beginnings of friendship. When Isabella returned to Mantua the two ladies corresponded, at first formally, then with growing warmth that led over the years to a genuine regard.

The city of Lucrezia's husband was in many ways a forbidding place for a stranger. Ferrara lay in a desolate landscape, as much salt marsh as

OPPOSITE Cardinal Giuliano della Rovere (in scarlet robes), the future Pope Julius II, wit Pietro and Girolamo Riario (standing on the left) at Sixtus IV's appointment of Platina as Vatican Librarian. Julius was sixty when he became pope but his features and bearing had lost none of their force in the thirty years since Melozzo had painted him as cardinal with his uncle

OVERLEAF 'The Feast of the Gods' (detail), Bellini mythological marriage painting, commissioned by Alfonso d'Este and completed in 1514. After their desperate struggle against Julius II, the Este were finally enjoying a reversal of papal policy toward Ferrara, and Leo X had reinstated Alfonso as defender of the faith. Ippolito d'Este who had negotiated the marriage contract presides over the feast as Mercury, the messenger of the gods. The goddess holding the quince, the symbol of matrimony, is thought to be a portrait of Lucrezia, her husband Alfonso in the role of Neptune. The infant Bacchus is the young Ercole, while the poet Bembo takes the part of a thin Silenus and Bellini himself is in attendance.

TEMPLA DOMVM EXPOSITIS·VICOS·FORA·MOENIA·PONTES·
VIRGINEAM TRIVII QVOD REPARARIS AQVAM·
PRISCA LICET NAVTIS STATVAS DARE COMMODA PORTVS·
ET VATICANVM CINGERE SIXTE IVGVM·
PLVS TAMEN VRBS DEBET·NAM QVAE SQVALORE LATEBAT·
CERNITVR IN CELEBRI BIBLIOTHECA LOCO·

plain, where flat vistas dissolved eventually into distant mists. The bleak territory was traversed by the River Po, and crossed by many canals. In the north of the city stood the huge, gloomy red hulk of the Castello Estense, assigned by the duke to be the home of Alfonso and Lucrezia. This stronghold of unrelieved severity, with jutting battlements and towers, brooded gigantically over the whole city, casting long shadows over the dark moat fed by waters of the Po. Within the castle was the spot where, not a century before, Niccolò d'Este had caused his son Ugo and his stepmother Parisina to be executed for adultery. These old memories reminded Lucrezia to beware of infidelity in the house of Este. Oppressed by the past, Lucrezia could expect little pleasure in the present. From the high battlements of the Castello Estense, studded with her husband's cannon, she looked out on one side to the well-cultivated but monotonous, malarial plains, and on the other to the unfriendly city. In rooms grown mouldy from parsimony and neglect she was forced to haggle with her father-in-law about the provision for her retinue and the size of her domestic allowance. Though she let many followers go, a stubborn instinct for self-preservation made her keep her Spaniards, among whom was her favourite, the flirtatious Angela Borgia Lanzol. The wearisome argument about household expense went on until, as she had done before in a time of unbearable stress, Lucrezia escaped, retreating into the convent of the Poor Clares at Corpus Domini. She returned with the matter still unresolved. She was pregnant and depressed. Her husband, though gratified at the thought of an heir, generally avoided her, at work in gun-foundry or brothel. In a cold, wet summer she caught the malaria that was endemic in the low-lying river plain. Summoned by the worried duke, Alfonso hurried home from the camp of the French king and for the first time looked on his wife with kindly eyes. Distressed both by her condition and by the possible loss of his child, he stayed by her bedside and tended her 'most lovingly'. Duke Ercole lent his own doctor, an admirable physician who had treated Alfonso's syphilis; he was joined by the pope's private physician, and as if this combination were not enough, Cesare sent from the Romagna the famous Gaspar Torella and four other doctors. Lucrezia responded to treatment and by the end of July was recovering well. On the 28th, her brother Cesare, on a flying visit to the French king in Milan, burst into her sickroom in disguise and frightened her

Lucrezia Borgia. As the Duchess of Ferrara, Lucrezia became known for her piety and good works. The Chevalier Bayard described her as a glorious princess, for she is beautiful and good, gentle and amiable to everyone'.

into a relapse. 'She immediately began to have stomach pains,' wrote her doctor, 'followed by a dysenteric flux and a fever that caused us much thought.' In the next month she grew worse, her body was wasting, her hands and feet swollen, and she bled frequently from the nose. On 5 September, seriously ill, with Alfonso helping to attend her, she was delivered of a still-born baby girl.

Lucrezia had experienced little joy in Ferrara. She took some comfort from the presence of her Spanish ladies, and more from the steadfast

The city of Ferrara, dominated by the forbidding Castello Estense, assigned to be the home of Alfonso and Lucrezia.

affection of her brother Cesare. In all his bitter, selfish life, he seemed to love only his mother Vanozza and his sister Lucrezia. As he had come to her when she had fever, so he rushed to her again in the perilous days after her miscarriage. He was the one who held her while the doctors bled her, and he remained to cheer her with jokes and stories. They had not been together much in the past, and were not to be so at all in the future, but there was always a close affinity between them. In the midst of his conquests, he gave her all the support he could, and the certainty of his revenge tempered the meanness of the Este family towards her. She for her part loved and admired her brother, and after his fall argued tirelessly in Ferrara for his freedom.

In the first year in Ferrara, Lucrezia had one other gallant and friend. Ercole Strozzi, the lame court poet, had flattered her and made her laugh, and having a mistress in Venice, brought from that great mart of the eastern trade routes the small luxuries that Lucrezia's extravagant heart always craved and her husband did not provide. She was still estranged from Alfonso, though he had acted well during her confinement and illness. She retired once again to the convent of the Poor Clares, and then, at the invitation of Strozzi, went to his villa at Ostellato, to recuperate in country air. Here she met another poet, the Venetian Pietro Bembo. Soon there passed between the young poet and the lady, starved of love and still only twenty-three, those ardent gallantries inevitable in a Renaissance court. Bembo praised her musical ability and wrote five hexameters on the subject of her bracelet. After several weeks of poetic adulation, Lucrezia responded with an encouraging letter.

In January 1503 she was still at odds with her husband, still without any sign of the child he had promised her. But she began to take heart from the attention of Bembo and life became altogether more pleasant. She appeared in public once more in jewels, and ornately dressed. The courtesies blossomed on each side. In the summer they began to correspond in a lovers' code, swearing the usual felicities when together and panting with the usual torment when apart. The tone was high and poetic, with no hint of sublunary lusts. Then Bembo caught a fever and withdrew to Ostellato. In August, malaria gripped the unhealthy city of Ferrara and Lucrezia fled to a villa at Medellana. Within a few days she heard that her father was dead.

Alexander had never forgotten his daughter. 'We think night and day', he had written, 'in what way we can increase and help your condition.' He made several plans to visit her in Ferrara, the last being in the summer of 1503; but always some piece of urgent business prevented him, and on the last occasion he was overtaken by death. As a child of the family, she had her place in Borgia schemes; yet though the pope might order her life with the heartlessness of the politician, he still watched over her with the fondness of a parent. It was necessary that she should go to Ferrara; but having placed her there, Alexander was anxious for her health and happiness. He did not expect that Alfonso should love his wife, but he was pleased when he heard that at least her husband spent his nights with her. 'He is young,' the pope told the envoy, 'during the day he goes where he likes, as is his right.' So long as the pope lived there was a measure of safety for Lucrezia. Alexander was too important and his son Cesare too dangerous to offend. All Italy knew the closeness of the Borgia ties, that an injury to one was likely to be avenged by another. But with her chief protector gone, what could she expect? Cardinal Ippolito brought the news of her father's death to Medellana. She put out the candles and refused to eat, withdrawing into the gloom of a house draped in black. Grieving for her father, she had cause also to weep for her future, stranger in an unfriendly city, with an indifferent husband and a grasping father-in-law.

Duke Ercole let it be known that he welcomed the death of Alexander. He claimed that the Borgias had not treated him fairly, and for this he blamed Cesare. 'He was never frank with us,' the duke told his envoy in Milan. 'As he was inclined to Spain and we remained good Frenchmen, we had little to look for either from the pope or his son. Therefore, this death caused us little grief, as we expect only evil from the advancement of the duke.' The whole of Italy shared Ercole's relief, and the exulting of the enemy looked ominous for Lucrezia. Bembo, coming to Medellana with words of sympathy, found her weeping on the floor in a black gown in a black-hung room and went away with the words unsaid. But in the following weeks he was able to comfort her, so much so that he became known as 'Lucrezia's Bembo'. Helped by the poet's touching devotion she began to live again and saw that her state was not as insecure as she had feared. She had brought Duke Ercole the benefit of a very large dowry, which he was loath to have to return.

TOP The Venetian poet Pietro Bembo whose attentions made Lucrezia's life in Ferrara more bearable: 'Who would not extol a woman so beautiful, so elegant, and in no way narrow-minded?' he wrote soon after his first meeting with Lucrezia.

BELOW *L'amorino bendato* or the blindfold cupid, with the initials F P H F F, the lovers' code used in Lucrezia's correspondence with the poet Bembo.

OPPOSITE The lock of Lucrezia's hair that inspired Bembo to write 'Every day you find some new way to fan my ardour. Today you did this with what had once adorned your lovely brow.'

The charm of her personality was beginning to break down animosity towards her. In particular, the danger of the confinement and her heart-felt grief at the loss of her child had shocked Alfonso and his father into some realization of her worth. Though they did not change their gruff, uncommunicative ways, they were better disposed towards her. And finally, since Venice had immediately thrust into the Romagna on the death of Alexander, Ercole decided that Cesare was a safer neighbour than his old, powerful Venetian enemy.

With her own position improving, Lucrezia did what she could for the rest of her family. For the past year she had provided funds for her son Rodrigo of Bisceglie and for little Giovanni Borgia, the *infans Romanus*. But from the distance of Ferrara there was nothing that she could do for them now. Their guardian removed them from Rome to the safety of Naples, and they disappeared from her life. Nor was there much she could do for Cesare. She pestered Duke Ercole to help him and wrote a pleading letter to the King of France. But both those politic men were biding their time and were not to be moved by a woman's tears. Strive as she might, her brother went on to his doom, betrayed by the frailty of the Borgia inheritance. By the end of 1503 Lucrezia had returned from Medellana to her red fortress in Ferrara. Her idyll with Bembo was coming to an end. He had been summoned back to Venice and she would not find it easy to meet him in the future amid the public spies of her husband's city. Bembo was a romantic swain, and his high-flown protestations were sweet consolation for an ardent young woman afflicted with a dour bore for a husband. But her destiny lay in Ferrara and she knew the perils of infidelity. She became reconciled to her fate and, free from the overpowering influence of Pope Alexander, began to form her own life. She had been granted, in fact, a fortunate release.

Duke Ercole died on 25 January 1505. Alfonso, who was away on one of his many foreign journeys, hastened home from England to claim his duchy. At once, he placed Lucrezia at the head of a court delegated to hear citizens' petitions, a recognition of her ability and a mark of confidence in the new duchess. Duke Alfonso needed as much competent help as he could get, for Venice was still aggressively expanding in the Romagna and Pope Julius was fiercely determined to make all papal fiefs obedient to his will, even if that meant attacking such long-established and secure vicariates as Bologna and Ferrara. Alfonso could not feel easy in his duchy, and his disquiet was increased by his own unsociable isolation and by the ambition of his more personable brothers. Another cruel chapter in the long history of Este violence and treachery was written when Cardinal Ippolito and his bastard brother Giulio fell out over Angela Borgia Lanzol, Lucrezia's favourite lady-in-waiting. On 3 November 1505, an enraged Ippolito ordered his servants to put out the eyes of his rival, which they gladly attempted to do, though the doctors managed to save some of Giulio's sight. Alfonso could hardly condone this atrocious act, but since he needed Ippolito's suave skills and influence in the Church he allowed the crime to go unpunished. In revenge, Giulio plotted with his brother Ferrante for the overthrow of Alfonso and the murder of Ippolito. The cardinal's extensive network of spies soon heard of the plot. Alfonso was informed, and this time acted with brutal swiftness. The brothers were apprehended and condemned, and the lesser conspirators executed. On 12 August 1506, Giulio and Ferrante were led to the scaffold in front of the duke, the duchess and all the court. At the last moment, Alfonso granted leniency and commuted the sentence to life imprisonment. And if this event did not warn Lucrezia of the raw violence of Este passions, two years later her first Ferrarese friend, the limping poet Ercole Strozzi, was discovered murdered near the Pareschi Palace, with his hair torn out and his body stabbed through twenty-two times. No guilt was ever proved but good evidence pointed at Duke Alfonso.

Into this ugly masculine world, Lucrezia introduced light and grace. Her husband, in his rustic clothes, had no time for art and culture; gunnery, fortifications and the difficulties of government took up all his days. Lucrezia was not naturally learned – her sister-in-law Isabella Gonzaga had more brilliant attainments, being a fluent Latinist which Lucrezia was not. But she was bilingual in Italian and Spanish; a list of her books included devotional and religious works in both languages and a small, worthy crop of poetry and philosophy. But she had taste and a love of refinement found in all the Borgias. And since she had a lively appreciation of the graces and amusements of a court, she gladly took on the patronage of courtly arts expected of an Italian prince. Pietro Bembo remained her romantic servant until he left for the court of Urbino in 1506. In 1505 he dedicated his *Gli Asolani* to her, and in later years they corresponded with friendly complicity. She was on the

Isabella d'Este, Marchesa of Mantua. Until Lucrezia's marriage to Alfonso, Isabella had been the uncontested first lady not only of Mantua but also of her father's court of Ferrara. At first, she did her best to make Lucrezia miserable.

best terms with the scintillating stars who revolved around the courts of Mantua and Urbino: Baldassar Castiglione and Aldo Manuzio were her friends. The famous poet Ariosto, who entered the service of Cardinal Ippolito in 1503, paid her rare compliments in *Orlando Furioso*, compliments that went beyond the need of a poet to flatter a great lady. She also began to refashion the ducal palaces, where so much had become decrepit through the neglect of Duke Ercole. She brought the painters Bartolomeo Veneto and Giovanni Bellini from Venice and set them to work with the local artist Benvenuto Garofalo.

Amid the attractions of art, Lucrezia could not forget the worries of the state. Alfonso continued his many wanderings, leaving Lucrezia to govern as regent with the help of Cardinal Ippolito. So long as Cesare was in prison, she also had her own troubles, and her efforts on behalf of her brother led her into another romantic attachment. Francesco Gonzaga, Marchese of Mantua, was the only Italian prince prepared to make some attempt to help, and the warmth of her gratitude pleased him. When Lucrezia lost another child in 1505 – her son dying after a month – Francesco invited her to recover in Mantua, since Alfonso was once again away. Gonzaga was an ugly, talented man, with a fascination for women, who had grown tired of the detachment of his able but cold wife Isabella. A flirtation with the young, warm-hearted Duchess of Ferrara amused him, and he lavished on her the attentions of an accomplished courtier who had seen much of the world. Again, it is not known if their affair went beyond romantic friendship; for one thing Lucrezia was recovering from a difficult childbirth and from the loss of a baby. Gonzaga later passed on to other women, but he and Lucrezia remained true friends, even after the first reason for their coming together was removed by the death of Cesare in 1507. Lucrezia took this death with stoical dignity and, having now less reason to see Gonzaga, was recalled to duty by thoughts of her brother's mortality. Alfonso, who had tolerated her indiscretions out of carelessness or ignorance, at last fathered a son and heir in 1508. The duchess knew now that her place was irrevocably with her Este husband and her son Ercole, and she entered into the affairs of Ferrara with wholehearted Borgia determination, giving her adopted city the benefit of her Borgia capacity for administration and hard work.

ucrezia with her ladies-ı-waiting presents her ın Ercole to Saint Maurelius, protector of errara. The birth of a ın and heir in 1508 ssured the future of the Iouse of Este and made ucrezia's position secure.

In 1508, five months after the birth of Lucrezia's son, Julius II instigated the League of Cambrai, and thus directed against Venice an alliance of the great European princes. This papal act brought down on
Italy a terror and a chaos far worse than the woes of the first French
invasion in 1494. Ferrara, a papal fief and a natural enemy of Venice,
was induced to join the League, and Duke Alfonso was invested with
the standard of the Church, which pleased the aspiring artilleryman.
For five years Lucrezia was duchess of a warring state, often regent for
an absent husband, and subject to all the distressful change of fortune
that the war brought with it. She was entering her thirtieth year. 'She
put aside the vanities to which she had been accustomed since child-
hood,' wrote Alfonso's biographer. She proved herself a good administrator – very much her father's daughter – with a steady hand at the
helm in the midst of the worst storms. For with the rapid change so
characteristic of Italian policy, Julius made peace with Venice in 1510
and turned his ferocity on the French. 'These French', he told the
Venetian envoy, 'are trying to make me nothing but their king's chaplain. But I mean to be pope, as they will find out to their discomfort.'
But Ferrara had always been a loyal ally of the French, and soon Duke
Alfonso found himself, with only fitful help from France, facing the
full might of Pope Julius. Alfonso's cannon won the famous victory of
Ravenna, on 1 April 1512, but it was so expensively purchased that it
finished the French in Italy. Alfonso was reduced to a desperate defence
of Ferrara against the armies of the pope when he was luckily relieved,
in February 1513, by the sudden death of the grim old warrior-pontiff.

Lucrezia emerged serenely from these years of trial. For those who
knew her she had outlived her Borgia notoriety. The people of Ferrara
praised her for pious works, for founding convents and hospitals; she
had become 'the good duchess'. Chevalier Bayard, the French knight
famous for his courtesy, wrote of her:

> She is a pearl in this world. I venture to say that neither in her time, nor for
> many years before, has there been such a glorious princess, for she is beautiful
> and good, gentle and amiable to everyone. And nothing is more certain than
> this: that though her husband is a skilful and brave prince, the gracious
> princess has been a great service to him.

She could rest on her reputation for the few years left to her. Towards
the end of 1518 Lucrezia was pregnant again. Childbearing had always

been difficult for her. She had lost two of the duke's babies and had borne him four sons and a daughter. Once again there were complications in the pregnancy. In March 1519, hearing that her old admirer Francesco Gonzaga had died, she sent his widow a touching letter of consolation. In June, Lucrezia gave birth to a girl, a poor, weak, undersized baby who did not live long. She felt her own end was near, but she did not fret, having sailed into the harbour of security. She had at last the affection of her husband, the high regard of her citizens, and the comfort of the Church. On 22 June 1519, she wrote to Pope Leo X, taking leave of life with serene resolution:

> So great is the favour which Our Merciful Creator has shown me that I approach the end of my life with pleasure, knowing that in a few hours and having received for the last time all the holy sacraments of the Church, I shall be released. Though a sinner, I desire as a Christian to ask your Holiness, in your mercy, to give me all possible spiritual consolation, and the blessing of your Holiness for my soul. Therefore I offer myself to you in all humility, and commend to your mercy my husband and my children, all of whom are your servants.

Two nights later Lucrezia Borgia died, in the presence of her husband Duke Alfonso. A gentle woman with a warm nature, a sinner indeed but more sinned against, Lucrezia had at the end, by the offering of a good life, redeemed in a small measure some of the evil of her family.

CHAPTER EIGHT
THE BORGIA LEGACY

N 26 NOVEMBER 1507, POPE JULIUS II ANNOUNCED that he would no longer inhabit the Borgia apartment in the Vatican. The Pinturicchio portraits of Alexander and his family haunted him, reminding him perpetually of 'those Marranos of cursed memory'. Giovanni Borgia, the *infans Romanus*, and Rodrigo of Bisceglie, Lucrezia's son, were stripped of their duchies; Pesaro was restored to Giovanni Sforza; the Orsini and the Colonna were handed back their castles. The six cardinals of the Borgia family who remained in the Sacred College lay low, content to hold quietly whatever benefices they could retain; they owed their peaceful survival to their Spanish blood and to the renewed importance of Spain. Only Cardinal Francesco Borgia stood against Julius and in 1511 joined an attempt to depose the pope at the Council of Pisa. The wrathful Julius had him stripped of his office, and he died soon after of apoplexy. 'All the Borgias', said an enemy triumphantly, 'have been uprooted from the soil and thrown out like poisonous plants, hated by God and noxious to man.'

The Borgia men and women were gone, but their effects remained. In particular, time could not erase so easily the acts of Alexander and Cesare. The conquest of the Romagna had been a political experiment of real interest and historical consequence. For the first time, the whole territory was consolidated into a unified principality, governed in the interests of the papacy, and governed well. Traditionally, the Romagna had been a sorry land, in economic decline, where petty, embattled lords could do little but cling to their papal vicariates against the encroachment of greater powers. With remarkable energy and in a very short time Cesare had changed the state of the land. The sceptical and impartial Florentine historian Guicciardini, who himself became civil

ala delle Scienze e delle Arti Liberali, the room in he Borgia Apartment hat Alexander used as a tudy. It was here that his reasure was discovered fter his death.

governor of the region fifteen years after Cesare's death, admitted that Borgia 'had put in charge of those people men who had governed with so much justice and integrity that the duke was loved by the population'. For one so capable of defying convention and bursting apart established forms, Cesare imposed a cautious, even conservative government. He did little to disturb the accepted organization of life in both country and town, but concentrated instead on efficient administration and swift, even-handed justice. And to help this good work along he laid plans for law courts, a university and municipal buildings in his capital at Cesena. He also knew the value of good communications; he ordered his engineer Leonardo da Vinci to remodel the port for Cesena and construct a canal to connect it to the capital. Since he ruled for such a short time, it was not possible that all Cesare's plans should come to fruition. But he sowed seeds and Pope Julius reaped the harvest. The attempt of Borgia in the Romagna was the inspiration of Julius. He intended to make just such a conquest as Cesare had done, but with the one crucial difference that this time the Church would hold the land directly, not through the intermediary of a papal *nipote*. Despite his bloodthirsty wars, his fearsome anger and his unsaintly ways, Julius has been praised for providing by force some solution to the age-old problem of the pope's temporal possessions in Italy. 'Formerly,' wrote Machiavelli, 'any insignificant baron despised the papal power; now a king of France stands in awe of it.' This was praiseworthy work, Machiavelli added, but it was only done because the pope followed the example and built on the achievements of the Borgias:

> Julius found the Church strong, in possession of all the Romagna, the Roman barons reduced to impotence, and the factions wiped out by the chastisements of Alexander. He also found means to accumulate money in a way that had never been practised before Alexander. These things Julius not only followed but improved upon; he intended to take Bologna, ruin the Venetians, and drive the French out of Italy. All these enterprises prospered with him and, the more to his credit, he did everything to strengthen the Church and not to profit any private person.

Although Alexander wanted to aggrandize his family, he had no desire to hurt the Church. It is a nice irony of his unholy pontificate that so much of what he did for the selfish interests of the Borgias rebounded to the profit of the Church. The Church, Machiavelli wrote, became 'the heir to all his labours'. But Alexander also did good work knowingly for the papacy and for Rome, since he was fully conscious of his duties as a Renaissance patron. Alexander came to a city in the process of transformation from unhealthy medieval huddle to a city of grandeur, with orderly spaces, determined avenues, and resounding buildings. The task had been started long before, in the time of Pope Martin V; Nicholas V and Sixtus IV, in particular, had hurried it along, and Alexander also played his part. Most of his building work was in Trastevere, the part of the city which contained the Vatican and had grown to bursting with the renewed importance of the papal court and the vast expansion of the Church administration. In this area Sixtus had driven through one wide avenue, the Borgo; Alexander cut another one, the Via Alessandrina, to run parallel to it. A papal Bull of 1500 gave privileges to all those who built houses in the new street. He caused gates to be rebuilt, some fountains to be put up, and another in the Piazza of St Peter to be adorned with the Borgia emblem of gilded bulls. Well aware of the importance of the Castel Sant'Angelo in times of trouble, Alexander commissioned Antonio da Sangallo to improve the fortress

LEFT Castel Sant'Angelo, repaired and improved by command of Alexander.

RIGHT Civita Castellana, built by Antonio da Sangallo, the palace-fortress that was both a summer retreat and a vital defence of the Via Flaminia.

with the latest advances in the science of fortification. The interior was also remodelled, providing large storage tanks for water and oil, a granary to hold 185 tons, and five new underground dungeons. The work was said to cost 85,000 ducats and the pope took a keen interest in the progress. In 1497 lightning struck the angel above the castle, ignited a magazine, and destroyed the upper buildings. When they were rebuilt, since form and adornment went together in the Renaissance mind, Alexander had Pinturicchio decorate the new rooms in his antique style, and in one of the towers the same artist also painted representations – now lost – of the events of Alexander's pontificate.

Around St Peter's and the Vatican Palace, Alexander did nothing grand on his own account, preferring to carry through respectfully the plans of his predecessors. The rooms in the Vatican known as the Borgia apartment were built by Nicholas V, but in these seven rooms Pinturicchio and his assistants painted for Alexander a series of large, declamatory frescoes, crowded with a lively iconography in which the Virgin Mary competed with astronomy and Jewish symbols with the Seven Liberal Arts, while portraits of the Borgias and the menacing presence of the Borgia bull paid deference to the patron and his family. Onto the Borgia apartment was built a large square tower, more a defensive bastion than papal living quarters, though it contained, in the upper storey, Alexander's private chapel. Outside the Vatican, Alexander was once again a completer of other men's plans. He continued work on several Roman churches, restored the city walls, and rebuilt the Sapienza in the university. It is said that he used the first gold brought from the Americas for the roof decoration of Santa Maria Maggiore.

The Borgia emblem.

An admirer of grandeur, a lover of spectacle and theatre, Alexander gave no evidence of sympathy with the work of scholars and humanists. He was not against them, but in an agitated, scheming pontificate he had more need of *condottieri* and castle builders than critics, Latinists or antiquarians. He preferred to answer immediate needs and was a great patron of military architects, expending large sums as a cardinal at Nepi, Soriano and Subiaco, and further sums when he became pope at Tivoli, Sermoneta, and particularly at Civita Castellana where Antonio da Sangallo built him a palace-fortress that was both a summer retreat and a vital defence of the Via Flaminia. But Alexander's genial interest in the arts, though he planned no monumental designs like Nicholas or Sixtus, was an encouragement to others. Rome was in the throes of change, and the pope was there to assist it on the way. Antonio Pollaiuolo continued work on the tombs of Sixtus and Innocent; Michelangelo carved his Pietà for Cardinal La Grolaye; the French, the Spaniards and the Germans built commemorative churches. Cardinal Castellesi erected his palace in the Borgo. Della Rovere, a great patron even before he became Julius II, commissioned from Giuliano da Sangallo a palace near San Pietro in Vincoli. And Raffaele Riario, the richest of the cardinals, completed and extended the famous Cancellaria, the palace which Rodrigo Borgia had fashioned for himself out of the old papal chancery. When Bramante first came to Rome in 1499, he began the architectural career that was later to adorn Rome so resplendently with a modest commission from Alexander for a city fountain.

On the spiritual side, the failings of Alexander were too painful to be missed. But however bad his own conduct, however much his example encouraged the worst in others and hurried the Catholic Church down the long slide to the Reformation, he never lost his real, though misguided, concern for the unity of the Church and the authority of the Universal Pastor. Time and his own selfish inclinations put the wrong tools in his hand, and he wielded them to the detriment of the Church. But it was remarkable, considering the qualities of the man and the turbulence of the reign, how he kept the Church under such firm control. The black spectre of schism haunted all the Renaissance popes. The captivity at Avignon, the Great Schism, the battles with the conciliar movement were recent, irksome memories. The threat of a Church Council was still a potent weapon in the anti-papal armoury of all great

Alexander VI presents the Bishop of Pesaro to St Peter. The bishop holds a flag which bears the arms of Alexander.

princes. When the idealist Christopher Columbus made his will in 1498, he so feared division in Christendom that he ordered his son to use his inheritance in support of a crusade 'or to help the pope if a schism in the Church should threaten to deprive him of his seat or his temporal possessions.' That Alexander avoided this danger so successfully was a tribute to his ability as politician and organizer; at a certain low administrative level the vast bureaucracy of the Church was run as efficiently as it had ever been. Hard work and good administration, however, did not explain completely Alexander's hold on the Church. He was, after all, a great cleric, though a flawed one, and he ruled with the true authority of a prince of the Church. He loved the holy theatre of the liturgy, enjoined strict observation of feasts and fasts, demanded church attendance from the cardinals, and delighted in a short, pithy style of preaching. He was a friend to the religious orders, yet a sharp critic of the slothful. He encouraged reform, promoted new foundations, and confirmed old rights and privileges. He was always a stout protector of the conventual life against any interference, either ecclesiastical or secular.

The theology of Alexander was orthodox. He was by nature a tolerant man, and particularly tolerant towards Jews whom he protected in Rome and elsewhere. If he turned against them, and the crypto-Jewish Marranos in later life, that was a lamentable political concession to the bigoted Catholic monarchs of Spain. But the Moslem infidel and the heretic could expect no charity from the pope. The crusading tax – the tenth – was collected rigorously, and though Alexander launched no general crusade and though malicious rumour had it that he diverted the crusading tax into the pockets of his family, he did distribute quite large sums to Venice, to the Empire and to Hungary, for resistance against the Turks. Against heresy he was more severe. Picards, Waldensians, Hussites, Utraquists, whether they lived in Lombardy, Germany, Bohemia or Moravia, received the attention of the Inquisition. Yet reconciliation not extermination was the ideal of this tolerant pope, and in the Eastern frontier lands, where heresy was strong, he gave the clergy special powers to receive the erring back into the true faith. His care for purity of doctrine in Germany, where heretical opinions were multiplying boldly, caused him, on 1 June 1501, to institute a censorship of books for the first time. All printed matter had to be submitted, under pain of excommunication and a large fine, to an ecclesiastical censor, 'so as to prevent anything from being printed that is contrary to the Catholic faith or ungodly or capable of causing scandal'. The attempt, as censorship usually does, rebounded against authority, and did nothing to delay the Protestant Reformation in Germany. But in an authoritarian age the attempt was not extraordinary, and argued that the pope had a true desire to preserve what he saw as a pure faith.

All this represented the negative, repressive side of Alexander's pastoral care. He was shown in a better light by his solicitude for nuns and by his devotion to the Virgin Mary. Coarse critics would expect Alexander to be a champion of women. And though it is quite obvious that he enjoyed the company of women for some not very noble reasons, it is also clear that he had a side to his nature that was at home and comfortable with women. The cult of the Virgin has been often damned as a grave superstition; but whatever are the theological rights of the matter, it was also an exaltation of woman and a valuable recognition of her dignity and place in an age barbarously dominated by men. In August 1500, to commemorate the Blessed Virgin, Alexander ordered the Angelus to be rung each day.

An intelligent sympathy appeared, too, in Alexander's approach to the great event of his pontificate – the discovery of America. When Columbus returned from the voyage of 1492, a quarrel very soon broke out between Spain and Portugal over the exploitation of the new lands. Both appealed to Pope Alexander, as the arbiter of Christendom, and the pope took this responsibility seriously. In May 1493, he issued three Bulls drawing a line of demarcation. Though the line was shifted 270 leagues to the west by the Treaty of Tordesillas in 1494, the papal decision formed the basis for all future negotiations between the countries of the navigators. Alexander may have favoured his native Spain, but his intercession was a statesmanlike determination of a knotty problem that allowed the exploration, which no pope could have stopped in any case, to go on without warfare between two important Christian kingdoms. Nor were these papal grants anything more than an indication of zones of influence to be respected by other European powers. They conferred no rights whatsoever over native populations; a concession to Portugal in 1497 expressly made the grant conditional on the free consent of the inhabitants. The robbery and enslavement of native Indians was chiefly the work of European monarchs and their servants. The pope saw exploration as a glorious means to evangelize pagans, spreading Christ's gospel, but he intended to do this by good works and preaching, not by the sword. The papal Brief given to Fray Boyl, the spiritual leader of Columbus' second expedition in 1493, was an enlightened encouragement of that good friar. Alexander had an imaginative vision of the fruits of exploration worthy of his Sacred Office. He saw them not as means to conquest, or as enterprises for the rape of distant lands, but as ventures for the propagation of the faith, and he declared that to be his intent in a Bull of 1501.

In better times Alexander would have been a better pope, having as he did remarkable qualities of intelligence, judgment and application. A man, armed by native talent, stands poised for good or bad, and by a twist of history may be damned or redeemed. The state of Church and papacy in fifteenth-century Italy was a cause for grief, but the sins had become so generally accepted that they were almost institutionalized. 'Those princes and republics', Machiavelli wrote with a nostalgia for ancient Roman virtue, 'which desire to remain free from corruption, should above all else maintain incorrupt the ceremonies of their religion and should always hold them in veneration; for there can be no surer indication of the decline of a country than to see divine worship neglected.' By this standard, Italy was manifestly corrupt, and it took more than mere intelligence to avoid it: it took moral probity, even saintliness. The early days of Francesco Guicciardini showed the silent process of evil at work. When Guicciardini was twenty his uncle, an archdeacon of Florence, died, leaving several profitable benefices. 'I wanted them,' the historian admitted in his *Ricordanze*,

> not to fatten on great revenues as most other priests do, but I thought that as I was young and had some letters it might be the way to become great in the Church, and I might one day hope to become cardinal. But my father determined not to have any of his sons a priest, though there were five of us, because he thought the affairs of the Church were decadent. He preferred to lose great profits in the present, and the chance to have an important son in the future, rather than bear the reproach of his conscience that he had made his son into a priest out of greed for wealth or lust for a great position.

Plucked from the easy path of Church preferment, Guicciardini was set on the straight road towards the realization of his talent as historian. There was no honest parent to perform this function for young Rodrigo Borgia. On the contrary, his way was made smooth by his uncle Calixtus and his great abilities led him to the corrupt rewards of a corrupt Church. 'The same arts had been employed by his predecessors,' Lord Acton wrote wisely, 'with less energy and profit. It was an unavoidable temptation, almost a necessity of his position, to carry them to the furthest excess.' What Pope Calixtus had done for his nephew Rodrigo, Pope Alexander did for his son Cesare, and that *nipote* grew terrifyingly into another kind of monster. But again, given the condition of the time, there was something almost inevitable in the process:

> There was [said Leopold Ranke, another great historian] but one point on earth where such a state of things was possible; namely, that at which the plenitude of secular power was united to the supreme spiritual jurisdiction. This point was occupied by Cesare. There is a perfection even in depravity. Many of the sons and nephews of popes attempted similar things, but none ever approached Cesare's bad eminence: he was a virtuoso in crime.

Guicciardini thought that in a world of expediency where all governments, including the rule of the Church, were violent, a man would

Maria Enriquez, widow of Juan Duke of Gandia, was convinced of Cesare's guilt as murderer of both Juan and Alfons di Bisceglie. She commissioned this altarpiece with Cesare (far right) raising his dagger to stab Juan in the back.

compromise with honesty and virtue not only to succeed but also to survive. The Borgias might have done differently in a different social and religious air, as the history of the family in the Spanish homeland demonstrates. When Alexander's son Juan, Duke of Gandia, was murdered in Rome in 1497, he left a wife in Spain with a small son, Juan, and pregnant with another child who became the daughter Isabella.

His widow Maria Enriquez cut all bonds with her Borgia in-laws, turned her back on Italy, sold her husband's Neapolitan estates, and planted her family solidly at Gandia, a Spanish matriarch in a Spanish duchy. And she managed her stony, sun-baked acres so well that her son Juan became a rich man. Her husband had been an immoral profligate, but Maria was grave, composed and pious. She became the great patroness of the churches of Gandia, with a particular affection for the convent of Santa Clara. As soon as her son was married and settled in the duchy, she retired into this quiet house of the Poor Clares taking her daughter Isabella with her. They were the first in a procession of Borja nuns, for in the next 200 years twenty-six young women of the family followed Doña Maria through the doors of Santa Clara, providing an almost unbroken line of Borja abbesses.

The third Duke of Gandia, therefore, grew up in a world radically different from the one inhabited by his Borgia relatives in Italy. The Borgias in Italy were landless opportunists, disenfranchised from their native country, living in a corrupt social order, dependent on favour and nepotism for their advancement. The Borjas of Gandia, though they owed their very existence to the dynastic scheming of Pope Alexander, became settled on their Gandia estate, attached to local soil, secure in their income, strictly and piously brought up. Duke Juan was a religious man, devoted to charity. It is said that he would drop all tasks to accompany the sacrament to the sick or dying, to comfort them in their suffering. But he was also a grandee of Spain, with a high sense of the rights and duties of the *hidalgo*, doubly related to the royal family through his mother and through his wife Juana, daughter of Ferdinand's illegitimate son. On the death of Juana he married again, and his two wives gave him seventeen children. He was also the father of a bastard son from the salad days of his adolescence.

His eldest son Francisco was born in 1510 and brought up within the narrow confines of the provincial duchy, bordered by Valencia to the north and Denia to the south. As a boy, Francisco showed a rather excessive religiosity which his father discouraged, insisting instead on proficiency in horsemanship, hunting, use of arms, and other manly pursuits. In 1520 two events broke the rural seclusion of Francisco's life and forced him into a wider world. First, his mother died; then the peasant revolt of the *Comuneros* swept over Gandia, sacked the ducal palace, and drove the family into temporary exile. The boy did not return, but entered the aristocratic household of his uncle Juan de Aragon, Archbishop of Saragossa, to learn the accomplishments of a knight and a courtier. In 1522 he became a page to the Infanta Caterina, sister of Charles V, and six years later, at the age of eighteen, he went to the imperial court at Valladolid. A handsome, dashing, talented lad, Francisco made a strong impression on the Emperor Charles and his wife Isabella, partly because Charles had an almost superstitious awe for Francisco's grandmother Maria, the royal nun of Santa Clara. In 1529 Francisco married a Portuguese lady, though his father objected to a foreigner bride, and seemed to be rising rapidly in the imperial household. When Charles went abroad a year later, he left Francisco de Borja as tutor and companion to his son Philip and administrator of the imperial household.

Francis Borgia. The life of the Borgia saint has never been able to counterbalance the legend of the Borgia pope and his son Cesare. The name Borgia will always be associated with sin rather than saintliness.

There was a certain obvious parallel between the progress of Francisco and that of his ancestor Alfons de Borja a century before. Alfons had made his way to the royal court, won the admiration of the king, and owed his career to royal patronage. Francisco, though starting from different circumstances, was following a similar course. But Alfons, although he was a cleric in minor orders, was at heart a worldly man seeking his fortune; whereas Francisco, a man who had begun with all the wordly advantages, was striving to pass through them, searching for some goal beyond wealth and rank and the friendship of the emperor. Even at Valladolid he mortified the flesh with a hair shirt and was derided by the gallants of the court for his chastity. He felt that strong religious influence descending in his family from Maria Enriquez. He was still the *hidalgo* Borja, a man of imperious temper, born to be obeyed, an accomplished knight and a talented administrator. But he was edging towards something else, beginning to make himself into the person known to history as St Francis Borgia.

In 1536 Francis went on campaign for the first time, accompanying Charles's army into Provence. He saw his great friend, the poet Garcilaso de la Vega, stoned to death attempting to scale the walls of a small fort near Fréjus. Soon after, Francis became sick, and in the course of a long illness turned more and more to spiritual reading. He went back to the court and in 1539 was placed in charge of the funeral arrangements for the Empress Isabella. He journeyed across Spain in high summer, taking the decomposing body to the final resting place in Granada. He was then appointed viceroy in Catalonia and given the task of subduing this restive province, with its independent Aragonese nobility who resented the dominance of Castile at the imperial court. Francis won a reputation as a stern, efficient governor, meting out peremptory justice, prepared to take horse and ride down malefactors himself, and hang them on the spot. But his responsibility was a penance. He was out of sympathy with the people he governed, and he had grown excessively fat, so that his belt went round three ordinary men. In 1543 his father died and Francis gladly resigned his viceregal post to return to the duchy at Gandia. The accumulation of weariness that had crept up on him in the world now encouraged him, in his retirement from great affairs, to turn more and more towards religion. He had already heard of the growing fame of his fellow Spaniard Ignatius Loyola, and in Barcelona had welcomed members of Ignatius' new Jesuit order. He began to correspond with Loyola, subjecting himself to a painful discipline, both mental and physical. He had a hearty thirst for wine, but reduced his intake by putting daily a drop of wax in his wine glass. With an ambition worthy of a duke, Francis persuaded a reluctant Ignatius to agree to the foundation of a college of Gandia which later blossomed into the first Jesuit university. In 1546, when his wife Eleanora died, Francis was free from the last worldly tie. He decided to enter the ranks of the Jesuits and began to study in secret since the duties of his dukedom did not allow him to make his decision known at once.

The remainder of Francis' life belongs properly to the history of the Jesuits and to the stories of sainthood. But Francis the new priest and Francis the old duke were never far apart. In 1550 he left for Rome to enter the Society of Jesus and to prepare for ordination into the priesthood. He was the most celebrated and influential recruit to the fledgling order, founded by Ignatius only ten years before. And Ignatius, a man of deep native practicality, intended to use this fortunate acquisition to the very best advantage. Francis retired to the Pyrenees to meditate and preach, but he was soon pitched back into the imperial court, becoming spiritual adviser to the emperor's daughter Juana and wielding as much influence in the world as he had ever done. The Borja boldness and pride were tempered by the conscious humility of the priest, but Francis was still a lordly man, an intimate of the Emperor Charles. Charles sent for him on his deathbed, and Francis preached the emperor's funeral oration in 1559. This standing at the royal court led to some resentment among the other Spanish Jesuits. Father Araoz, the Jesuit provincial in Castile, complained at the cavalier way in which Francis flew over the heads of the Spanish provincials. And it is certain that the patrician priest treated the old-fashioned, conservative Jesuits of the Spanish provinces with some condescension and impatience. When Ignatius Loyola died in 1556, hostility against Francis increased to the point where he fell under the ban of the Spanish Inquisition, was censured for tolerance towards Lutheran opinions, and had to be recalled to Rome by Ignatius' successor in 1561 to avoid further scandal in the peninsula.

The wayward qualities that made the Borgias so dangerous in Italy were never fully exorcized from the family in Spain, but only reined and held in check by a different sense of responsibility and a surer faith. Francis spoke of his long struggle with 'the two beasts of anger and lust', and he only kept his passions under control by severe penances. His half-brothers, Felipe, a knight of Montesa, and Diego, a cleric in Valencia, became involved in a bloody vendetta which caused them, in 1554, to murder the son of the viceroy of Valencia. They fled into exile and Francis did what he could to protect them, but he could not smooth the indignation of the court nor the outrage of the people. Some years later Philip II captured Diego and executed him. Carlos, the eldest son of Francis, also had the turbulent Borja blood flowing in his veins. He begrudged the family money that his father spent on charity, reluctantly contributed as little as he could to the college at Gandia, and refused point blank, as duke, to give the sum promised by his father for the Jesuit college in Rome. He assaulted a gentleman in the streets of Valencia and in the ensuing fight killed an opponent. The litigation that followed drew him into a long lawsuit that consumed much of the ducal income. The Borjas still felt the contrary pulls between the world and the spirit, and this appeared very clearly in the histories of Francis' brothers and sisters, the eighteen children of Juan, third Duke of Gandia. There were among them a saint, two cardinals, one archbishop and five nuns; but also a viceroy, soldiers and *conquistadores*, four girls married into the greatest noble houses of Spain, and a convicted murderer.

When Francis went to Rome in 1561 he became the right-hand man to the General of the order. And when Diego Laynez died in 1565,

Ignatius Loyola receiving Francis Borgia in Rome. St Francis was beatified in 1624 by Pope Urban VIII and canonized in 1671 by Pope Clement X nearly a hundred years after his death.

Francis was elected third General of the Society of Jesus. In the last seven years of his life he put all his considerable Borja energy and ability into the difficult work of stabilizing an infant Society already acquiring a reputation and responsibilities throughout the world as the spearhead of the Catholic Counter-Reformation. On the death of Pope Pius V, Francis was spoken of as a candidate for the Apostle's Chair. But there was no chance to see if Italy and the Church would have countenanced another Borgia pope, for Francis was a sick man, incurably ill with a lung disease. He died in Rome on 30 September 1572.

The Borgia Bull, from which Italy turned with aversion, became in Spain an emblem of sanctity. In the legends of the family, aversion has predominated to the exclusion of all memories of holiness. And with good reason. Alexander, though a Spaniard, was the archetype of the new religious man born of the Italian Renaissance. He was the great capitalist of the faith, the first pope to make all spiritual wares commodities in the worldly marketplace. This expediency brought forth the execrations of Luther, and it was against a characteristically Alexandrine Church that the German reformer began his revolt. Cesare Borgia, too, exuding such a menace and executing his plans with such dreadful efficiency, was only the brilliant culmination to a long line of Italian political development, and Machiavelli was surely right, in *The Prince*, to make Cesare the exemplar of a peculiarly Italian art. In time, he became one of the bogymen of history, which was a rare distinction; in England, Elizabethan schoolmasters shuddered at his name and advised their young charges to avoid the corruption of Italy. The supposed practices of Cesare's court became the commonplaces of the drama, implanting in susceptible northern minds the sinister image of Italian *virtù*:

> There is a Fate, that flies with towering spirits
> Home to the mark, and never checks it conscience.
> Poor plodding Priests, and preaching Friars may make
> Their hollow pulpits, and the empty aisles
> Of churches ring with that round word: But we
> That draw the subtle, and more piercing air,
> In that sublimed region of Court,
> Know all is good, we make so, and go on,
> Secured by the prosperity of our crimes.

And such was the naughty way of the world that very many young
gentlemen could not wait to rush to this iniquity. 'Many of our travellers into Italy', Roger Ascham sighed, 'do not eschew the way to
Circe's court, but go, and ride, and run, and fly thither.' They learned
there such vices, if we believe Robert Greene, as satisfied their liveliest
expectations: 'Being new come from Italy,' he wrote, 'where I learned
all the villanies under the heavens, I was drowned in pride, whoredom
was my daily exercise.'

How do the historical Borgias stand in relation to the myth? Vice and
cruelty to equal and go beyond them could be found in a dozen Italian
courts, large and small. Among great men, Ferdinand of Spain, Louis
of France and Ludovico il Moro were as calculating and faithless;
Ferrante of Naples was more faithless and far more depraved. As promoters of terror and harbingers of chaos, Vitelleschi, Sixtus IV and
Charles VIII outdid them – the first a prelate, the second a pope, and the
third a king. The prolonged, bloody wars of the respected Pope Julius
destroyed many more than the swift, effective campaign of the execrable
Borgias. The carnage at the battle of Ravenna alone very possibly killed
more than all the wars of Cesare.

Time makes no fine distinctions, just and unjust are tumbled in its
maw. Perfect vice is as rare as perfect virtue, and where the names of
so few last a generation it is perhaps better to be remembered for
notoriety than to be consigned to the general oblivion.

ELECT BIBLIOGRAPHY
F WORKS IN THE ENGLISH LANGUAGE

cton, Lord 'The Borgias and their latest storian', *Historical Essays and Studies*, ed. N. Figgis and R. V. Laurence. London)07

dy, C. M. *The Bentivoglio of Bologna.*)xford 1937

ellonci, M. *The Life and Times of Lucrezia*)rgia, tr. Bernard Wall. London 1953; lew York 1953 [tr. Barbara and Bernard Vall]

isticci, Vespasiano da *Lives of Illustrious Men of the Fifteenth Century*, tr. W. George 1d E. Waters. London 1926

3radford, S. *Cesare Borgia: His Life and* imes. London and New York 1976

3reisach, E. *Caterina Sforza, a Renaissance* Virago. Chicago 1967; London 1968

3urchard, Johann *At the Court of the Borgia*, :r. and ed. G. Parker. London 1963
—— *The Diary of John Burchard of Strasburg*, Vol. I: 1483-92, tr. A. H. Mathew. London 910
—— *Pope Alexander and His Court*, extracts from the Latin diary of Johannes Burhardus, ed. F. L. Glaser. New York 1921

3urckhardt, Jacob *The Civilization of the* Renaissance in Italy, tr. S. G. C. Middlemore; ed. L. Goldscheider. London 1951; New York 1954

Chamberlain, E. R. *The Fall of the House of* Borgia. London and New York 1974

Collison-Morley, L. *The Story of the Sforzas.* New York 1934; London 1937
—— *The Story of the Borgias*. London 1932; New York 1933

Comines, Philippe de *The Historical Memoirs of Philip de Comines*. London 1817

Creighton, M. *A History of the Papacy from the Great Schism to the Sack of Rome*, new edn, Vols IV and V. London and New York 1897

Erlanger, R. *Lucretia [Lucrezia] Borgia: A Biography*. New York 1978; London 1979

Ferrara, O. *The Borgia Pope, Alexander the Sixth*, tr. F. J. Sheed. New York 1940; London 1942

Gregorovius, Ferdinand *Lucretia Borgia*, tr. J. L. Garner. New York 1903; London 1948 [ed. L. Goldscheider]
—— *History of the City of Rome in the Middle Ages*, Vols I-VI, tr. A. Hamilton. London 1894-8; 2nd edn, 8 vols [VII and VIII tr. from 1st German edn], tr. G. W. Hamilton. London 1900-9

Guicciardini, Francesco *The History of Italy*, tr. S. Alexander. New York 1968; London 1969
—— *Maxims and Reflections of a Renaissance Statesman*, tr. M. Domandi. London and New York 1965

Machiavelli, Niccolò *The Prince* and *The Discourses*, introd. M. Lerner. New York 1940

Mâle, E. *The Early Churches of Rome*, tr. D. Buxton. London and New York 1960

Mallett, Michael *The Borgias: The Rise and Fall of a Renaissance Dynasty*. London and New York 1969

Masson, G. *The Companion Guide to Rome*, rev. edn. London 1980

—— *Italian Villas and Palaces*. London and New York 1959
—— *Italian Gardens*. London and New York 1961

Mathew, A. H. *The Life and Times of Rodrigo Borgia*. London 1912; New York n.d.

Pastor, L. von *The History of the Popes from the Close of the Middle Ages*, 14 vols, variously ed. F. I. Antrobus; R. F. Kerr. London 1922-4; St Louis, Mo., 1923

Pius II [Aeneas Sylvius Piccolomini] *Memoirs of a Renaissance Pope* [his] *Commentaries*, abridgment tr. F. A. Cragg. New York 1959; London 1960

Ranke, L. von *The Ecclesiastical and Political History of the Popes during the Sixteenth and Seventeenth Centuries*, 3 vols, tr. E. Foster; rev. G. R. Dennis. London 1907

Rolfe, F. W. [Frederick, Baron Corvo] *Chronicles of the House of Borgia*. New York 1962

Symonds, J. A. *Renaissance in Italy*, 7 vols. London 1875-85 [Vol. II: *The Revival of Learning* in various edns to 1929]

Vasari, Giorgio *Lives of Painters, Sculptors and Architects*, 4 vols, tr. Hinds; ed. W. Gaunt. London 1963
—— *The Lives of the Artists*, tr. G. Bull. London and New York 1965

Woodward, W. H. *Cesare Borgia: A Biography*. London 1913

Yriarte, C. *Cesare Borgia*, tr. W. Stirling. London 1947

ILLUSTRATIONS AND ACKNOWLEDGMENTS

The museums, firms and photographers who supplied the illustrations are kindly thanked for their cooperation and are listed below. If in any case the acknowledgment proves to be inadequate the producers apologize. In no case is such inadequacy intentional, and if any owner of copyright who has remained untraced will communicate with the producers a reasonable fee will be paid, and the required acknowledgment made in future editions of the book

Figures in **bold** type indicate pages opposite or between which colour plates are to be found

Endpapers woodcut of Rome. Istituto di Studi Romani, Rome

Frontispiece Photo: Scala, Florence

6 Spanish National Tourist Office, London. Photo: Josip Ciganovic

8-9 Drawn by Eugene Fleury. Alexander's

coat of arms. Photo: The Mansell Collection Ltd

11 'Miracles of St Vincent Ferrer'. Predella panel of an altarpiece by Cossa or his pupil Roberti. Vatican. Photo: Alinari, Rome

13 Medal of Pisanello. Museo Nazionale, Florence. Photo: Mansell/Alinari

19 Painter unknown. Photo: Soprintendenza per i Beni Artistici e Storici, Naples

21 Service de documentation photographique de la Réunion des musées nationaux, Paris

23 Attributed to Isara da Pisa and Francesco Laurana, *c* 1470. Photo: The Mansell Collection Ltd

24 Photo: the author

26 Cathedral of Valencia. Photo: F. Gil Carles, Valencia

28 From H. van Cleef's *Antiquities of Rome and Neighbourhood*. Victoria and Albert Museum, London

29 Photo: The Mansell Collection Ltd

31 Drawn by Eugene Fleury

32 Drawn by Eugene Fleury

36 Side panel of retable by Jaime Baco, or Jacomart. College of Játiva, Valencia. Photo: F. Gil Carles, Valencia

36-7 Sala dei Santi, Vatican. Photo: Scala, Florence

37 Pinacoteca Comunale, Siena. Photo: Scala, Florence

38 Engraving from H. van Cleef's *Antiquities of Rome and Neighbourhood*. Victoria and Albert Museum, London

42 Woodcut of Rome. Istituto di Studi Romani

45 Engraving from H. van Cleef's *Antiquities of Rome and Neighbourhood*. Victoria and Albert Museum, London

52 Maerten van Heemskerck, 1498-1574. Photo: Derrick Witty

53 Detail from a painting by Paolo Uccello, Palazzo Ducale, Urbino. Photo: Mansell/Anderson

54 Tomb in the crypt of St Peter's, Rome. Photo: The Mansell Collection Ltd

56 Siena Cathedral. Photo: Mansell/Alinari

61 Photo: The Mansell Collection Ltd

62 Fresco by Andrea Mantegna in the Camera degli Sposi, Palazzo Ducale, Mantua, 1474. Photo: Mansell/Alinari

63 Musée Condé, Chantilly. Photographie Giraudon, Paris

64-5 Detail of painting by Francesco di Giorgio. Archivio di Stato, Siena

70 Photo: Mansell/Alinari

73 School of Castiglia. Galleria del Prado, Madrid. Photo: Mansell/Anderson

74-5 Photo: the author

75 ABOVE Miniature attributed to Cosimo Tura. The Trustees of The Pierpont Morgan Library, New York. BELOW Manuscript illumination from Biblioteca Estense, Modena. Photo: Orlandini Carlo, Modena

76 Bernardino Pinturicchio. Duomo Libreria Piccolomini, Siena. Photo: Scala, Florence

77 Scene from Benozzo Gozzoli's 'Life of St Augustine'. Chiesa di S. Agostino, San Gimignano. Photo: Scala, Florence

78 Photo: Mansell/Alinari

79 LEFT Supposed portrait of Vanozza dei Catanei by Girolamo de Carpi. Galleria Borghese, Rome. Photo: The Mansell Collection Ltd. RIGHT Portrait of Vanozza dei Catanei, painter unknown. Congregazione delle Carità, Rome. Photo: J. Powell, Rome

82 Detail from Pinturicchio's 'Resurrection'. Photo: Mansell/Alinari

84 Photo: Mansell/Alinari

86 Detail from 'The Marriage of the Virgin' by Lorenzo da Viterbo. Chiesa della Verità. Photo: Mansell/Alinari

87 Photo: Mansell/Anderson

89 Attributed to Leonardo da Vinci. Ambrosiana, Milan. Photo: Mansell/Anderson

90-1 Drawn by Eugene Fleury. Medals: courtesy of the Trustees of the British Museum, London

92 From a missal of Alexander VI in the Vatican Library, Rome

93 Andrea Mantegna. Musée du Louvre, Paris. Photographie Giraudon, Paris

94-5 Detail from Pinturicchio's 'The Disputation of St Catherine'. Borgia Apartment, Vatican. Photo: Mansell/Alinari

99 Detail from Raphael's 'Transfiguration'. Pinacoteca Vaticana. Photo: Alinari, Rome

100 Courtesy of the Trustees of the British Museum, London. Photo: John Freeman

102 Courtesy of the Trustees of the British Museum, London

103 Portrait of a woman thought to be Lucrezia by Bartolomeo Veneto. Städelschen Kunstinstituts, Frankfurt

104 Gouache miniature by Jean Perréal, *c* 1495. Bibliothèque Nationale, Paris. Photo: Robert Harding Associates, London

105 Detail from Botticelli's 'Castigo di Fuoco celeste', Sistine Chapel, Vatican. Photo: Mansell/Anderson

106-7 Painting by Giuseppe Bezzuoli, Galleria Moderna, Florence. Photo: The Mansell Collection Ltd

108 Detail from Pinturicchio's 'The Disputation of St Catherine'. Photo: Mansell/Anderson

110 Portrait of Bernardino dei Conti. Brera, Milan. Photo: Mansell/Anderson

112 Painting (detail) by Francesco Iacovacci. Galleria Nazionale d'Arte Moderna, Rome. Photo: Mansell/Alinari

114-15 Woodcut from *Mer des Histoires* printed 1503. Bibliothèque Nationale, Paris

117 LEFT Detail from 'The Crossing of the Red Sea' by Piero di Cosimo. Sistine Chapel, Vatican. Photo: Alinari, Rome. RIGHT Portrait by Bronzino. Galleria Palatina, Florence. Photo: Mansell/Alinari

119 Photos: Mansell/Alinari

121 Engraving for the 1575 jubilee from *Speculum Romanae Magnificentiae*. Victoria and Albert Museum, London

124-5 Photo: Mansell/Anderson

125 Photo: Mansell/Anderson

129 Victoria and Albert Museum, London. Photo: Derrick Witty

133 Painter unknown. Museo di S. Marco, Florence. Photo: Mansell/Alinari

135 Portrait by Jean Perréal. Reproduced by gracious permission of Her Majesty The Queen. Photo: Robert Harding Associates, London

137 Portrait by Raphael. Galleria Borghese, Rome. Photo: Mansell/Anderson

139 Château of Blois, one of the wings built by Louis XII. Photo: Jeremy Whitaker

142 Portrait by Giorgione. Pinacoteca Comunale, Forlì. Photo: Mansell/Alinari

144 Manuscript illumination in Biblioteca Estense, Modena. Photo: Orlandini Carlo, Modena

147 Tempio Malatestiano, Rimini. Photo: Mansell/Anderson

151 Reproduced by gracious permission of Her Majesty The Queen

153 Portrait by Marco Palmezzani. Pinacoteca Comunale, Forlì. Photo: Mansell/Alinari

INDEX